Praise for

STRAIGHT UP FOOD

"TrueNorth Health Center has been teaching patients to eat an exclusively plant-food diet free of added salt, oil, and sugar for over 30 years. During this time the greatest challenge that our patients have faced is how to sustain the results they achieve through diet and fasting at TrueNorth once they return home. Cathy Fisher has helped solve this problem. Even the most resistant to dietary change will love her flavorful food and easy-to-follow recipes. This book can help save your life and the lives of the people you love."

—Alan Goldhamer, D.C., co-founder of TrueNorth Health Center and co-author of *The Pleasure Trap*

"Cathy Fisher is a very talented chef who has been helping people at the McDougall Program for many years to regain their lost health. Her recipes are delicious and easy to prepare, and we highly recommend that you prominently place *Straight Up Food* in your cookbook library."

—John McDougall, M.D. and Mary McDougall, national best-selling authors and co-founders of the McDougall Program

"Cathy Fisher is a gentle and beautiful force of nature. We work together at TrueNorth Health Center, and people often comment to me that her SOS-free (without added salt, oil, or sugar) recipes are the best they have ever tasted. I have to agree. Her simple yet flavorful approach to cooking is exquisite. You'll be very happy that you brought her cookbook into your healthy kitchen."

—Douglas Lisle, Ph.D., co-author of *The Pleasure Trap*

"The specialty of nutrition has been misunderstood for far too long. The future of health care worldwide requires a better understanding of a whole-food, plant-based diet and its enormous nutritional benefits. In making a transition to this dietary lifestyle, one of the biggest challenges is learning how to cook healthy food. Toward this end, I recommend Cathy Fisher's excellent cookbook, *Straight Up Food*."

—T. Colin Campbell, Ph.D., Jacob Gould Sherman Professor Emeritus of Nutritional Biochemistry Cornell University, co-author of the best-selling books, *The China Study* and *Whole*

"I love it! Plant-based, whole-food-focused, and no added sugar, oil, or salt—who knew healthy eating could be so easy and delicious!?"

—Michael Greger, M.D., FACLM, creator of NutritionFacts.org

"Cathy is unique in her ability to do what few other chefs are able to do: produce recipes that combine simplicity with great taste, and can meet the guidelines of whole-food, plant-based eating without any added salt, oil or sugar. Her recipes are a true gift to everyone who follows this way of living. I call her work 'elegant simplicity.'"

—Jeff Novick, M.S., R.D.N.

"Cathy Fisher's recipes are utterly appealing! They are easy to make with familiar ingredients, visually beautiful, and delicious in their flavor *and* flexibility. *Straight Up Food's* whole-food, plant-based recipes will help you unlearn lifelong bad eating habits so that you can feel and look your best!"

—Ann Crile Esselstyn and Jane Esselstyn, authors of *The Prevent and Reverse Heart Disease Cookbook*, and Caldwell B. Esselstyn, Jr., M.D., author of *Prevent and Reverse Heart Disease*

"As a professional chef who has followed a plant-based, SOS-free diet for almost 10 years, I can honestly tell you that Cathy's food is among the best I have ever tasted. You won't notice what is missing, only what is present: familiar-looking dishes that are full of flavor! If you don't believe me, try her Tu-No Salad, Creamy Coleslaw, or Carrot Cake. You can even serve her food to company—they won't believe that food this delicious is also healthy!"

—Chef AJ, host of the Foody TV show *Healthy Living* and author of *Unprocessed*

"Let's cut through all the hype and nonsense: Good health is the result of consuming natural foods without added salt, oil, concentrated sweeteners, or white flour. Cathy Fisher's cookbook, *Straight Up Food,* is your recipe for 'straight up' good health!"

—Joel Fuhrman, M.D., six-time *New York Times* best-selling author, including *The End of Diabetes* and *The End of Heart Disease*

"Cathy's recipes are always hearty, healthy, and full of flavor. I highly recommend *Straight Up Food* for your plant-based kitchen!"

—Brian Wendel, founder and president of Forks Over Knives

"The most powerful medicine I can prescribe for my patients is food, and Cathy's book is an excellent pharmacy to get that prescription filled!"

—James F. Loomis, M.D., Medical Director, Barnard Medical Center, Washington, D.C.

STRAIGHT UP FOOD

DELICIOUS AND EASY PLANT-BASED
COOKING WITHOUT SALT, OIL OR SUGAR

Cathy Fisher

Green Bite Publishing
SANTA ROSA, CA

Published by:
Green Bite Publishing
1585 Terrace Way #225
Santa Rosa, CA 95404
Contact: cookbook@StraightUpFood.com

Cover and interior design by Monica Thomas for TLC Graphics, www.TLCGraphics.com
Photographs by Cathy Fisher, www.StraightUpFood.com
Cover photo ©vicuschka, www.istockphoto.com
Page 233 photo, Cathy Stancil, www.CathyStancilPhotography.com
Page 17 photo, Angela Glasser

ISBN: 978-0-9976369-0-1 (paper)
ISBN: 978-0-9976369-1-8 (eBook)

First Edition
Printed in Canada

This publication contains the opinions and ideas of its author. It is intended to provide helpful information on adopting and sustaining a health-promoting, plant-based diet free of added salt, oil, and sugar. It is offered with the understanding that the author and the publisher are not rendering medical, health, or clinical treatment advice; this information is not meant to diagnose, treat, cure, or prevent any disease. Readers—in particular those with a diagnosed medical condition and/or who are taking medications (especially for high blood pressure or high blood sugar)—should consult with their doctor or other health professional before adopting any of the suggestions in this book or drawing inferences from them. The author and publisher disclaim all responsibility for any liability, loss, or risk that may be incurred as a consequence of the use and application of any of the information in this book.

CONTENTS

"Most deaths in the United States are preventable, and they are related to what we eat." —Michael Greger, M.D., *How Not to Die*

PREFACE

I wrote *Straight Up Food* to help fill a fast-growing demand for recipes that call for all plant foods without any added salt, oil, or sugar. This demand continues to grow as more people discover the powerful and direct correlation between what we eat and how we look and feel. This book will guide you in eliminating the foods that hinder good health, and it will teach you how to eat more of the foods that promote good health.

Recipes call for 100% plant foods: vegetables, fruits, whole grains, legumes, nuts and seeds, and contain no animal-derived ingredients: meat (beef, pork, fowl, fish, or seafood), eggs, honey, or dairy products (cow's milk, cream, butter, cheese, or yogurt). Recipes also emphasize the use of unprocessed foods.

My recipes contain no added salt, oil, or sugar, relying instead on subtler but naturally delicious sources of sodium, fat, and sweetness. The goal is not to give up flavor, but to eat great tasting food without sacrificing health. Additionally, these recipes are free of gluten (wheat, barley, rye), caffeine (coffee, chocolate), and peanuts, as well as any products derived from these items.

Each of us striving to change our dietary habits enters at a different point: some of us are brand new to dietary change while others are more experienced; some have sweeping goals for change while others have the smaller aim of simply "trying it on." Most people who choose to explore a new way of eating do it gradually while a few jump in all at once. Some people seek to *eliminate* salt, oil, and/or sugar from their daily diet (eliminating all three is called "SOS-free") while others seek merely to *reduce* their intake of salt, oil, and/or sugar. This cookbook is for anyone along these spectrums.

If you are new to a plant-based diet, I welcome you and encourage you to give the recipes in this book a try. After years of teaching these recipes to students in my classes—most of whom were new to this way of eating—I know you will be pleased with how flavorful and easy they are to make. These are not special "health-food" recipes; they are simply familiar favorites—such as Caesar salad, split pea soup, coleslaw, ranch dressing, and carrot cake—that have been given health-promoting makeovers.

The recipes and information in this book are based on the beliefs that (1) the type of food we consume—our human fuel—is the single most important factor in how we look and feel; (2) a truly health-promoting diet is one made up of all plant foods in an unprocessed or minimally processed state; and (3) each of us must take responsibility for our own good health by learning about and practicing the principles that support it.

> *This book will guide you in eliminating the foods that hinder good health, and it will teach you how to eat more of the foods that promote good health.*

FOREWORD BY MICHAEL KLAPER, M.D.

I have been practicing clinical medicine for over 40 years, and every day I battle the 21st-century scourges of obesity, diabetes, clogged arteries, and high blood pressure, which can lead to devastating heart attacks, strokes, cancers, and inflammatory and autoimmune diseases.

Most of my medical colleagues—internists, surgeons, cardiologists, rheumatologists, gastroenterologists, dermatologists, pediatricians, and radiologists—also struggle, valiantly but blindly, to treat these diseases using the most powerful pills and procedures known to medical science. They believe these diseases are caused by things such as genetics, environmental toxins, and life stressors.

However, as in the fable of the blind men and the elephant, where each man holds a different part of the animal and thinks that he understands the elephant's entire nature, most of today's health practitioners do not realize that they are, for the most part, treating various manifestations of the same malicious cause. The driving force behind all of our health afflictions can be summarized in three words: "It's the food!" These words are so important that I have a plaque in my office stating this simple but powerful truth.

The standard American diet, laden with meat, dairy, and packaged foods, has become toxic. Every few hours in Western societies, people flood their tissues with repeated tides of damaging fats, denatured proteins from cooked animal flesh, concentrated refined sugars, unnatural extracted oils, and a host of artificial flavorings, colorings, and preservatives that permeate our modern "fast food" cuisine. As this toxic brew courses through our arteries, blood vessels are clogged, obesity grows, inflammation is fanned, malignancies are spawned, and life-threatening diseases are manifested in almost every organ of our bodies.

Through my lectures and writings, I let my colleagues know that the majority of people sitting in their waiting rooms each morning are there because they are sick from what they are eating. And until this reality is recognized and this root cause is effectively addressed, my colleagues will continue to treat symptoms rather than remove causes. Their patients will remain sick, their procedures will generate devastating medical expenses, and their joy in practicing medicine will evaporate.

All of the formidable tools and technologies available to me and my colleagues pale in comparison to the single most effective force to cure disease: a plant-based diet made up of unprocessed or minimally processed foods. When people transition to this health-supporting style of eating, medical miracles become commonplace: elevated blood pressure normalizes, blood cholesterol falls to safe levels, inflammation subsides, arteries become unclogged, skin lesions clear up, bowel function becomes normal, and people regain lost vitality and look healthier.

But a health-promoting, plant-based diet is of value only if my patients actually eat it. And for many people, if not most, who have been raised on a diet of meat, dairy, and packaged foods, such a transition can seem daunting, if not impossible. This is where I rely on the work of one of my most powerful allies, my friend and colleague Cathy Fisher. A master of tastes and textures, spices and seasonings, Cathy's "straight up food" is the magic ingredient that gets my patients to take that most important step of actually putting health-promoting food into their mouths and enjoying it!

An essential step toward healing occurs when one of my skeptical patients takes that first bite of one of Cathy's simple but elegant dishes, savors the aromas and flavors, and says, "Oh, if this is healthy food, I can eat *this*!" My patients' health and lives change for the better from that moment on. You will find her recipes familiar and easy to prepare. Very importantly, her soups, stews, and casseroles can be frozen and then reheated for a convenient and nourishing meal.

Yes, I am a doctor who advocates a plant-based diet, but I also love to eat delicious food. And I can testify that Cathy's meals never fail to delight. I get to sample many of the demonstration dishes that she prepares as a cooking instructor at TrueNorth Health Center in Santa Rosa, California, where I am a staff physician (lucky me!). The dishes in this book are never overpowering or too sweet. Cathy makes artful use of seasonings and clever cooking techniques to bring out the delectable flavors that nature has placed in nourishing whole vegetables, fruits, grains, legumes (beans, peas, lentils), and nuts and seeds.

If you are facing a health challenge, or if you just like to eat fabulous food that will leave you feeling satisfied and guilt-free, you are holding the key in your hands. I urge you to explore these wonderful recipes and make them part of your daily food program. Your body will respond with glowing health, and your taste buds will welcome the light, clean flavors and textures that greet you with each dish.

I view Cathy Fisher as one of the most important colleagues on my healing team, and I am pleased to recommend this valuable volume to you. I wish you good health and great eating!

Michael Klaper, M.D.
www.DoctorKlaper.com

"Unfortunately, in the great majority of cases, both physicians and patients are looking for health in the wrong place. It is rarely the case that something needs to be added to the patient's body. Instead, dietary excesses need to be subtracted." —Doug Lisle, Ph.D. and Alan Goldhamer, D.C., *The Pleasure Trap*

PART ONE

GETTING STARTED

INTRODUCTION

If you were given the choice between eating delicious food that *compromised* your health and eating delicious food that *promoted* your health, which would you choose? The question seems almost too silly to ask. Of course you'd choose delicious food that promoted good health—who wouldn't?

But many of us, even though we understand that eating healthier would greatly benefit us, find it challenging to turn our desire for a health-promoting lifestyle into day-to-day reality. We get stuck before we start for three main reasons: (1) We think that changing how we eat will be too hard to learn and sustain: "It's easier to keep doing what's familiar." (2) We think we will miss our favorite foods too much: "Healthy food won't taste good." (3) We anticipate the scrutiny of our new lifestyle (and ourselves) by others: "I don't want to be the oddball." For some of us one of these reasons rings true, and for others it's all three.

Well, I bring you good news on all fronts.

Beefless Stew (page 118)

As for the difficulty of adopting and sustaining a healthier way of eating—in this case, a 100% plant-food diet free of added salt, oil, and sugar ("SOS-free")—this cookbook will guide you with kindness and clarity. I have written this book to support *you* by including dishes that are familiar, ingredients that are easy to find, and instructions that are easy to follow. I have also included practical tips and information on transitioning to and successfully sustaining this lifestyle. This is not a complicated gourmet cookbook—this is a "let's make really good food so we can feel really good" cookbook!

If you are concerned that healthy food will not taste good and that you will miss your favorite dishes, let me put you at ease with two very important points. First, after a period of consistently eating the dishes in this book (and others like them), your taste buds will adjust, and you'll begin to find them far more flavorful and appealing. The key is allowing your taste buds this important adjustment period. Second, the recipes in this book do not sacrifice flavor for health. You will learn to prepare familiar dishes that taste great, even without meat (beef, pork, fowl, fish, or seafood), honey, eggs, dairy (cow's milk, cream, butter, cheese, or yogurt), salt, oil, or sugar.

The third objection can be the most challenging for many of us: "What will people think?" We humans are most comfortable being with others who act the same way we do, value the same things we do, and eat the same way we do. In these familiar circles, we feel validated, supported, and accepted. We risk losing these connections when we decide to walk a path that is different, especially when it comes to how we eat.

However, if you have a serious interest in changing your eating habits to improve your health and appearance, you will find that the courage, confidence, and tools necessary to navigate these often frustrating social waters will unfold gradually as you continue to learn and practice, much like the process of learning a foreign language.

In the past I have taken solace in recalling this saying: "Sometimes the people around you won't understand your journey. They don't need to; it's not for them." Living a life of discomfort and ill health for others (to avoid their scrutiny and disapproval) is no way to live. Building your "health courage" and creating your new lifestyle take patience and practice, two things that are fortunately followed by another important P word: progress!

Most of us who have been eating this way for a while now sing a similar tune: We love eating even more now than we used to when we ate the overly greasy, salty, sugary, processed American diet. It's true—we're not just saying this to trick you. It may be hard to imagine a healthy diet that excites you and tastes delicious. But rest assured, you can become less dependent on health-compromising foods when they're no longer a part of your everyday meal routine, and you replace them with healthier options that taste great.

Burrito Bowl (page 53)

It is true that some people live long lives despite their consistently unhealthful eating habits. But it's likely most of them did not feel vibrant, strong, and joyful in their mid to later years, but rather tired, weak, and frustrated with the state of their declining bodies and minds.

Growing up, I was frequently reminded by my elders that the most precious thing in life is my health, for without it, the best that life has to offer will move out of my reach. I'd seen this happen in their lives and knew I wanted something different. I didn't want to set myself up for a medicated life, bouncing back and forth between doctors' offices and hospitals, a reality that has unfortunately become commonplace for many of today's older (and, increasingly, younger) Americans. I didn't want to find myself in a position where I felt hopeless *and helpless* about my health. So in 1999 I decided to learn a new language: the language of human nutrition.

Contrary to popular belief, the human body was not designed to operate as a painful, broken-down system as we get older. Old age in itself is not supposed to leave us unable to function and enjoy life. If you're feeling uncomfortable, or downright miserable, this is likely your body's way of

3

letting you know it's struggling to keep you moving forward and that something isn't right. In most cases, what your body is asking for is the correct fuel in the form of what you eat. This fuel can have a profound effect on how you feel and look. And it's never too late to change how you eat, no matter how old, sick, or overweight you may be.

You will find this book particularly interesting if (1) your health has been in the dumps for a while and you're ready to try a dietary approach to healing, (2) you're ready to swap dieting for a lifelong healthy *lifestyle*, (3) you're a parent who is concerned about feeding your family in today's world of overly engineered and processed foods, or (4) you're already eating a vegetarian or wholly plant-based diet but want to clean things up even further. If you fit into one of these groups, you will gain a great deal from this book. If you don't fit into one of these groups, you are likely an open-minded, self-loving person who is striving to feel and look your best. I'm confident that you, too, will find value in these pages.

Physicians, researchers, dietitians, and other professionals have written a great deal about why a plant-based lifestyle that emphasizes unprocessed or minimally processed foods is optimum for human health. Many of these people—through their websites, books, lectures, and videos—have been my teachers and mentors, and it is their body of work that I base my teachings and recipes on. Working closely with Alan Goldhamer, D.C., John McDougall, M.D., Michael Klaper, M.D., and Jeff Novick, R.D., in particular, has shaped my work and my understanding of true health and how to achieve it for a lifetime. (For more information about their work and that of others, see Resources on page 230.)

The recipes and information in this book will help you provide your body with the fuel it was designed to run on most effectively: plants! Adopting a plant-based diet is no longer the sole domain of "alternative" family members and friends; it is for *anyone* who is interested in maintaining or regaining his or her good health.

~ *Cathy Fisher*

Sweet Potato-Pecan Pie (page 174)

Note: *Significantly changing your diet can have a powerful effect on your body. Therefore, it is recommended that you discuss any plans for dietary change with your doctor, particularly if you are taking medications for high blood pressure or high blood sugar.*

THE FOOD

The recipes in this cookbook were created during my many years of teaching cooking classes at TrueNorth Health Center in Santa Rosa, California, where the motto is: "Real health comes from healthful living." Founded by Dr. Alan Goldhamer, TrueNorth is one of the few well-established, medically supervised fasting centers in the world. It also advocates an exclusively plant-based diet where the majority of calories come from unprocessed (or minimally processed) plant foods without any added refined salt, oil, or sugar, known as "SOS-free."

The way of eating described in this book is really a *lifestyle* since it's most effective and enjoyable when adopted for the long term. This is in contrast to a *diet*, which may conjure up memories of short-lived attempts to change how we eat to lose weight, often entered into with negativity and self-doubt. For practicality's sake, I do use the word "diet" in this book to refer to overall styles of eating—"plant-based diet," "standard American diet," etc.—and not to short-term dietary changes. In addition, "plant-based" in this book refers to a diet made up entirely of plants, not just a portion.

Plant-based professionals all have their own recommendations for eating more or less of certain plant foods. While most of them recommend a very similar overall dietary pattern, you will not find two plans or paths that are exactly the same. But the great thing about plant-based diets is that most of them will bring you better health than the standard American diet (SAD) that most Americans are living on today. More specifically, adopting any plant-based diet that emphasizes unprocessed or minimally processed foods is going to put you far ahead healthwise.

So, the question is: how far do you want to go? If you seek *dramatic* changes in your health and/or appearance, *dramatic* changes in your dietary habits will be your best prescription. This way of eating does not seem dramatic to me anymore since I've been following it for many years now, but if it's new to you, it may seem a bit radical. However, when you compare it with options like taking blood pressure medication for a lifetime, having open heart surgery, or getting stents inserted into your arteries to keep them open, changing the way you eat is actually far less radical.

Clean arteries and a clean bill of health blossom from practicing a clean lifestyle, in which diet is paramount. Through the recipes in this book, you will increase your consumption of the foods that are widely accepted to promote good health and eliminate your consumption of those known to hinder good health (especially in the excessive amounts that most people tend to consume them nowadays). In summary, the recipes in this book are based on the following diet:

> *If you seek dramatic changes in your health and/or appearance, dramatic changes in your dietary habits will be your best prescription.*

5

1. 100% plant foods: starchy and nonstarchy vegetables, fruits, whole grains, legumes (beans, peas, lentils), and nuts and seeds, with an emphasis on consuming these foods unprocessed or minimally processed.

2. No animal-derived foods or ingredients, including meat (beef, pork, fowl, fish, seafood), eggs, honey, or dairy products (cow's milk, cream, butter, cheese, yogurt).

3. No added salt, oil, or sugar ("SOS-free").

4. No packaged or prepared foods (or beverages) that contain refined flours, chemical preservatives, or artificial colors or flavors. (And, of course, no salt, oil, or sugar.)

5. No glutenous grains (wheat, rye, barley), caffeine (coffee, chocolate), or peanuts and their products (peanuts are a very common allergen).

Let's look at this diet in more detail.

A plant-based diet naturally promotes health because plants are full of vitamins, minerals, antioxidants, phytochemicals, and other health-promoting nutrients that keep us alive and thriving. Plant foods also contain fiber (animal foods do not), which helps eliminate excess fat and cholesterol (among other harmful substances) from the body. The ample fiber and water in plant foods also help our bowel elimination to be regular and easy. In addition, plant foods are generally lower in calorie density than animal foods and overly processed foods, which helps keep us from overeating and gaining weight.

Particularly nutrient-dense plant foods include leafy green vegetables, such as spinach, kale, and Swiss chard; colorful vegetables, such as carrots, broccoli, and bell peppers; as well as mushrooms, lentils, and sweet potatoes. Eating a diet made up of a variety of plant foods, while taking in adequate daily calories, can result in a body that is slim, energetic, attractive, and disease-free. Let us also take comfort in knowing that many of our planet's largest animals—elephants, rhinos, horses, moose—get all the nutrition they need to grow big and strong by eating only plants.

Animal foods, however, generally offer fewer micronutrients and more fat and protein than are healthful. Animal foods also do not contain the health-promoting antioxidants and phytochemicals that plants do, and they are usually higher in calorie density. This imbalance can be harmful to health. High-calorie foods that are low in nutrient density include animal foods, and overly refined and processed foods, particularly fast food, packaged snack food, bread, cheese, oil, and soda.[1]

When we make getting enough protein and/or calcium our main reasons for eating animal foods, we can pay the price of good health. Plant foods such as nuts, seeds, greens, grains, and legumes deliver more than enough protein and calcium to keep plant-based eaters vibrantly healthy.[2,3] Animal food marketing efforts have taught us to be afraid of not getting enough protein and calcium and, therefore, that we should regularly buy and consume their products. But we must remember that they are not in business to care about consumer health; they are in business to make money. It's nearly impossible to become deficient in protein and calcium if you are eating a varied diet of plant foods and taking in enough calories every day.[4, 5]

So, why not just bypass the compromised packages of overly processed foods and animal products—which not only harm our health, but in their production also harm animals and our natural environment[6]—and get almost everything we need from the complete package of plant foods? As nutrient delivery systems go, getting what we need from plants rather than animals is simply more efficient and makes more health sense.

There is one vital nutrient that a plant-based diet does not supply, and that is vitamin B12. Most people who consume a plant-based diet opt to take a daily or weekly B12 vitamin supplement since B12 is essential to health. People who eat animal foods usually get adequate B12 since the animals they have consumed have synthesized B12 from ingested bacteria. But since plant-based eaters don't consume animal foods, and since our modern-day food is so thoroughly cleansed of bacteria, they can become B12-deficient. (For an article covering this issue in more detail, search the Internet for "Vitamin B12 Recommendations for Vegans" by Drs. Alan Goldhamer and Doug Lisle.)

The TrueNorth diet also avoids gluten and, therefore, so do my recipes. Whether or not to consume gluten (a protein found in wheat, rye, and barley) has become a hot topic in nutrition discussions. While most people can tolerate gluten, many others have sensitivities to it and encounter joint pain, gut discomfort, and sinus problems after consuming it.[7] People with celiac disease (about 1% of the population) have extreme sensitivities to gluten, causing their immune systems to attack their intestinal linings, resulting in inflammation, malabsorption, pain, and other symptoms. (People with Hashimoto's thyroiditis, the most common form of hypothyroidism, can also be affected by gluten, but in this case the immune system attacks the thyroid gland.)

Given these issues, and that TrueNorth patients come to the center to clean out their bodies and eat the heathiest diet possible, gluten is off the menu. And since gluten most commonly shows up in overly processed foods loaded with refined flour, salt, oil, and sugar (such as bread, cookies, cakes, crackers, and flour tortillas), it's not difficult for health seekers to avoid gluten on this program. However, if you are not concerned about gluten in your own diet, simply strive to consume wheat, rye, and barley as unprocessed or minimally processed grains.

If you are used to eating the standard American diet, you may imagine this way of eating to be limiting or boring, but nothing could be further from the truth. You may be thinking, "If you eliminate meat, dairy, salt, oil, sugar, and wheat, what's left?" I assure you, there is *plenty* left; you are just not as familiar with these foods and their preparations yet. But becoming familiar with them, through this book, will open your eyes to a wonderful new world of eating pleasure and improved health.

SOS-FREE

Since this cookbook is distinct in its absence of salt, oil, and sugar, let's delve a little more deeply into why these ingredients are not used. "SOS-free" means that no salt, oil, or sugar have been added to the food at any stage of preparation. Going SOS-free continues to grow in popularity as more people strive to reduce or eliminate these ingredients for health reasons.

My own immersion into SOS-free eating began in 2010 when I started teaching cooking classes at TrueNorth Health Center. I had already been eating a plant-based, oil-free diet for about 10 years, but I was still using salt and sugar in my cooking and baking. However, I wanted to be sure that my recipes followed the TrueNorth guidelines, so I started eating SOS-free all the time.

After about a month of not adding salt and sugar to my meals (and long before, oil), my taste buds got used to not having them, and I no longer missed them. I learned how to flavor my food with fresh and dried herbs and spices instead of salt, how to cook and roast vegetables and make salad dressings without oil, and how to substitute oil and sugar in baking. Soon I began to prefer SOS-free food, and when I ate food with added salt, oil, and/or sugar, the amounts tasted excessive.

Many people find that forgoing added salt, oil, and sugar can be a challenge. This is because all three products are highly concentrated, the results of excessive refining and processing by food manufacturers. The more salt, oil, and sugar we eat, the more intense our cravings can become (due to their ultra-concentrated states).[8, 9] But take comfort in knowing that our taste preferences have all been acquired, meaning they were developed at some point in our lives and, therefore, can be undeveloped and replaced by new preferences.[10]

While it's true that our taste buds are naturally designed to seek out saltiness, richness, and sweetness, when the sources of these flavors have been unnaturally concentrated and are consumed in excess, the body's desire for them goes into overdrive.[11] This leads us to seek out the foods that contain the most salt, oil, and sugar (like bread, cookies, pastries, crackers, potato chips, candy, soda, and condiments).[12]

One of the hardest foods for people to give up is cheese, and why wouldn't it be, with its sky-high concentrations of fat and salt, sending our brains into a hyperstimulated tizzy of bliss. After I stopped cooking with salt, oil, and sugar, it became easier to discern an enjoyable SOS-free meal from a "tizzy of bliss" meal. While the bliss felt good in the short term, it would always leave me feeling tired and heavy soon after and, in general, less conscious about what I was putting into my mouth.

Some people feel that the consumption of salt, oil, and/or sugar in small amounts, or only during the transition away from the standard American diet (SAD), is fine if that's what it takes to get others to adopt a plant-based diet. This may work for some people, but for others it can be difficult to keep these three highly concentrated ingredients to small amounts since they can easily become addictive. This frustrating "push-pull" is one of the reasons people choose to shift to an SOS-free diet. Forgoing these three ingredients entirely has worked better for many people than consuming them in moderation. Moderation results in slower and fewer improvements in health and appearance, and it reminds your brain that these intense flavors are still within reach and keeps begging you for more, driving you crazy. If you view moderation as eating just a little less than what you're used to, that won't get you very far in your efforts to become healthier and lose weight.

Today's food culture of being able to eat whatever we want, whenever we want has also made it difficult for people to limit their intakes to "just a little." This has led to 70% of American adults being overweight or obese (about 36% are obese).[13] When alcoholics or smokers try to quit, having just one drink or one cigarette a day does little to eliminate their cravings or the overall habit; it only leaves them frustrated and wanting more. Giving up salt, oil, and sugar can feel the same way for many people, a state that TrueNorth Health Center calls "the pleasure trap." (Read the excellent book, *The Pleasure Trap*, for more about this).

Today's food culture of being able to eat whatever we want, whenever we want has also made it difficult for people to limit their intakes to "just a little."

Nutritionally speaking, we do not need to add salt, oil, and sugar to our food; we can get everything we need simply from eating a wholesome, plant-based diet. The body's actual needs for sodium and fat are, in fact, pretty low (less than the amount of sodium in one-quarter teaspoon of salt a day and less than 10% of daily calories from fat).[14]

We do, however, benefit from consuming plenty of carbohydrates (70 to 90% of daily calories), which are our primary source of energy (from complex carbohydrates like potatoes, rice, corn, green and yellow vegetables, and fruits). But when it comes to sugar (a carbohydrate) we want to steer clear of overly concentrated, simple sugars, such as white table sugar (sucrose), corn syrup, maple syrup, honey, and agave,[15] as well as white flour products (which are not only stripped of their nutrients but also typically loaded with salt, oil, and sugar). Instead, we want to embrace complex carbohydrates and the naturally occurring sugars found in them. (Although widely misunderstood, these naturally packaged sugars do not adversely affect blood glucose or other health factors, such as type 2 diabetes, when consumed intact.[16])

SALT

We Americans love our table salt (also known as "sodium chloride," which is 40% sodium and 60% chloride), but mostly we get our salt from all the packaged foods we eat: canned foods (pasta sauce, vegetables, soups, and broths), condiments (dressings, ketchup, gravies, and sauces, especially soy sauce), breads, meats, dairy products (cheese, milk, yogurt), snack foods (cookies, chips, crackers, cereals), and fast foods.[17] Restaurant food is also very high in salt (the more salt, oil, and sugar the restaurant adds, the more we come back). Even some medications contain salt.

While most people can tolerate a little bit of salt with no ill effects, we are not a nation of people who like consuming "just a little bit"—we are a nation of excess; and when our salt intake reaches levels that are excessive, our health can be negatively impacted.

According to a 2016 report by the CDC (Centers for Disease Control and Prevention), 89% of adults and over 90% of children exceeded recommendations for sodium intake between 2009 and 2012.[18] And among adults who are hypertensive (having high blood pressure), 86% exceeded the upper limit of dietary sodium per day. The report also notes that excess sodium intake increases people's "potential risk of stroke and coronary heart disease mortality."

So how much sodium is too much? The USDA Dietary Guidelines recommend a tolerable upper limit of 2,300 mg (about 1 teaspoon of salt) or less per day. No more than 1,500 mg sodium (a little over a half teaspoon) has been recommended for older people (over 51), African Americans, and people with high blood pressure, diabetes, or chronic kidney disease. A recommended safe *minimum* of sodium is set at 500 mg per day.

If you consume a salt-free diet, you needn't worry that you're not getting enough sodium because even without adding salt to your food, you will still get plenty of sodium, as it occurs naturally in plants. As long as you consume a variety of plant foods and adequate daily calories, you will get all the minerals necessary for good health.

> As long as you consume a variety of plant foods and adequate daily calories, you will get all the minerals necessary for good health.

You may say, "But I like salt, and it enhances the flavor of my food. Plus sea salt is natural." These are three reasons we cling to our salt habit. Of course we like it; it's the whole "tizzy bliss" thing again, and we've been using it all of our lives, so it's comforting. As a flavoring, too much salt can actually mask the flavors of our food; remove the salt and you will begin to appreciate the food itself more. (It's also been suggested that adding salt to our food causes us to overeat fatty foods.[19])

Many people believe sea salt to be particularly nutritious, but while it may be prettier than common table salt and contain a few more minerals, it's still hazardously high in sodium, and we can still easily overconsume it.

The human body does need some sodium to function correctly. Our kidneys regulate the amount stored and released so that just the right balance is maintained. But if the kidneys become exhausted and cannot excrete sodium (due to heart or kidney disease, diabetes, overall poor health, or excess consumption), it begins to build up in the system, which results in the retention of water, causing higher blood volume and thereby putting more pressure on our heart and arteries.[20] Common health concerns associated with too much salt in the bloodstream include high blood pressure, stroke, and an increased risk for heart disease, osteoporosis, and stomach cancer.[21, 22]

In my own effort to consume much less sodium, I have made the following shifts: (1) I eat out less often; (2) when I do eat out, I choose restaurants where I know I can order dishes that contain no salt or very little; (3) I strive to buy packaged foods that do not contain salt or have just very low amounts; and (4) I do not add salt (or other high-sodium condiments) on top of my food or during preparation. I don't even keep salt in the house anymore. And this goes for anything I am trying to avoid: if I don't want it in my body, it doesn't come into my house.

We mainly consume oil because it has become a habit that we've developed over time, and it's a comforting one, so it's not easy to give up.

OIL

There are many reasons to avoid adding oil to food, but let's start with the most indisputable one first: oil is 100% fat, which makes it the most calorie-dense food there is. One tablespoon of oil contains about 120 calories (15 grams by weight), which is significant when compared to the same weight of other high-calorie foods like sour cream (about 27 calories) and Brie cheese (about 50 calories).[23] If you are trying to lose weight and be kind to your blood vessels, removing oil from your diet is an essential first step.

Additionally, since oil contains no fiber or water (which helps us to feel full), we have a tendency to overconsume it, and thus our efforts to lose weight are made that much more difficult. Excess weight has been shown to promote inflammation, inhibit immune function, and increase the risk for heart disease, high cholesterol, diabetes, and cancer.[24]

As oil enters our bloodstream, our blood vessels come in contact with it and over time become damaged. Our circulation slows (raising blood pressure), and as oil builds up in our arteries, it forms potentially dangerous plaques[25] that can lead to heart disease, the number-one killer in the U.S.[26] Damaged blood vessels also put men at risk for impotence.[27]

Also, because the fat in oil has been extracted from its original food source, it is now unprotected, making it more prone to becoming rancid through oxidation (prolonged exposure to oxygen), inhibiting freshness and degrading food. Oil that has been oxidized also contains free radicals, which can damage the body and contribute to cancers.[28]

The bottom line is that the oils we believe to be healthy, including olive, coconut, and flax, do not promote health and are best left off our plates since all oils have been stripped of fiber and most of the nutrients that originally existed in the intact food (the olive, the nut, the seed). Fish oil is another hot topic. Consumed by health seekers for its DHA and EPA content, fish contain these omega-3 fats only because they ate plants that contain them. A whole-food, plant-based diet supplies plenty of omega-3 fat without the health consequences of eating animal protein and ocean contaminants.

"But it tastes good!" Not really. We don't drink a cup of oil for a very good reason: it doesn't taste good on its own. In fact, oil has come to be the glue that keeps salt stuck to our food, but if we're not using salt, this is yet another reason to ditch the oil. Oil is always added to or combined with other foods since we respond to its creamy texture (fat), not its flavor. We mainly consume oil because it has become a habit that we've developed over time, and it's a comforting one, so it's not easy to give up.

We do need to consume a small percentage of fat as part of a healthy diet, but the body responds better to the naturally occurring fats found in plant foods—as Mother Nature packaged them—not as highly refined and concentrated oils. Wild animals do not need to consume oil to be healthy and neither do human animals. We just think we do based on cultural tradition and because oils have been marketed to us relentlessly (as most manufactured food products have) since there is so much money to be made from them.

Your taste buds will adapt after a while, usually within a few weeks, and you will get used to not having oil at all. This is where you must have faith and patience.

It may be hard to imagine going without oil when cooking vegetables, making salad dressings, and baking, but it is not as hard as you think. Once you decide you are going to ditch the oil from your everyday diet, the fear of giving it up starts to fade as you learn simple techniques for preparing food without it (see Cooking without Oil on page 195).

And remember, your taste buds will adapt after a while, usually within a few weeks, and you will get used to not having oil at all. This is where you must have *faith and patience*. A transformation will be taking place that you may not even notice, as your body becomes cleaner and your blood begins to flow more efficiently without all the oil clogging the pipes.

SUGAR

Sugar exists naturally in most plant foods to some degree, and from these plants refined sugars are made. Food manufacturers then sell this refined substance as pure sugar or add it to the packaged foods and beverages we buy at the grocery store. However, as is the case with salt, Americans are getting too much sugar. According to the USDA, total per-capita sugar consumption in the U.S. (2011-2012, for males and females age two and older) reached 96 pounds a year[29] (that's about a quarter pound per day)!

Refined sugar is an empty-calorie food, meaning it has little to no nutrients. And much like the concentrated nature of salt and oil, refined sugar is very easy to overconsume, often leading to weight gain, a factor for disease. We find the highest amounts of sugar in packaged foods, such as sugar-sweetened beverages (sodas, sports drinks, juice drinks), snack foods (cookies, candy), condiments (jams, sauces, dressings), breakfast cereals, and canned foods.

The sugars in bananas and apples, on the other hand, are packaged exactly as nature intended, along with all of their accompanying nutrients, fiber, and water. This ensures that the sugars will gradually absorb into the bloodstream so that we will not be immediately hungry for more and we won't overeat. Whenever the sugars from foods are extracted and refined—as in table sugar from beets, or corn syrup from corn—the opposite effect can occur. The human body does not require any added sugar for health; therefore we could get by without consuming it at all. But don't confuse this with not being able to have anything sweet.

If you're in the mood for something sweet, look to fruit to satisfy your craving. If this sounds terribly boring, fear not: your taste buds will adapt, and soon you will delight in a piece of fruit instead of a cookie for a snack, or cut-up fruit over your morning oatmeal instead of white or brown sugar. In my opinion, sugar is the easiest of the three (salt, oil, sugar) to substitute and not notice a difference in flavor, particularly in desserts and baked goods.

Instead of refined sugars, I often use apples, applesauce, peaches, strawberries, bananas, dates, and/or raisins in my desserts. A fruit cobbler sweetened with a few dates is just as tasty as one made with refined sugar. However, it's important to understand that certain fruits can have very high concentrations of natural sugars ("sugar density").[30] One pound of dates contains 298 grams of sugar, and one pound of raisins contains 265 grams of sugar, quite a bit more than one pound of apples (47 grams of sugar) or one pound of bananas (55 grams of sugar). For this reason, I eat lower-sugar-density foods more often than I do higher-sugar-density foods. For example, I eat fresh fruit every day, but I eat dates and prepared desserts just once in a while, mainly on special occasions.

THE RECIPES

The two comments I hear most often from my students are, "Your recipes are easy to prepare," and "This tastes really good!" I love to hear this feedback because I truly value simplicity *and* eating delicious food at every meal.

The recipes in this book are easy from every angle. Most will (1) be easy to recognize as familiar, (2) be easy to prepare, (3) call for easy-to-find ingredients, and (4) be easy to adapt to *your* tastes—all things helpful in transitioning to a new way of eating.

In addition, most of the recipes will appeal to your friends and family who don't already eat a plant-based diet. This is because the recipes will sound and look familiar to them and, most importantly, taste great. Someone may say to you, "This needs salt." That's fine; they probably add salt to their food on a regular basis and can add it if they want to (the craving for salt decreases after we stop consuming it). But I rarely hear people say "This needs oil," or "This needs white sugar." People don't notice the absence of these two ingredients and how they've been substituted with more health-promoting options; they just notice how much they enjoy the food.

In fact, I often hear students in my classes remarking that they *prefer* these healthier dishes to those they have grown used to eating. I believe this is because we are so accustomed to eating foods that are overly processed and made with excessive amounts of salt, oil, and/or sugar that we've been missing out on the amazing natural flavors of simple foods. Worrying that you won't enjoy the taste of "healthy" food should be put out of your mind; healthful food preparations have come a *long* way.

The recipes in this book will appeal to veteran plant-based eaters as well as those new to this way of eating; however, the organizational style of the book lends an extra hand to the latter group in the following ways.

Each section (Soups and Stews, Salads, Main Dishes, Desserts, etc.), contains an introduction to the basics of that recipe category at the beginning of each chapter.

As for the recipes themselves, each begins with a brief introduction to give you an idea of what to expect from the dish. Many recipes also include shopping tips to help you find the healthiest, most appropriate ingredients for that recipe. I also note preparation and cooking times, as well as serving and volume amounts, to help with meal planning.

Many of the ingredients listed include more than one type of measurement since we all approach preparing recipes a little differently. I don't mind an instruction like "1 medium red bell pepper, chopped," but others may prefer a more precise instruction like "1½ cups chopped bell pepper." So you will find both measures in many instances. Every effort has been made to be as clear and helpful as possible without drowning you in information.

In general, the recipes are very flexible, and a little more or less of this or that than the recipe calls for is usually fine. Baked dessert recipes, however, should be followed more precisely, as any digressions can affect how the dish bakes and rises, and ultimately how it looks and tastes.

All recipe instructions have been numbered to help you keep your place, and like the ingredient listings, they have been clearly written with newer cooks in mind. When there are separate preparations within one recipe—as with many salads that also call for a separate dressing—they have been clearly broken out and labeled.

Many of the recipes include notes offering ingredient alternatives as well as extra information on preparation techniques. Many also feature brief unsolicited quotes, from Straight Up Food blog followers, that are informative, inspiring, and often humorous.

TAILORING RECIPES TO YOUR TASTES

Cookbook recipes are typically developed by one chef according to *his or her* taste preferences. So do not feel shy about adjusting any of the recipes in this book to fit *your* tastes. Recipe editing by home cooks is very common and, in fact, encouraged since you're more likely to keep eating the dish if you make it the way *you* like it.

For example, should you come across an ingredient that you cannot eat or don't like, feel free to omit it or make a substitution. Don't let one ingredient keep you from making a dish that appeals to you. I like to think of recipes as starting points or templates, from which I can make adjustments, sometimes out of necessity or just because I'm feeling creative. New cooks, however, may feel more comfortable following recipes exactly, at least the first time around.

If you like spicy food, for example, feel free to add your favorite ground chili pepper or some chopped jalapeños to a dish. If you're trying to avoid all or just certain nuts and seeds, leave them out, reduce the amount, or use a type of nut or seed that works for you (white beans are also a great low-calorie nut replacement in blended salad dressings). Keep notes of any changes you make right in the book or on sticky notes so you can replicate the same results next time if you wish.

It will take some time to adjust to eating food that is prepared differently. But just as we learned our eating habits as kids and young adults, we can unlearn them in the process of forming new, healthier habits. The surest way of making this transition successful is to keep the most health-compromising foods (meat, dairy, salt, sugar, oil, and overly processed fare) out of your diet (and kitchen) entirely, as moderation often just serves to keep us tied to them, sabotaging our efforts to leave them behind and improve our health and appearance.

CALORIE COUNTING AND NUTRITIONAL BREAKDOWNS

Counting calories is not required on a plant-based diet like this one, since the majority of foods are low in calorie density and high in water and fiber—meaning you'll get full and stop eating before you can overdo it on calories. But I know that many people like calorie counting and knowing the nutrient breakdowns of recipes, so I have included this information starting on page 220. You can also find information on reading food labels on page 206.

KITCHEN TOOLS

You don't need a lot of fancy kitchen tools to prepare the recipes in this book, but I do recommend the following basic items to make cooking more efficient and enjoyable. To see all of my favorite cooking tools and products, visit *StraightUpFood. com* and click "Store."

BLENDERS

I use my blender most often for making dressings, sauces, and gravies. I also use it to grind seeds and nuts, to grind whole grains (like rolled oats and millet) into flour, and to process dates and other dried fruit. My primary blender is a Vitamix (a powerful home blender that costs between $300 and $500), and I also have a small but powerful Tribest Personal Blender (about $75), to do quick, small-volume jobs. (If you're on a tight budget, you can get by with the smaller Tribest alone.)

CUTTING BOARD

Recommending a cutting board seems obvious, but I have been in so many kitchens (professional and home) where the cutting boards should have been replaced long ago. I encourage you to use a good cutting board that is not stained or warped. I prefer an 18×12-inch wood cutting board for most of my cooking because I like the feel of it when chopping, but I use plastic at times too. Give yourself the gift of a nice, new cutting board; it will make cooking so much more enjoyable.

KNIVES

Knives come in a wide variety of sizes, qualities, and prices. I recommend having at least an 8-inch chef's knife, a smaller 5- or 6-inch utility knife, and a paring knife. The most important thing about knives is to keep them sharp. This, like having a good cutting board, will make cooking so much more fun, as well as efficient and safe. You can sharpen your knives at home with a sharpening stone or a manual or electric sharpener, or send them to your local cutlery shop for service. Search "knife sharpening" on YouTube to learn how to sharpen your own knives at home.

FOOD PROCESSOR

Even if you have a blender, I still recommend a food processor. A blender is most often used to create a very smooth consistency (as with gravy, frosting, or sauce) while a food processor allows for a more coarse consistency (as with hummus or salsa). A food processor also has attachments that allow for chopping, shredding, slicing, and grating. Food processors come in many sizes. I recommend at least an 11-cup bowl; I love my 14-cup model.

POTS AND PANS

Most handy will be a large soup pot (6 to 8 quarts), a smaller sauce pot (2 quarts), and a frying or sauté pan (11 inches). I use mostly stainless steel pots and pans, but I have a quality nonstick frying pan for things like veggie burger patties, hash browns, and pancakes since I don't use oil to prepare my pans. If you have a large family, you may want larger pots and pans, but these sizes are generally fine when cooking for one to four people.

Cathy in the kitchen

BAKING

Baking pans (metal) and dishes (glass) sized 9×13-inch and 8×8-inch are staples. A 12-cup muffin pan and a standard 9×5-inch loaf pan are also handy to have in the cupboard. Many people prefer metal pans for things they want to cook up drier, firmer, and with crusty edges (including muffins and cookies) and glass dishes for moister food (such as casseroles and cobblers).

Aside from the above items, I also use many smaller kitchen tools, such as a sharp potato peeler, a lemon juicer, a garlic press, measuring spoons and cups, parchment paper, and silicone spatulas. I also keep certain tools on hand for when I'm making something special, including a waffle iron, rotary cheese grater (using nuts instead of cheese), french fry cutter, mandolin (produces thin, consistent slices), and an immersion blender to create creamy soups.

NOTES AND TERMS

Teaching cooking classes on a weekly basis and blogging for many years has given me the opportunity to field almost every possible question about plant-based eating and cooking. To address many of them, I have put together this alphabetical list of terms, interwoven with notes and tips to help you navigate any unfamiliar terrain. I located it up front, rather than toward the end, as I recommend you read through it once before embarking on the recipes. This will provide you with a broad understanding of this way of eating and cooking and, therefore, make your transition easier and more enjoyable.

BAKING SODA AND BAKING POWDER

Both of the leavening agents baking soda and baking powder are used in baked goods, and both are very high in sodium (around 450 mg per teaspoon for baking powder and 1,200 mg for baking soda). But, luckily, both can be found sodium-free. Hain makes a sodium-free baking powder, and Ener-G makes a baking soda substitute, both of which may be purchased at natural grocery stores or online. To confirm that your baking powder is still active, stir ¼ teaspoon into ½ cup of warm or hot water. If you see bubbling or fizzing, then it is still potent and usable. To test baking soda, stir ¼ teaspoon into ½ cup of warm or hot water along with ¼ teaspoon of vinegar, and look for the same reaction.

CARDAMOM

Cardamom is a wonderfully aromatic spice that is often used in Asian and Indian cooking. You can buy it as pods, seeds, or preground. I usually buy preground, but when I want extra flavor, I buy the seeds and grind them with my small Tribest blender or a coffee grinder. Cardamom can be found wherever spices are sold.

DATES

I use whole fresh or dried fruits in my cooking instead of sugar, and dates are my favorite. Dates are a wonderful source of sweetness, and their flavor is similar to brown sugar or maple syrup. If you don't have access to Medjool dates (my favorite), Deglet Noor dates may also be used (they are not quite as sweet and are smaller and drier in texture. I advise using about twice as many Deglet Noor dates as Medjool). Where dates are called for in the ingredient lists, I have also noted the measurement in ounces since dates come in different sizes (the ounces measure will always be the most accurate). If you want more or less sweetness in a recipe, simply adjust the dates by one or two in either direction. If you buy already pitted dates, be sure to chop each one in half or quarters since sometimes the very hard pits have been missed in processing.

DESSERTS

As a dessert fan, I strive to create sweet treats that are delicious but also health-promoting. All of my dessert recipes call for fruits to sweeten them (dates primarily, but also bananas, applesauce, and raisins). Even though the fat and sugar in these desserts come from unprocessed or minimally processed foods, I still view them as occasional treats, rather than everyday indulgences. When I want something quick and sweet, I eat some fruit and reserve prepared desserts for special occasions.

FLOUR

If I need flour for a recipe, I grind rolled oats and millet in my blender. High-speed blenders do a great job of quickly grinding whole grains into flour. If you're not used to doing this, you may be hesitant, but I encourage you to try it. Grinding your own flour results in better-tasting dishes, and you can quickly make the exact amount needed, thereby avoiding storing bulky bags of flour in the cupboard. If you've already purchased whole-grain flour from the store, you can try using it; however, the recipes in this cookbook have not been tested with it, so results may vary.

FREEZING FOOD

Generally, the foods that freeze best are batch-cooked dishes, like soups or stews, because they won't dry out when reheated. Baked cakes, muffins, and waffles may dry out a little, but they still freeze well. Cooked legumes (peas, lentils, beans), nuts, and seeds also freeze well. I try to eat my frozen foods within three months for the best flavor (write the date of freezing on each container).

Foods you may want to avoid freezing are high-moisture raw fruits and vegetables, like apples, oranges, cucumbers, and lettuce. After thawing, these raw foods will not taste as good since the texture will have changed. However, fresh berries and cut-up bananas do freeze well. I also tend to avoid freezing creamy foods, cooked pasta, and rice. If you're not sure how something will freeze, give a small amount a try and see how it goes, or search the question online.

GARLIC

I use both fresh and dried garlic in my recipes, with fresh used most often for recipes that are raw (hummus, pesto sauce, salad dressings) or quickly cooked in a frying or sauté pan (like vegetable stir-fries), and dried with boiling vegetables and for dishes that are cooked longer (soups, stews, casseroles).

When using dried garlic, I prefer the granulated form since it does not clump like powder can when added to hot liquid (such as with soup). But feel free to use whatever you like or have on hand. Everyone has their own affinity for garlic, so use (or don't use) what feels right to you. A helpful conversion guideline is 1 fresh clove = 1 teaspoon chopped = ½ teaspoon minced or flaked = ¼ teaspoon granulated = ⅛ teaspoon powder.

GLUTEN

None of the recipes in this book calls for glutenous grains (wheat, rye, barley) or their products. (See Oats in this section for more about gluten sensitivity, as well as page 7 for more information on gluten.)

GRAINS

Nonglutenous grains, such as rice, corn, oats, and millet, are used in many of my recipes, from breakfast porridge to meatless main dishes to desserts. Since these unprocessed (intact) and minimally processed grains are a more health-promoting choice than refined grains (which have been stripped of their outer bran and/or the germ), I recommend them whenever possible. When buying packaged grain-based foods, look for those that list the grain as whole, rolled, cracked, or stone ground.

HERBS AND SPICES

Fresh and dried culinary herbs and spices are important additions to meals but especially when forgoing salt, the most commonly used seasoning in American cooking. The recipes in this book call for easily found herbs and spices. I encourage you to become familiar with those that are used often, as well as a few that are less commonly used. Through making these recipes, you will naturally develop an understanding of how to use different herbs and spices. (For a more thorough discussion of herbs and spices, see page 197.)

INGREDIENT LISTS

The best way to determine which packaged foods are healthiest is to read the ingredient list. What you're looking for is a list with just a very few easily recognizable ingredients—things you could plant and grow yourself (for example, tomatoes and oregano vs. sorbitol or potassium bromate). The ingredients are listed in order of weight, so there is more of the first ingredient than any other, and conversely, there is less of the last ingredient than any other.

I always try to buy packaged foods that contain no added salt (or high-sodium ingredients like miso, tamari, soy sauce, liquid aminos), sugar (in any of its many forms), or oil of any kind. I also look for packaged foods with not more than five ingredients. For example, canned diced tomatoes with one ingredient (tomatoes); soy milk with two ingredients (soy beans, water); corn tortillas with three ingredients (corn, lime, water); and mustard with four ingredients (water, vinegar, mustard seeds, spices). See page 206 for more on label reading.

LOW-FAT

This book is not a "low-fat" cookbook, but you can easily modify most of the recipes to make them lower in fat and calories. The highest-fat plant foods I use are nuts, seeds, and avocados, and often they are optional, or I provide substitution options. If you are not overweight and do not have any heart disease-related health issues, small amounts of higher-fat plant foods are generally fine. I do not use any oil in my recipes since oil is refined and overly processed, is 100% fat, and is very calorie dense (120 calories per tablespoon). For more information about oil, see page 11. For guidelines on cooking without oil, see page 195.

MILLET

Millet is a nonglutenous grain that is very mild in flavor. Along with oats, I occasionally use millet flour in baking. Even when ground and baked, it has a slightly crunchy texture (like cornmeal), which is delicious. It is yellow and round, and can be found most often in natural grocery stores, either packaged or in the bulk food section. It can also be ordered online. If you don't have millet on hand, you can try substituting cornmeal.

NONDAIRY MILK

When a recipe calls for nondairy milk, I leave it up to you which kind to use (soy, rice, almond, etc.), as I find it makes little difference in most cases. If there is a specific type of milk that I like in a recipe, I have noted this. I tend to buy organic soy milk most of the time since I can easily find it without added salt, sugar, and oil (I like Westsoy and Eden brands). I also strive to purchase only organic soy (and corn) products since their conventional forms are most often genetically modified (a technology whose long-term safety in humans has yet to be proven). Most other nondairy milks contain at least some salt, oil, and/or sugar. It's tricky to find brands without all three of these ingredients, as well as other ingredients that are not health supporting (like caramel color, carrageenan, artificial sweeteners, "natural" flavors, and the like). I often make my own nondairy milk at home since it's so easy (see pages 35–36).

NUTS AND SEEDS

I am aware that many people are striving to avoid high-fat, calorie-dense nuts and seeds, usually for weight-loss or sensitivity reasons. Toward this, feel free to eliminate them, reduce the amount listed, or substitute with something else (like white beans instead of cashews in salad dressings or sauces). Additionally, nuts are often interchangeable in a pinch, so try pecans if you can't find walnuts, or macadamia nuts if you don't have cashews. I buy raw (not roasted), unsalted nuts and seeds, which are healthier options. They can usually be found in the bulk food section of natural grocery stores.

OATS

I use old-fashioned rolled oats most often in my recipes and sometimes quick-cooking oats (but not instant oats, which are more processed and often contain added salt and sugar). While oats are not glutenous by nature, they often contain glutenous particles (from contact with machines that also process gluten-containing grains, such as wheat). Some people who are allergic or sensitive to gluten choose not to consume oats for this reason while others with gluten sensitivity can consume oats without issue. (True celiacs, however, can experience serious symptoms from even a single molecule of gliadin, a component of gluten.) You can buy packaged "gluten-free" oats (which have not been processed with gluten-containing grains) in many natual grocery stores as well as online.

Oats come in many forms. Oat groats are intact, unprocessed grains with only their hulls removed (the germ, bran, and endosperm are still retained). Steel-cut oats are oat groats that have been chopped. Rolled oats are oat groats that have been steamed, flat-rolled, and lightly toasted. These are also known as "old-fashioned" oats. Further processing of the rolled oat flakes results in smaller flakes, known as "quick oats."

ORGANIC FOOD

I buy organically grown food whenever it is available at the grocery store or farmers' market. Even though organic food may not always be visually perfect, it is grown with fewer and less toxic chemicals, and the taste is often more flavorful. Organic food can sometimes (but not always) cost more than conventional food, but since fresh nutrient-dense food is a priority for me, I budget for it. If you are not able to buy organic food, due to cost or availability, buying conventional produce, grains, beans, nuts, and seeds is still a healthier choice than not eating these foods at all.

PARCHMENT PAPER

Parchment paper (or baking paper) is a disposable paper that is manufactured to withstand high oven temperatures, and food does not stick to it. It is used in place of oil in preparing pans for foods that would otherwise stick, such as cookies, cakes, and roasted vegetables. Parchment paper is found near the aluminum foil in grocery stores. You can also buy parchment cupcake liners, which seem to work better than regular paper liners when cooking without oil. Silicone bakeware and mats are also available, and they are washable and reusable. Some people do get by with using high-quality, nonstick metal bakeware without parchment paper. Visit "Resources" at *StraightUpFood.com* to learn how to line a pan with parchment paper.

If you prefer not to expose your food to aluminum foil, look for Reynolds Wrap Pan Lining Paper, with foil on one side and parchment paper on the other.

PLANNING MEALS

There are many meal preparation suggestions that can be extremely helpful. Key among them are menu planning, shopping less frequently, using an organized shopping list, preparing key components on the weekend (or whenever there is more time), and cooking in double and triple batches. See page 200 for more suggestions on meal planning. Also, to see photos of my own simply prepared meals (mostly made without recipes), visit the "My Meals" section of my website *(StraightUpFood.com)* or visit my Facebook page and click "Photos" *(Facebook.com/StraightUpFood)*.

PROCESSED FOOD

Processed food—any food that has undergone a change of character—varies by type and degree. For example, corn can range from fresh on the cob (unprocessed) to corn flakes (highly processed), and nuts can range from raw in their shells (unprocessed) to roasted, salted, and sweetend (processed). We process food at home when we chop, blend, bake, or cook it, but this level of processing is usually much less than the processing done by food manufacturers.

The human body loves unprocessed and minimally processed foods—foods that are as close to how nature made them as possible. The recipes in this book call for a handful of processed store-bought foods, such as nondairy milk, corn tortillas, mustard, and baking powder, but the overall emphasis is on unprocessed or minimally processed foods, whenever possible.

QUINOA

Quinoa (pronounced "keen-wa"), a small seed native to South America, is usually counted as part of the grain family since it has a similar nutritional profile. It has a nutty, earthy flavor and can be used in place of rice, added to salads, or eaten as a hot breakfast cereal. It cooks up fluffy in 15 to 20 minutes (see page 30).

REFRIGERATING FOOD

Fresh foods do not contain the preservatives common to many packaged foods, so they do not stay fresh in the refrigerator as long. It depends on the food, but items such as homemade salad dressings, prepared salads (like potato salad), and beans do not stay fresh long, so I make a point to eat them within two to five days. Smelling food usually lets you know if it's too old. Certain foods do not require refrigeration, including whole onions, bananas, avocados (until they are very ripe), garlic, winter squashes, tomatoes, and potatoes (keep in a cool, dark cupboard). You can buy special bags made to keep produce fresher longer; just search "green produce bags" online.

SOAKING FOOD

I often soak nuts, seeds, and dates in water or nondairy milk to soften them so they will blend more easily. Most of my recipes call for a minimum soaking time of 15 minutes, but you can go longer if you like (if I soak anything overnight, I cover the bowl and put it in the refrigerator). If you have a high-powered blender, like a Vitamix, you can sometimes get away without soaking at all, but I usually soak my nuts and dates anyway to ensure a very smooth final texture. Denser nuts, such as almonds, require a longer soaking period than softer nuts like cashews and pecans. Dates can range from very soft to very hard (if they were stored in the refrigerator or freezer, or are just on the dry side) so feel free to adjust the soaking time based on the state of your dates.

SOS-FREE

"SOS-free" stands for salt-, oil-, and sugar-free. Foods and recipes considered SOS-free have become more popular with people who are striving to eliminate or drastically reduce their intake of these three ingredients. None of the recipes in this book calls for the addition of table salt or sea salt, or high-sodium products, such as soy sauce, tamari, or miso. All the packaged items in the recipes, such as canned beans, frozen vegetables, baking powder, and baking soda, can be found salt-free in stores or online. I do not use oil in these recipes. I also do not use any white or brown sugar or other concentrated sweeteners, such as honey, agave, or maple syrup. I use only fresh and dried fruit to add sweetness.

SOY

None of the recipes in this book calls for soy sauce since even the low-sodium variety is very high in salt, and also contains wheat (tamari is a soy sauce made with little or no wheat, but it's still very high in sodium). I do not use any soy-based margarine, mayonnaise, or oil. I also avoid highly processed soy foods, such as soy-based hot dogs, burgers, and cheeses. In addition, none of these recipes calls for any plain tofu since it's high in fat and I'm not a big fan of the taste. But feel free to use it if you like it (most likely in place of nuts or seeds in dressings or sauces). Just be sure to read the label to make sure it does not contain any undesirable ingredients.

SUGAR
I do not use refined and/or concentrated sweeteners in my recipes, such as white or brown sugar, honey, maple syrup, agave, molasses, corn syrup, and stevia. I instead sweeten my recipes with dates, bananas, applesauce, and raisins. Most often I use dates (Medjool or Deglet Noor) since they are so naturally high in sugar and taste so good (see Dates in this section).

SWEET POTATOES AND YAMS
Interestingly, sweet potatoes and yams are not related. They are two different species of root vegetable. The orange-reddish "yam" and the golden-tan sweet potato that we find in U.S. grocery stores are actually two different varieties of sweet potato, but the orange-red ones were named "yams" to distinguish the two. True yams, which we don't often see in the U.S., are native to Africa and Asia, and are large and starchy with brown, bark-like skin.

TAHINI
A new jar of tahini (sesame seed paste) will have a layer of oil on top due to separation after sitting. I pour this off and discard it instead of stirring it in. Look for tahini that has just one ingredient: ground sesame seeds.

VANILLA
I use both vanilla extract and vanilla beans/seeds in my recipes, but mostly the extract because it's more convenient. (Most extracts contain alcohol, but you can also find them alcohol-free.) Measurements for both options are provided in this book's ingredient lists (one teaspoon of extract is approximately equivalent to one vanilla bean's worth of seeds).

VEGETABLE BROTH
I use water instead of packaged vegetable broths in my savory recipes (soups, stews, and stovetop cooking) because it's convenient and inexpensive. Store-bought vegetable seasoning cubes or boxed broths are loaded with salt (even the low-sodium options), so I avoid them altogether. In my experience, by the time a dish is done cooking and all of the herbs, spices, and vegetables have intermingled for a while, the resulting flavor is delicious. However, see page 164 for a recipe if you'd like to make your own vegetable stock or broth ("broth" means that seasoning has been added; "stock" is without seasoning).

ZESTING
Zesting removes the very top layer of the peel from a lemon, orange, or lime. Citrus zest is used to add more flavor and aroma to a dish (be sure to zest your citrus before juicing it). There are a variety of zesting tools available, but my favorite is a very sharp, fine-toothed grater called a Microplane, which you can find wherever kitchen tools are sold. You can also use it to finely grind whole nutmeg and grate fresh ginger. (Some cheese graters also have a small-toothed section on the side that you can use for zesting, but they won't be as sharp as a Microplane.)

RECIPES

"You don't need to eat foods from animals to have enough protein in your diet. Plant proteins alone can provide enough of the essential and non-essential amino acids, as long as sources of dietary protein are varied and calorie intake is high enough to meet energy needs." —John McDougall, M.D., *The Starch Solution*

BREAKFAST

BREAKFAST BASICS

The key to a health-promoting breakfast is to find one that you love, and then eat it over and over. Most of my morning meals are fairly repetitive, and are based on a basic template of fruit and cooked whole-grain cereals.

- **Fruit:** Each morning I cut up a bowl of my favorite fruit: usually an apple and a banana, and sometimes one or two more pieces that look good at the grocery store or farmers' market, such as a peach, nectarine, pear, mango, kiwifruit, or some berries or pineapple.

- **Whole grains:** Each morning I also eat a bowl of hot whole-grain cereal. Many boxed (dry) cereals on the market advertise their health benefits (often derived from a handful of laboratory-synthesized vitamins and minerals), but in my efforts to move away from overly processed and packaged foods, dry cereals have given way to hot unprocessed or minimally processed grains, such as oatmeal, steel-cut oats, quinoa, buckwheat, millet, or brown rice. I add some cinnamon and nutmeg on top, and then pour on some nondairy milk (I vary here as well, with soy, rice, almond, pecan, or oat milk). Sometimes I eat my sliced fruit on top of my hot whole-grain cereal instead of having it separately. This hearty fruit and grain breakfast helps keep me full and satisfied until lunch.

- **Vegetables:** Some people like to take a more savory approach to breakfast, opting for a big bowl of vegetable soup, a baked potato or yam, a green salad, or steamed vegetables and greens (kale, chard, etc.), and that's fine. Consuming a varied plant-based diet *overall* is what counts most, not "balanced" individual meals. Your body doesn't care if you're having beets or bananas for breakfast. It takes in nutrients constantly, assimilates them as needed, and knows how to keep you healthy, as long as you provide it with its preferred fuel: unprocessed or minimally processed plant foods.

- **Special breakfasts:** I reserve more decadent breakfasts for special occasions, such as when family is visiting, around the holidays, or on the occasional Sunday morning. I might whip up a batch of pancakes, waffles, hash browns, or blueberry muffins, as well as some homemade ketchup or date syrup. You don't need to give up special breakfasts, but it's best to regard them as once-in-a-while treats since they are typically more processed and higher in calories.

- **Advance preparation:** If you find yourself saying, "I just don't have time for breakfast," try embracing a bit of planning (I know, "ugh," but it works). Decide the night before or even the week before what you'll be eating for breakfast, thereby eliminating any excuse for not eating a healthy morning meal. Or you can actually prepare your breakfast the night before so that in the morning you can eat it quickly at home or take it with you.

- **The bottom line:** The only real rule about breakfast is that it should be composed of plant foods that *you* enjoy eating. Experiment with the recipes and ideas in this chapter to discover what works best for your schedule and taste buds—and then keep making and eating those things over and over.

5-Minute Oatmeal (page 30) with bananas and strawberries

HOT WHOLE-GRAIN CEREALS

A bowl of hot whole-grain cereal in the morning can keep you full and satisfied until lunchtime, and there are many options to choose from.

I like to eat a variety of hot cereals, so I rotate between oatmeal, steel-cut oats, brown rice, and quinoa. And occasionally I cook up something a little different, like millet or amaranth. Some people like to eat the same hot whole-grain cereal (such as oatmeal) every single morning, and that is fine. But there are so many delicious hot cereal options out there that I encourage you to try some new ones.

I add cinnamon and nutmeg to the top of my hot cereal, as well as a bit of nondairy milk. Sometimes I'll add a tablespoon of chopped walnuts or ground flax seeds, or some raisins, sliced banana, or seasonal fruit. The combinations are endless.

I remember trying nondairy milk for the first time and thinking that it tasted odd. But the more I used it on my cereal, the more I got used to it, and now I love it (and it's much gentler on my stomach than cow's milk). The same thing happened with sugar:

my oatmeal tasted pretty bland without a little brown sugar or maple syrup added on top, but nowadays I don't miss it at all. The cinnamon, nutmeg, and sliced fruit are completely satisfying on their own.

On the following pages are descriptions of and cooking instructions for a variety of hot whole-grain cereals: oatmeal, quinoa, brown rice, millet, amaranth, and buckwheat (no glutenous grains, such as wheat, rye, or barley, have been included). The cereal grains will be sufficiently cooked when they are tender and all or most of the cooking liquid has been absorbed. Cooking times and measurements may vary slightly, depending on your stovetop, cookware, and personal tastes.

Each instruction yields about 1 cup of cooked cereal, enough for one hearty serving. You can find all of the dry/uncooked grains either in packages in the cereal or baking aisle or in the bulk-food section of your grocery store.

A special note about oats: Although oats do not contain gluten by nature, they can include trace amounts due to being processed in or around machinery that also processes glutenous grains, such as wheat. If you don't want to take the chance, buy "gluten-free" rolled oats and steel-cut oats.

Brown Rice (page 31) with raisins

5-MINUTE OATMEAL

This oatmeal is made with hearty "old-fashioned" rolled oats, which are processed by steaming oat groats and then rolling them flat, thereby making the dry oats easy to store and quick to prepare.

Bring **1¼ cups of water** to a boil in a medium saucepan over high heat, uncovered. Stir in **½ cup of old-fashioned rolled oats**. Reduce the heat to medium-low, then cover and simmer for 5 minutes or so. (For creamier oatmeal, bring the water and oats to a boil together at the start.) Makes 1 cup.

1-MINUTE OATMEAL

This oatmeal is made with "quick-cooking" oats, which are processed in the same way as old-fashioned oats but are rolled even thinner and then coarsely chopped, making

them even quicker to cook. ("Instant" oats, by comparison, are also rolled but are then cooked and dried. Instant oatmeal usually comes in individual packages with added sugar and salt, so it's best to avoid it.)

Bring **1 cup of water** to a boil in a medium saucepan over high heat, uncovered. Stir in **½ cup of quick-cooking oats**. Reduce the heat to medium-low, then cover and simmer for 1 minute or so. (For creamier oatmeal, bring the water and oats to a boil together at the start.) Makes about 1 cup.

STEEL-CUT OATMEAL

Steel-cut oats, also known as "Irish oats," are oat groats that have been chopped into pieces with steel blades (Scottish oats, by comparison, have been "ground" into a meal). Cooked steel-cut oatmeal results in a chewier texture than regular oatmeal.

Bring **1½ cups of water** and **⅓ cup of steel-cut oats** to a boil in a medium-large saucepan over high heat, uncovered. Reduce the heat to low, then cover and simmer for 25 minutes. I like to stir this oatmeal once toward the end since it tends to separate a little and stick to the bottom of the pan. I also like to use a larger saucepan to cook these oats since they love to boil up and over the edge, even on low heat. Makes about 1¼ cups.

QUINOA

The texture of cooked quinoa is light and fluffy, and the flavor is nutty and earthy. Quinoa can be found in different colors, including yellow, red, and black. Quinoa is especially popular with people who are gluten-free and seeking plant foods that are particularly high in protein.

Bring **1 cup of water** and **½ cup of dry/ uncooked quinoa** to a boil in a medium saucepan over high heat, uncovered. Reduce the heat to low, then cover and simmer for 20 minutes. Makes about 1 cup.

BROWN RICE

Brown rice is simply white rice that has not been milled, and therefore each grain retains its nutrient- and fiber-rich germ and bran. Eating brown rice for breakfast is highly underrated, in my opinion. People are often surprised that I eat rice for breakfast, but I love it because it has a naturally sweet taste, and it fills me up for quite a while.

Bring **1 cup of water** and **½ cup of dry/ uncooked brown rice** to a boil in a medium saucepan over high heat, uncovered. Reduce the heat to low, then cover and simmer for 45 minutes for long-grain rice or 50 minutes for short-grain rice. Remove it from the heat and let stand for 10 minutes with the lid still on, which makes the rice fluffier. Makes about 1¼ cups.

MILLET

Uncooked millet looks like small, yellow bird seed and, in fact, is a common ingredient in bird seed. But don't let that keep you from eating it. Millet cooks up fluffy with a slightly corn-like flavor and is very filling.

Bring **1 cup of water** and **⅓ cup of dry/ uncooked millet** to a boil in a medium saucepan over high heat, uncovered. Reduce the heat to low, then cover and simmer for 30 minutes. Makes about 1 cup.

AMARANTH

Amaranth is a tiny seed that when cooked has an earthy, nutty flavor. Cooked amaranth has a slippery yet slightly crunchy, pudding-like texture. Both the texture and flavor took me some time to get used to, but now I enjoy amaranth as part of my breakfast rotation.

Bring **1¼ cups of water** and **½ cup of dry/ uncooked amaranth** to a boil in a medium saucepan over high heat, uncovered. Reduce the heat to low, then cover and simmer for 25 minutes. Stir once or twice during cooking, since it tends to separate. Makes about 1¼ cups.

BUCKWHEAT

Buckwheat, which is not related to wheat, comes as toasted or untoasted (raw) groats. The toasted variety is known as "kasha." Both are fluffy and nutty in flavor when cooked, with the toasted type being especially flavorful.

Bring **¾ cup of water** to a boil in a medium saucepan over high heat, uncovered. Stir in **¼ cup of buckwheat groats**. Reduce the heat to low, then cover and simmer for 20 minutes. Makes about 1¼ cups.

From the blog

"New favorite way to make oatmeal! I used your recommended cardamom, added the dates, 1 grated apple, 1 chopped banana. Oh so good! Love the cardamom flavor!" —*Kristine*

BAKED OATMEAL WITH APPLES AND RAISINS

PREPARATION
about 15 minutes

COOKING TIME
30 minutes

SERVES
4 to 6 (or makes
16 snack bars)

Baked oatmeal is delicious for breakfast or as a snack bar when cooled. Baking oatmeal results in a spongy texture, much like bread pudding. It's easy to make and customize with your favorite fruits and spices.

Shopping tips: If you are using commercial nondairy milk, look for brands with the fewest ingredients and no added oil, salt, or sugar. Make sure your raisins have not had oil or sugar added to them.

2½ cups old-fashioned rolled oats

1¾ cups unsweetened nondairy milk (or water)

1 large apple, cored and chopped (peeled or unpeeled)

½ cup raisins

1½ teaspoons cinnamon

½ teaspoon ground nutmeg

1. Preheat the oven to 375°F. Line an 8×8-inch baking pan with parchment paper.

2. Stir all of the ingredients (oats, milk, apple, raisins, cinnamon, and nutmeg) together in a medium bowl.

3. Spread the batter evenly into the pan, and bake uncovered for 30 minutes or until lightly browned. To serve for breakfast, spoon into bowls with a little nondairy milk. To serve as snack bars, allow to cool completely before cutting into 16 squares.

NOTES

Instead of an apple, try a banana, pear, or a cup of pineapple, raspberries, strawberries, and/or blueberries.

To further sweeten this dish, blend 2 ounces pitted and quartered dates (3 to 4 Medjool or 6 to 8 Deglet Noor) with the nondairy milk before mixing.

A favorite variation of mine is to substitute 1½ cups of sliced strawberries and ¼ teaspoon of ground cardamom for the apple, raisins and nutmeg.

CREAMY RICE CEREAL

I loved creamy rice cereal when I was a kid. And until recently, I didn't know it was so easy to make, by simply grinding dry/uncooked brown rice in a blender (high-speed blenders work best for this). And it tastes just as good as I remember.

Shopping tips: If using commercial nondairy milk, look for brands with no added salt, oil, or sugar, and the fewest ingredients possible. Make sure your raisins have not had oil or sugar added to them.

PREPARATION
about 5 minutes

COOKING TIME
8 minutes

SERVES
2 (makes about 2 cups)

2 cups water

½ cup dry/uncooked brown rice

¼ cup raisins (optional)

1½ cups unsweetened nondairy milk (optional)

Sliced fruit of choice (optional)

Cinnamon and ground nutmeg (optional)

1. Place the water into a medium saucepan over medium-high heat.

2. Grind the rice in a high-speed blender until it resembles sand (beware: this gets loud!).

3. Gradually whisk the ground rice into the water just as it begins to boil. Immediately reduce the heat to low, add the raisins (if using), and cover. Cook for 5 to 8 minutes, stirring once or twice (if it is too thick, just stir in a bit more water). Serve plain or with nondairy milk, sliced fruit, cinnamon, and/or nutmeg.

NONDAIRY MILK

Nondairy milk describes any milk made from a plant. Any type of milk, whether animal or plant, is composed mostly of water, but it's the fat in milk that we crave most.

You can make nondairy milk from a wide variety of nuts, seeds, and grains. Some types of nondairy milk (such as almond and pecan) look just like cow's milk because they are high in fat and thus whiter in appearance. Other nondairy milks (such as oat and rice) have a thinner, more translucent appearance because they are lower in fat.

You may ask, "Why would I want to make my own nondairy milk when I can simply buy it?" There are two reasons: (1) homemade nondairy milk tastes better and is fresher than store-bought, and (2) you know exactly what's in it and what's not.

Additionally, many people choose to consume only nondairy milk because their digestive systems cannot break down lactose, the sugar found in cow's milk (this condition is called "lactose intolerance"). Other people abstain from cow's milk for ethical reasons, not wishing to participate in exploiting cows and their calves. A cow's breast milk is a substance that is neither nutritionally required nor beneficial for human health.

High-fat, high-protein cow's milk is specifically designed to quickly grow newborn calves, who will gain about a pound and a half per day and increase their weight by eight times or more in their first year. In reality, after calves (and all mammals, including humans) are weaned, they no longer have any nutritional need for their mother's breast milk.

Most grocery stores today carry at least a few types of nondairy milk, but it can be a challenge to find them without added salt, oil, sugar, or other additives. When I do buy nondairy milk from the store (usually sold in 32-ounce cartons), I read the ingredient list to find one that has the fewest ingredients. I most often end up buying any brand of soymilk that contains only organic soybeans and water. For people who avoid soy, however, this gets trickier, and making your own nondairy milk becomes an excellent alternative.

I primarily use nondairy milk as a condiment on hot grain cereals or in baked desserts, not as a stand-alone beverage. My guess is that you will love the taste of homemade nut, seed, and grain milks more than their store-bought versions. In general, I do my best to buy nuts and seeds that are unsalted, and if I can also find them raw (unroasted), this is an extra bonus. Following are the basics you'll need to know to make your own nondairy milk:

- **You'll need a strainer:** Some nondairy milks, such as almond milk, require straining (after soaking and blending) in order to separate the liquid from the pulp; but softer nuts and seeds, like cashews and sunflower seeds, do not require straining. I recommend a reusable nylon mesh nut-milk bag made just for this purpose, which you can order from my online store or find in natural grocery stores for around $10.

- **You'll need a blender:** High-speed blenders (like the Vitamix or Blendtec) work best for making nondairy milks, especially when using harder nuts, such as almonds. But you can also get by with a standard home blender; you may just need to blend your nuts or seeds a little longer.

- **You'll need a canning jar or other storage container:** For storing nondairy milk, I like to use a 32-ounce (4-cup) glass canning jar. I like these larger jars because they hold the same amount of nondairy milk as quart-sized cartons in the store. Any kitchen storage container will work, but I like the canning jars best.

- **You may want more flavor:** While almond and pecan milks have a naturally sweet flavor all on their own, other milks, such as grain milks, are less flavorful and may benefit from the addition of a half teaspoon of vanilla extract and/or a few dashes of cinnamon. Sometimes I also blend in half of a banana, a few strawberries, or a pitted date (you can do this before or after straining). Experiment and find the flavors that you like best.

- **You may be in a hurry:** When I have not planned ahead to soak and make nondairy milk, and discover only in the morning— when I need it—that I am out, I blend up a whole or partial batch without soaking first. But soaking is the preferred method because it allows for increased absorption of nutrients, aids in digestibility, and lends itself to more complete blending.

Almond Milk (page 37) with nut-milk bag

ALMOND OR PECAN MILK

My favorite nuts to use, when making nondairy milk, are almonds and pecans. They have a naturally sweet flavor and are bright white in color, which makes them an excellent first-time nondairy milk choice for people who have only ever had cow's milk.

Shopping tips: Look for nuts that are unsalted and unroasted. Almonds with brown skins are fine since the skins will be separated out after blending and straining.

PREPARATION
about 5 minutes
(not counting
soak time)

COOKING TIME
0 minutes

MAKES
about 4½ cups

2½ ounces almonds or pecans (or about ½ cup)

1 cup water (for soaking)

4 cups water (for blending)

1. If using almonds, place them into a small bowl with 1 cup of water, then cover and let soak in the refrigerator overnight. If using pecans (which are a softer nut), place them into a small bowl with 1 cup of water, then let soak for an hour or two.

2. Drain off and discard the soak water, and place the nuts into a blender with 4 cups of fresh water. Blend on high speed for 30 to 60 seconds until the nuts are thoroughly broken down.

3. Hold a nut-milk bag over a large bowl and pour the water-nut mixture through the bag. Squeeze the bag (gently at first when full), wringing it until all of the water has filtered through and only the dry, chalky pulp is left. Discard the pulp (or see Notes at right).

4. Pour the bowl of milk into a 32-ounce canning jar or other container. Taste it, and if it's too rich, add some water; if it's not rich enough, make a note for next time to use less water. It will keep for about four days in the refrigerator. The milk will have separated after sitting so be sure to shake it well before using.

NOTES

I don't usually save my pulp, but if you're interested in finding a use for yours, search "uses for nut milk pulp" online.

Other nuts and seeds. For other nuts, try walnuts, hazelnuts, pistachios, and cashews. For seeds, try sunflower, sesame, and hemp. Use the same process above, and find the balance of water and nuts/seeds that tastes best to you.

OAT OR RICE MILK

The difference between nut or seed milk and grain milk is that grain milk is lower in fat (and calories) and the color is not as white. On the plus side, grain milk is cheaper to make than nut milk, and it is a great option for people who must avoid nuts and/or seeds in their diet. The recipe below explains how to make oat milk, with instructions on how to make rice milk in step 5.

PREPARATION
about 20 minutes

COOKING TIME
0 minutes

MAKES
4 cups oat milk
6 cups rice milk

¼ cup steel-cut oats, rinsed

4 cups water

½ teaspoon vanilla extract (or seeds from ½ vanilla bean)

1. Place the oats and water into a blender, and set aside for at least 15 minutes.

2. Blend on high speed for 20 to 30 seconds.

3. Hold a nut-milk bag over a large bowl and pour the water-oat mixture through the bag. Squeeze the bag (gently at first when full), wringing until all the water has filtered through. Discard any pulp or residue that remains.

4. Pour the bowl of oat milk into a 32-ounce canning jar (or other storage container). Taste it, and if it's too rich or thick, add some water; if it's not rich or thick enough, make a note for next time to add less water. Add the vanilla, and stir. It will keep for about four days in the refrigerator. The milk will have separated after sitting so shake it well before using.

5. To make rice milk, place 1 cup of *cooked* brown rice (see Note) into a blender with 6 cups of water and blend thoroughly. After straining through the nut-milk bag, pour into two canning jars or other storage containers.

NOTE

To make 1 cup of cooked brown rice, bring ½ cup of dry/uncooked brown rice and 1 cup of water to a boil in a medium saucepan over high heat, uncovered. Reduce the heat to low, then cover and simmer for 45 minutes for long-grain rice or 50 minutes for short-grain rice. Remove from the heat and let stand for 10 minutes with the lid still on.

GRANOLA

Finding commercial granola that does not contain oil is nearly impossible. This is a food that can be perfectly delicious, and still crunchy, without added oil. Making your own homemade granola is easy, and you don't even need a food dehydrator. Serve over hot cereal or with fruit.

Shopping tips: Look for dates in the bulk food section or packaged near the raisins. Make sure your raisins have not had oil or sugar added to them.

PREPARATION
about 15 minutes

COOKING TIME
55 minutes

SERVES
4 to 6 (makes
about 3½ cups)

½ cup water

4 ounces pitted dates (7 to 8 Medjool or 14 to 16 Deglet Noor), chopped

1½ teaspoons vanilla extract (or seeds from 1 to 2 vanilla beans)

1¼ teaspoons cinnamon

½ teaspoon ground nutmeg

2 cups old-fashioned rolled oats

½ cup raisins

½ cup sliced almonds (optional)

1. Place the water, dates, vanilla, cinnamon, and nutmeg into a blender and set aside for at least 15 minutes (so the dates can soften).

2. Preheat the oven to 250°F. Line two baking sheets with parchment paper, and set them aside.

3. Combine the oats, raisins, and almonds (if using) in a medium bowl.

4. Blend the dates, vanilla, cinnamon, and nutmeg until smooth. Pour this into the bowl of oats, raisins, and nuts, and stir well.

5. Spread the granola evenly between the two baking sheets, breaking up any large clumps. Bake for 30 minutes.

6. Remove the baking sheets from the oven and shuffle the granola around with a spatula. Return to the oven (but switch racks for even browning) for 20 to 25 minutes more, or until lightly browned. Completely cool the granola for maximum crunchiness.

NOTE
Try unsweetened fruit juice (orange, tangerine, or apple) instead of water for added sweetness and flavor.

From the blog

"Making hash browns this way is a real game changer! I wouldn't have thought to use a spiralizer, but it makes all the difference. Thank you!" —*Tiffany*

OIL-FREE HASH BROWNS

Hash browns are typically fried in oil, but eliminating the oil is easy when you use a quality nonstick pan and know the best way to cut the potatoes. You can grate the potatoes, as is traditional, but using a spiral vegetable cutter (see Note) is the best way to go. This recipe yields two moderate servings but double the recipe for two large servings (each filling a dinner plate).

PREPARATION
about 5 minutes

COOKING TIME
10 to 14 minutes

SERVES
2 (makes 2
hash browns)

2 small Yukon Gold potatoes (about 3 inches long), peeled
Better Ketchup (optional; page 152)
½ medium, ripe avocado, sliced (optional)
Ground black pepper

1. Slice each peeled potato by using the coarse blade of a spiral vegetable cutter (see Note) or grate the potatoes using the larger holes on a traditional cheese grater. Pat dry the cut potatoes between two paper towels to remove most of the moisture (this will help prevent sticking and will promote browning).

2. Preheat a large nonstick frying pan to medium heat (no oil or water is needed). Place the sliced or grated potatoes into the hot frying pan, spreading the sliced potatoes evenly into a 1-inch layer or the grated potatoes into a ½-inch layer.

3. Cook for 5 to 7 minutes with the lid partially off (this promotes thorough cooking and a crisp surface), occasionally lifting a corner of the hash browns with a spatula to make sure they're not getting too brown (if so, reduce the heat). When the hash browns are a medium brown, flip them and cook for 5 to 7 minutes more, still with the lid partially off. As with the first side, check the underside occasionally so it does not overbrown.

4. Serve immediately, seasoned with a little pepper. A side of ketchup and sliced avocado also adds a bit of richness and flavor.

NOTE
Spiral vegetable slicers can cut any firm fruit or vegetable (apples, carrots, beets, zucchini) into a variety of ribbon-like widths, but they really shine with potatoes on their way to becoming hash browns. The sliced potatoes cook up lighter since air can more easily move between the strands, thereby avoiding the gluey texture of traditional hash browns. The slicer I use is in my online store, the Benriner Cook Helper Slicer ($33), but many other brands are also available.

OATMEAL-LEMON PANCAKES

So many of my students say they like these pancakes even more than "regular" pancakes, and now these *are* their regular pancakes. These cakes rise nicely and fill your kitchen with a wonderful lemony aroma. For best results, read the tips on page 43 first.

Shopping tips: To avoid excess sodium, use sodium-free baking powder and soda. Look for dates in the bulk food section or packaged near the raisins. If you are using commercial nondairy milk, look for brands with the fewest ingredients, as well as no added oil, salt, or sugar.

PREPARATION
about 20 minutes

COOKING TIME
2 to 4 minutes per pancake

SERVES
2 to 4 (makes about 12 small or 6 larger pancakes)

2 cups unsweetened nondairy milk (plus more to thin batter as it sits)
2 ounces pitted dates (3 to 4 Medjool or 6 to 8 Deglet Noor), chopped
1½ cups old-fashioned rolled oats
½ cup cornmeal
1½ teaspoons baking powder
½ teaspoon baking soda
½ teaspoon cinnamon
1 tablespoon lemon zest (from 1 medium lemon; see Pancake Tips on next page)
3 tablespoons lemon juice
Sliced fruit, such as bananas, strawberries, or blueberries, to top pancakes (optional)
Finely chopped walnuts to top pancakes (optional)
1 recipe Strawberry-Date Syrup (optional; page 50)

1. Place the nondairy milk and dates into a small bowl, and set aside for 15 minutes (so the dates can soften).

2. Grind the rolled oats into flour with a blender. Transfer to a medium bowl, and whisk in the cornmeal, baking powder, baking soda, and cinnamon. Heat a nonstick frying pan or griddle to medium heat (not high).

3. Pour the soaking dates and milk into the blender, and blend until smooth.

4. Add this mixture to the bowl of dry ingredients, along with the lemon juice and zest, and whisk until smooth.

5. When a water droplet sputters on the surface of the frying pan or griddle, it is ready: pour ¼ to ½ cup of the batter onto the surface (no oil is needed), and cook until bubbles form around the edges and on top, and the underside is medium brown (1 to 2 minutes). Flip the pancake and cook for another 1 to 2 minutes. (As the batter sits, it may thicken so add a little more milk as needed.)

6. Serve pancakes immediately with one or all of the optional toppings: sliced fruit, chopped walnuts, and/or Strawberry-Date Syrup.

PANCAKE TIPS

- **Use a high-quality, nonstick frying pan** for these pancakes, since there is no oil in the batter or on the pan's surface to help prevent sticking. A quality nonstick pan also produces more evenly cooked and browned pancakes.

- **If you do not have (or do not want to use) nonstick cookware,** you can also bake the pancakes in the oven. Line a baking sheet with parchment paper, and bake at 400°F for 5 to 10 minutes before flipping them and baking for another 5 to 10 minutes. Baking does not yield the same deep brown color that you get from using the frying pan, but the pancakes will still taste great.

- **Use a silicone (not plastic) spatula** with a large, flat surface and tapered edge for best pancake-flipping results.

- **To zest a lemon,** use a very fine-toothed grater (a Microplane), grating or "zesting" only the yellow outer skin while avoiding the white pith below it. Be sure to always zest your citrus before juicing it.

From the blog

"My five-year-old, three-year-old, and I loved these pancakes! I cooked all of them at one time, even though we didn't eat them all in one sitting. I left them on the counter to cool, and all morning the kids kept running by for a 'fly-by' bite." —*Monica*

WAFFLES

Making waffles without oil is pretty unheard of, but oil-free waffles are indeed possible and completely delicious. This recipe works for both classic (small-well) and Belgian (large-well) waffle irons. Before you begin, review the recipe and the Waffle Tips on the next page.

Shopping tips: To avoid excess sodium, use sodium-free baking powder. Look for dates in the bulk food section or packaged near the raisins.

PREPARATION
about 20 minutes

COOKING TIME
3 to 5 minutes per waffle (depending on type/size)

SERVES
2 to 3 (for 6-inch waffles, makes 5 to 6 classic or 3 to 4 Belgian)

2 cups unsweetened nondairy milk (plus more to thin batter as it sits)

1 ounce pitted dates (2 Medjool or 4 Deglet Noor), chopped

1 ounce raw, unsalted cashews (about ¼ cup) or 2 tablespoons almond butter

1½ cups old-fashioned rolled oats

½ cup cornmeal

2 teaspoons baking powder

½ teaspoon cinnamon

Sliced fruit, such as bananas, strawberries, and/or blueberries, to top waffles (optional)

1 recipe Strawberry-Date Syrup (optional; page 50)

Extra cashews to grate on top (optional; see Note)

1. Place the nondairy milk, dates, and cashews or almond butter into a small bowl, and set aside for at least 15 minutes (so the dates and nuts can soften).

2. Grind the rolled oats into flour with a blender. Transfer to a medium bowl, and whisk in the cornmeal, baking powder, and cinnamon. Plug in your waffle iron and set it to medium or medium-high (I use a 6-inch, round waffle iron with this recipe).

3. Pour the soaking ingredients (milk, dates, and cashews or almond butter) into the blender, and blend until smooth.

4. Add this mixture to the bowl of dry ingredients and whisk until smooth. Allow the batter to rest for one minute. (Add a little milk, as needed, between cooking the waffles, as the batter will thicken.)

5. Pour ½ to ¾ cup of batter into the center of a heated waffle iron for classic waffles or ¾ to 1 cup for Belgian waffles; no oil is needed on the irons. Close the lid and cook until the indicator light shows that they have finished cooking (refer to your waffle iron's manual). All waffle irons will vary slightly, but generally classic waffles cook in 3 to 4 minutes and Belgian waffles in 4 to 5 minutes (see Waffle Tips on next page).

6. Serve immediately, topped with sliced fruit, Strawberry-Date Syrup, and/or grated nuts.

NOTE
Use a rotary cheese grater to grate some cashews (or any nut) on top of your cooked waffles for a little extra richness without going overboard on fat.

WAFFLE TIPS

While I have seen many no-oil waffle recipes, that description usually applies to the batter only, not the waffle iron. Some cooks still spray or rub their waffle iron with a little cooking oil, but if you're trying to avoid all oil, that won't do. The addition of cashews or almond butter in this recipe helps to keep the waffles from sticking, but you may want to consider these tips for greater success:

- **Use a waffle iron with a nonstick coating,** preferably an iron that has never been oiled before (since the oily residue may encourage sticking). If you have a nonstick waffle iron that is very old, consider buying a new one, as they're pretty inexpensive (about $35). Waffle iron instructions usually say to oil the surface the first time but disregard that.

- **Read the manufacturer's instructions** to get a more accurate estimate of how long waffles should take to cook in your particular unit. Each waffle iron is a little bit different.

- **Set the heat at medium.** Each waffle iron is different so experiment with the heat setting that works best for yours. Mine has five heat settings (5 is hottest), and I find that setting it to 4 works best.

- **To promote easier removal,** pour in just enough batter so that the edges of the waffle come to the edge of the iron without spilling over (otherwise the waffle becomes tricky to remove, and may want to split in half).

- **When the "done" light comes on, lift the lid slowly (beware of escaping steam).** If it just doesn't want to open, give it another 30 to 60 seconds and then try again. Even when the waffles are done, sometimes the lid still requires a firm tug to get it to separate from the waffle since we are not using oil. Slightly overbaked waffles are preferable to underbaked waffles (which can result in a gooey, sticky mess).

- **Always be prepared with a fork to help release the waffle from the iron.** Your waffles may stick a little, and the halves may start to come apart. Gently pry the edge of the stuck side off the iron with a fork, and the two sides will fall back together and still taste great.

- **To keep your waffles warm as you make them,** transfer them to a baking rack in the oven, set to 250°F.

- **Have patience,** and find the amount of batter and the heat setting that work best for your taste and your waffle iron, and make a note for next time.

POTATO-VEGGIE SCRAMBLE

This scramble makes a hearty, colorful breakfast. I usually make this for special occasion breakfasts since it takes some time to prepare.

Shopping tips: To avoid excess sodium, look for canned beans with no added salt (or cook your beans from scratch). Instead of buying ketchup and salsa, which are full of salt and/or sugar, consider making your own ketchup (page 152) and salsa (page 153).

PREPARATION
about 35 minutes

COOKING TIME
35 minutes (baking potatoes), 10 minutes (stovetop)

SERVES
4 (makes about 8 cups)

1½ pounds white potatoes, unpeeled, cut into ½-inch cubes (about 4½ cups)

1 medium yellow or white onion, chopped (about 2 cups)

1 medium red bell pepper, seeded and chopped (about 1½ cups)

5 medium white or cremini mushrooms, sliced (about 2 cups)

1½ teaspoons finely chopped garlic (about 2 medium cloves)

1 tablespoon dried Italian herb seasoning

1 teaspoon paprika or smoked paprika

1 can cooked navy or other white beans (15 ounces; about 1½ cups), drained and rinsed

1 cup halved cherry or grape tomatoes

3 cups packed spinach leaves or coarsely chopped Swiss chard

Better Ketchup (page 152) and/or Fresh Tomato Salsa (page 153) (optional)

1. Preheat the oven to 400°F. Line a large baking sheet with parchment paper.

2. Spread the potatoes out evenly on the baking sheet and bake for 15 minutes. Remove from the oven and flip the potatoes with a spatula (this does not have to be precise). Return to the oven, and bake for 20 to 25 minutes more, or until tender and lightly browned.

3. About 10 minutes before the potatoes are done, place 1 tablespoon of water into a frying pan over medium-high heat. When the water starts to sputter, add the onion, bell pepper, and mushrooms, and cook while stirring for about 3 minutes. Stir in the garlic, Italian seasoning, and paprika, adding a little water, as needed, to prevent sticking.

4. Decrease the heat to medium-low and stir in the beans, tomatoes, and greens. Cover and cook for 5 minutes, or until the greens have wilted, stirring once or twice. Toss in the hot cooked potatoes last, and serve immediately as is or with Better Ketchup and/or Fresh Tomato Salsa.

NOTE
This scramble is also delicious served in steamed corn tortillas topped with salsa and avocado.

BLUEBERRY MUFFINS

Lemon zest and ground cardamom give these muffins a dreamy flavor and aroma. Oat and millet flours produce a muffin that is hearty and filling while dates and applesauce lend sweetness and moistness without refined sugar and oil.

Shopping tips: To avoid excess sodium, use sodium-free baking powder. Look for dates in the bulk food section or packaged near the raisins. If you are using commercial nondairy milk, look for brands with the fewest ingredients, as well as no added oil, salt, or sugar.

PREPARATION
about 25 minutes

COOKING TIME
30 minutes

MAKES
12 muffins

8 ounces pitted dates (12 to 14 Medjool or 24 to 28 Deglet Noor), chopped

1¼ cups unsweetened nondairy milk

1½ cups old-fashioned rolled oats

¾ cup dry/uncooked millet

2 teaspoons baking powder

½ teaspoon ground cardamom (or see Notes)

½ cup applesauce

1 teaspoon lemon zest (see Notes)

1 cup fresh or unthawed frozen blueberries (to go into batter)

2 ounces walnuts, chopped (about ½ cup; optional)

½ cup fresh or unthawed frozen blueberries (to go on top)

1. Place the dates and nondairy milk into a small bowl, and set aside for at least 15 minutes (so the dates can soften).

2. Preheat the oven to 350°F. Line a standard 12-cup muffin tray with paper cupcake liners (parchment paper liners are preferable).

3. Grind the rolled oats and millet into flour with a blender (30 to 40 seconds; millet is hard). Transfer to a medium bowl, and whisk in the baking powder and cardamom.

4. Pour the soaking dates and milk into the blender, and blend until smooth.

5. Pour the date mixture into the bowl of dry ingredients, add the applesauce and lemon zest, and mix just until all the dry ingredients have disappeared (the batter will be thick).

6. Gently fold in the blueberries and chopped walnuts (if using). Don't overmix or you'll have purple muffins.

7. Fill each muffin cup with an even amount of batter. Use the ½ cup of extra blueberries to top each muffin with a few just before baking (make sure to push them in at least halfway so they won't roll off during rising).

8. Bake for 25 to 30 minutes until the tops have begun to brown. (These are hearty muffins, so they will not rise very much.) Set aside to cool before serving.

NOTES

If you do not have cardamom, you can use 1½ teaspoons of cinnamon instead.

To zest a lemon, use a very fine-toothed grater (like a Microplane), grating or "zesting" only the yellow outer skin, avoiding the white pith below it.

From the blog

"These muffins are super flavorful! I love the crunchiness of the millet. I have made them twice so far, and both times they were a big hit with family and friends!" —*J. Lavin*

STRAWBERRY-DATE SYRUP

PREPARATION
about 20 minutes

COOKING TIME
0 minutes

SERVES
4 (makes about
2 cups)

I love this syrup on pancakes and waffles because it's sweet but not "tooth-tingling" sweet like maple syrup. It also works well with a variety of fresh fruits (see Notes).

Shopping tip: Look for dates in the bulk food section or packaged near the raisins.

1½ cups water

4 ounces pitted dates (7 to 8 Medjool or 14 to 16 Deglet Noor), chopped

½ cup sliced strawberries

1. Place the water, dates, and strawberries into a blender, and set aside for at least 15 minutes (so the dates can soften).

2. Blend until a smooth, pourable consistency is reached (add more water, as needed, to thin, but the syrup will thicken as it sits). Serve over pancakes (page 42) and waffles (page 44).

NOTES

Instead of water, you may also use fruit juice (or a mixture); I love fresh tangerine juice in this syrup.

Instead of strawberries, try raspberries, blueberries, kiwifruit, peaches, and mango.

Use any leftover syrup over fruit or oatmeal.

SALADS

SALAD BASICS

Salads can be almost any combination of raw and/or cooked plant foods. I offer many delicious salad recipes in this chapter. But if you're like me, most of the time you just throw together salads based on what you have at home, so here are a few tips along these lines.

Simple is okay: Don't skip eating a salad because you have only a few ingredients on hand—simple salads are delicious. For example, romaine lettuce with some sliced cucumber and cherry tomatoes, dressed with a squeeze of lime juice is very tasty (see page 73 for tips on making your own dressings). Even if you don't have lettuce, you can still make a chunky "lettuce-less" salad by chopping up ingredients such as cucumber, radish, carrots, and cabbage, and adding a handful of garbanzo beans.

Mix it up: Avoid getting in a salad rut by mixing up your usual ingredients. When it comes to salad greens, for example, vary between romaine, butter, and red-leaf lettuces (or mix them), and occasionally add some spinach leaves, arugula, baby beet greens, or chopped kale as a secondary green. If you always buy green bell peppers, try a red or orange one (green bell peppers are less ripe; you'll find the red and orange peppers much sweeter). And every once in a while, choose a salad ingredient that you've never tried before.

Plan ahead: Many people find that washing and portioning their lettuce (or all of their salad ingredients) when they get home from the grocery store, makes salad preparation much easier in the days to follow. Another way to go is to make two servings each time you prepare a salad; you will be *thrilled* at your next meal that you don't have to drag all the bags of produce out of the fridge again.

Make a "main-dish" salad: I often eat a salad by itself as a meal by making it a bit larger and adding some hearty ingredients, such as cooked beans (black beans and garbanzo beans are my favorites), cooked long-grain brown rice or quinoa, a chopped leftover baked potato or yam, or a toasted corn tortilla cut into bite-size pieces.

Add a little sweetness: Don't be afraid to add a little sweetness to your salads. Sliced apples, pears, or strawberries are wonderful. A sectioned grapefruit or orange can be very tasty while at the same time adding a light dressing. A little sliced mango, nectarine, or pineapple can also be fun, and don't forget about grapes, blueberries, and raspberries.

Vary how you cut your vegetables: Preparing your salad vegetables in different shapes and sizes can really perk up your salads. Instead of cutting your carrots into discs, try grating them, peeling them right into your salad (with a vegetable peeler), or using a spiral slicer to make "carrot ribbons." We adults tend to forget that the shape of our food can produce a different appeal, but kids have always known this.

BURRITO BOWL

Burrito bowls have come into fashion as more people cut out refined carbohydrates, in this case the flour tortilla. This filling dish can be a meal in itself. It is flavorful, colorful, easy to make, and the simple lime juice dressing is just right. (See photo on page 3.)

Shopping tip: To avoid excess sodium, look for canned beans with no added salt (or cook your beans from scratch).

PREPARATION
about 20 minutes

COOKING TIME
45 minutes
(to cook rice)

SERVES
4 to 6 (makes
about 12 cups)

2 cups water

1 cup dry/uncooked long-grain brown rice (or 3 cups cooked)

4 cups thinly sliced romaine lettuce

1 can cooked black beans (15 ounces; about 1½ cups), drained and rinsed

1 cup thinly sliced green cabbage

1 cup chopped tomatoes (I like halved cherry or plum tomatoes)

1 cup corn kernels (thaw first if frozen)

1 cup loosely packed cilantro, coarsely chopped

½ cup finely chopped red onion

1 medium, ripe avocado, chopped (optional)

⅓ cup lime juice

1. Bring the water and uncooked rice to a boil in a medium saucepan over high heat, uncovered. Reduce the heat to low, then cover and cook for 45 minutes. Remove from the heat and let stand for 10 minutes with the lid still on.

2. Toss the rice, lettuce, beans, cabbage, tomatoes, corn, cilantro, onion, avocado (if using), and lime juice together in a large bowl (the cooked rice and beans may be added warm or cold).

NOTES

When tomatoes aren't in season and don't taste very good, you can substitute 1 medium red bell pepper, seeded and chopped (about 1½ cups).

If you have access to fresh, organic corn, cut the kernels right from the cob. They do not need to be cooked; raw corn is delicious!

For cilantro objectors, feel free to substitute fresh basil or parsley.

If you are making this recipe ahead of time, add the avocado and lime juice closer to serving time.

FRUIT SALAD WITH FRESH MINT

PREPARATION
about 15 minutes

COOKING TIME
0 minutes

SERVES
2 to 4 (makes
about 5 cups)

If you've never had fresh mint in your fruit salad, you are in for a treat! This is the recipe I use at home, which makes about 5 cups; but if I'm going to a potluck or picnic, I will double it. Below the recipe is a list of fruits and "extras" so you can create your own unique fruit salads.

1 cup cubed watermelon (remove any seeds)

1 apple, cored and chopped (peeled or unpeeled)

1 orange, peeled and chopped (remove any seeds)

1 cup fresh blueberries

1 cup sliced strawberries

1 peach or nectarine, pitted and chopped

1 large kiwifruit, peeled and chopped

1½ teaspoons finely chopped fresh mint

1. Toss the watermelon, apple, orange, blueberries, strawberries, peach or nectarine, kiwifruit, and mint together in a large bowl. Eat within one or two days.

FRUIT OPTIONS:

apples, apricots, bananas, blackberries, blueberries, cantaloupe, cherries, figs, grapefruit, grapes, kiwifruit, mango, nectarines, oranges, papaya, peaches, pears, persimmons, plums, pomegranates, raspberries, strawberries, tangerines, watermelon

FRUIT SALAD EXTRAS:

Other herb options: Add 1 to 2 tablespoons of finely chopped fresh basil or parsley.

Zest: Add some freshly grated ginger, or lemon or lime zest to your salad (a little goes a long way). A Microplane grater (which has very small but sharp holes) works best for zesting. Be sure to always zest your citrus before juicing it.

Spices: Sprinkle a little ground cinnamon, nutmeg, allspice, pumpkin pie spice, or Chinese 5-spice on your fruit salad.

For a light, juicy dressing, stir 1 to 2 tablespoons of orange, lime, grapefruit, tangerine, or lemon juice into your fruit salad. (Meyer lemons are extra flavorful.)

CABBAGE SALAD WITH MUSTARD-LIME DRESSING

This modest-sounding salad always gets rave reviews in my classes. The beans and thinly sliced cabbage create a hearty salad, and the light dressing is simple yet flavorful.

Shopping tip: To avoid excess sodium, look for canned beans with no added salt (or cook your beans from scratch).

PREPARATION
about 25 minutes

COOKING TIME
0 minutes

SERVES
6 (makes about ⅔ cup dressing and 10 cups salad)

For the salad:

4 cups thinly sliced green cabbage

2 cups grated carrots (about 2 medium)

1 can cooked garbanzo beans (15 ounces; about 1½ cups), drained and rinsed

1 medium red bell pepper, seeded and chopped (about 1½ cups)

1 medium cucumber, peeled or unpeeled and sliced (about 2 cups)

2 ribs celery, sliced (about ⅔ cup)

3 green onions, white and green parts, thinly sliced

¼ cup chopped fresh basil

1 medium, ripe avocado, chopped (optional)

Mustard-Lime Dressing:

½ cup lime juice

¼ cup mustard (I like Dijon or stone ground)

1 medium clove garlic

1. Place the cabbage, carrots, beans, bell pepper, cucumber, celery, green onions, basil, and avocado (if using) into a large bowl.

2. Place the dressing ingredients (lime juice, mustard, and garlic) into a blender, and blend until smooth.

3. Toss the dressing and the salad.

NOTE
To create an even more colorful salad, substitute 1 cup of red cabbage for 1 cup of the green cabbage.

From the blog

"My kids and I had this for lunch today, and it was soooo good! Amazingly fresh and flavorful, perfect for a hot summer day! And it was quick and easy to throw together; I love that!" —Talia

SPINACH-MANGO SALAD

This light, colorful, and fruity spinach salad is a refreshing alternative to everyday green salads. It calls for fresh fennel, which can be found at most grocery stores. Fennel has a distinctive flavor reminiscent of black licorice, that pairs nicely with the mango and lime juice.

PREPARATION
about 25 minutes

COOKING TIME
0 minutes

SERVES
4 to 6 (makes about 9 cups)

6 cups baby spinach leaves (loosely packed)

2 cups baby arugula leaves (loosely packed)

1 large mango, peeled, seeded, and chopped

1 grapefruit, peeled and cut into sections (with seeds removed)

1 medium cucumber, peeled or unpeeled and sliced (about 2 cups)

½ cup thinly sliced fresh fennel

2 green onions, white and green parts, sliced

¼ cup finely chopped fresh basil

1 medium, ripe avocado, chopped (optional)

1 tablespoon vinegar (I like apple cider)

¼ cup lime juice

1. Thoroughly wash the spinach and arugula, pat it dry with paper towels, and place it into a large bowl. (If you are not using baby spinach and baby arugula, you may want to coarsely chop larger leaves.)

2. Add the mango, grapefruit, cucumber, fennel, green onion, basil, and avocado (if using) to the bowl of spinach and arugula. Add the vinegar and lime juice, and toss.

NOTES

Arugula is a peppery-tasting salad green that can be found in loose-leaf form or bunches in most produce sections. If you cannot locate any, use more spinach in its place.

If you cannot find fresh fennel, you may substitute with celery. I like using a small handheld or regular sized mandolin to achieve very thin slices of fennel and celery.

TU-NO SALAD

Garbanzo beans are an ideal substitute for canned tuna when it comes to creating a health-promoting tuna salad. You can serve this salad by itself or on top of a green or spinach salad, spooned into romaine or endive leaves, or as a filling in steamed corn tortillas.

Shopping tip: To avoid excess sodium, look for canned beans with no added salt (or cook your beans from scratch).

PREPARATION
about 25 minutes

COOKING TIME
0 minutes

SERVES
4 to 6 (makes about 1 cup dressing and 5 cups salad)

For the salad:

2 cans cooked garbanzo beans (15 ounces each; about 3 cups total), drained and rinsed

3 ribs celery, sliced or chopped (about 1 cup)

¼ cup finely chopped red onion

¼ cup finely chopped fresh basil

1 medium, ripe avocado, chopped (optional)

Cashew-Mustard Dressing:

½ cup water

2 ounces raw, unsalted cashews (about ½ cup)

3 tablespoons lemon juice

2 tablespoons mustard (I like Dijon or stone ground)

2 teaspoons vinegar (I like apple cider)

1 medium clove garlic

2 to 3 teaspoons kelp granules (optional; see Notes)

1. Place all of the dressing ingredients (water, cashews, lemon juice, mustard, vinegar, garlic, and kelp, if using) into a blender, and set aside for at least 15 minutes (so the cashews can soften).

2. Place the garbanzo beans into a food processor and pulse until the beans are broken but still flaky (do not overblend). Transfer the beans to a large bowl and add the celery, red onion, basil, and avocado (if using).

3. Blend the dressing ingredients until smooth, adding a little water as needed. Stir the dressing into the salad. Serve as is or see the serving suggestions above.

NOTES

Adding kelp granules lends a seafood flavor to this salad (although it's great without it, too). You can find kelp granules in the spice aisle of the grocery store.

For a lower-fat dressing, substitute ¾ to 1 cup cooked white beans for the cashews.

From the blog

"I rate my recipes with 3, 4, or 5 stars so that I can recall how much I liked them. I literally gave this recipe 500 stars!" —Tom

CAESAR-Y SALAD

Caesar salad is traditionally made with many ingredients that are not particularly health-promoting, mainly eggs, cheese, oil, salt, anchovies, and oil-soaked croutons. This recipe shows that you can still enjoy the tangy, sweet flavors of this beloved salad in good health.

PREPARATION
about 20 minutes

COOKING TIME
0 minutes

SERVES
4 to 6 (makes about 9 cups salad and 1 cup dressing)

For the salad:

1 large head romaine lettuce (about ¾ pound), coarsely chopped

1 medium red bell pepper, seeded and chopped (about 1½ cups)

1 medium, ripe avocado, chopped (optional)

1 ounce raw, unsalted cashews or walnuts, ground (about ¼ cup; for optional garnish)

Ground black pepper

For the dressing:

½ cup water

2 ounces raw, unsalted cashews (about ½ cup)

2 tablespoons lemon juice

2 tablespoons mustard (I like Dijon or stone ground)

1 tablespoon raisins

1 medium clove garlic

1 teaspoon dried Italian herb seasoning

1. Place all of the dressing ingredients (water, cashews, lemon juice, mustard, raisins, garlic, and herbs) into a blender, and set aside for 15 minutes (so the cashews can soften).

2. Place the lettuce, bell pepper, and avocado (if using) into a large salad bowl.

3. Blend the dressing ingredients until smooth. Pour the dressing over the salad and toss well. Season with pepper to taste, and garnish with ground cashews or walnuts, if desired (see Notes).

NOTES

For a lower-fat dressing, replace the cashews with ¾ to 1 cup of cooked white beans.

To achieve the look of finely grated parmesan cheese, use a rotary cheese grater to add a dusting of walnuts or cashews to the top of each salad plate.

When tomatoes are in season, I use 2 cups chopped instead of the bell pepper.

As a crouton substitute, try some Roasted Garbanzo Beans (page 144).

POTATO SALAD

The most common reaction I get from people trying this salad for the first time is, "It tastes like potato salad!" This healthful version of potato salad is just as comforting and satisfying as traditional versions, but without any eggs, oil, or salt.

PREPARATION
about 20 minutes

COOKING TIME
25 minutes

SERVES
6 to 8 (makes about 9 cups salad and 1 cup dressing)

For the salad:

3 pounds red potatoes, unpeeled, cut into about ¾-inch chunks (about 9 cups)

3 ribs celery, sliced or chopped (about 1 cup)

½ cup finely chopped red onion

1 medium, ripe avocado, chopped (optional)

2 tablespoons chopped fresh dill

For the dressing:

½ cup water

2 ounces raw, unsalted cashews (about ½ cup)

3 tablespoons lemon juice

2 tablespoons mustard (I like Dijon or stone ground)

1 medium clove garlic

½ teaspoon ground cumin

1. Place all of the dressing ingredients (water, cashews, lemon juice, mustard, garlic, and cumin) into a blender, and set aside for at least 15 minutes (so the cashews can soften).

2. Cover the potatoes with cold water in a large pot and bring to a boil over high heat, uncovered. Reduce the heat to medium-high, and continue to cook until the potatoes are tender but not falling apart when pierced with a knife, about 15 to 20 minutes. Drain and rinse under cold water.

3. Place the cooked potatoes, celery, red onion, avocado (if using), and dill into a large bowl.

4. Blend the dressing ingredients until smooth. Stir the dressing into the salad. Serve immediately or after chilling for an hour.

NOTES

You can use any kind of potato, but red potatoes are traditional since they hold together well and look nice.

You can use 1 teaspoon of dried dill instead of fresh, but there's nothing like fresh herbs in a salad.

For a lower-fat dressing, substitute ¾ to 1 cup of cooked white beans for the cashews.

MACARONI SALAD

Traditional macaroni salad dressings usually call for white sugar and mayonnaise (full of oil and eggs), but in this recipe we'll use dates and cashews instead.

PREPARATION
about 25 minutes

COOKING TIME
15 minutes

SERVES
6 to 8 (makes about 7½ cups salad and 1¼ cups dressing)

For the salad:

2 cups dry/uncooked elbow macaroni (use rice, corn, and/or quinoa pasta if you avoid gluten)

1½ cups grated carrots (1 to 2 medium)

1 medium red bell pepper, seeded and chopped (about 1½ cups)

3 ribs celery, sliced or chopped (about 1 cup)

½ cup finely chopped red onion

½ cup chopped fresh parsley

¼ cup chopped fresh basil

1 medium, ripe avocado, chopped (optional)

Sweet Mustard Dressing:

½ cup water

2 ounces raw, unsalted cashews (about ½ cup)

1 ounce pitted dates (2 Medjool or 4 Deglet Noor), chopped

3 tablespoons lemon juice

2 tablespoons mustard (I like Dijon or stone ground)

1 medium clove garlic

1. Place all of the dressing ingredients (water, cashews, dates, lemon juice, mustard, and garlic) into a blender, and set aside for at least 15 minutes (so the cashews can soften).

2. To make the pasta, cook the macaroni according to the package instructions. Drain and rinse with cool water, and set aside.

3. Place the carrots, bell pepper, celery, red onion, parsley, basil, and avocado (if using) into a large bowl.

4. Blend the dressing ingredients until smooth. Stir the dressing and cooked pasta into the bowl of salad ingredients. Serve immediately or after chilling for an hour.

NOTE
For a lower-fat dressing, substitute ¾ to 1 cup of cooked white beans for the cashews.

CREAMY COLESLAW

This recipe was inspired by my mom's coleslaw, which features apples and raisins. Coleslaw makes a great side dish for soups and stews.

Shopping tip: Make sure your raisins have not had oil added to them, a common practice to keep them from sticking together.

PREPARATION
about 20 minutes

COOKING TIME
0 minutes

SERVES
6 (makes about
8 cups salad and
1 cup dressing)

For the salad:

3 cups chopped green cabbage

1¾ cups grated carrots (1 to 2 medium)

1½ cups diced apple (1 to 2 medium), peeled or unpeeled

1 cup chopped red cabbage

½ cup raisins

¼ cup finely chopped red onion

For the dressing:

½ cup water

2 ounces raw, unsalted cashews (about ½ cup)

2 tablespoons mustard (I like Dijon or stone ground)

1 tablespoon vinegar (I like apple cider)

1 medium clove garlic

1. Place all of the dressing ingredients (water, cashews, mustard, vinegar, and garlic) into a blender, and set aside for at least 15 minutes (so the cashews can soften).

2. Place all of the salad ingredients (green cabbage, carrots, apple, red cabbage, raisins, and onion) into a large bowl.

3. Blend the dressing ingredients until smooth. Pour the dressing over the salad and toss well.

NOTES

For a little variation, add ¼ cup of thinly sliced radish, celery, or fresh fennel, or ½ cup of chopped bell pepper, broccoli, cauliflower, or pineapple.

For a lower-fat dressing, substitute ¾ to 1 cup of cooked white beans for the cashews.

From the blog

"I just made this, and it is fantastic! I think my fiancée may eat the whole batch before we make it to dinner, and he's not even vegan, and he doesn't like traditional coleslaw." —*James*

CURRIED SWEET POTATO SALAD

This potato salad is distinctive, daring, and delectable—one of my favorite recipes!

PREPARATION
about 30 minutes

COOKING TIME
15 minutes

SERVES
6 to 8 (makes about 8½ cups salad and 1 cup dressing)

For the salad:

2 pounds sweet potatoes, peeled and cut into ¾-inch chunks (about 6 cups)

2 cups coarsely chopped fresh spinach leaves

2 ribs celery, sliced or chopped (about ⅔ cup)

½ cup raisins (brown or golden)

½ cup sliced almonds (plus extra for garnish; optional)

4 green onions, white and green parts, sliced

Creamy Curry Dressing:

1 teaspoon orange zest

½ cup water

2 ounces raw, unsalted cashews (about ½ cup)

¼ cup orange juice

1 teaspoon curry powder

1 medium clove garlic

1. To start the dressing, zest the orange first before juicing it. Set the zest aside.

2. Place all of the dressing ingredients, except the orange zest, into a blender and set aside for at least 15 minutes (so the cashews can soften).

3. To make the salad, place the sweet potatoes into a soup pot and cover them with water. Bring to a boil over high heat, uncovered. Reduce the heat to medium-high, and cook until the potatoes are tender but not falling apart when pierced with a knife, about 10 to 15 minutes. Drain and rinse under cold water, and set aside.

4. Once the potatoes have thoroughly drained, place them into a large bowl, along with the spinach, celery, raisins, almonds, and green onions.

5. Blend the dressing ingredients until smooth. Stir the orange zest into the blended dressing with a fork (but don't blend it). Then stir the dressing into the salad. Serve warm or chilled, plain or topped with sliced almonds.

NOTE

For a lower-fat dressing, substitute ¾ to 1 cup of cooked white beans for the cashews.

From the blog

"I love the fresh OJ with the curry, and the almonds and celery add a nice crunch." —*Jen*

BLACK BEAN AND YAM SALAD

Black beans, yams, and quinoa come together beautifully in this filling and colorful salad.

Shopping tips: To avoid excess sodium, look for canned beans with no added salt (or cook your beans from scratch). When buying Mexican or taco-style seasoning, look for salt-free blends in the spice aisle, not a "taco seasoning" packet.

PREPARATION
about 35 minutes

COOKING TIME
30 minutes

SERVES
8 (makes about 9 cups salad and ⅓ cup dressing)

For the salad:

2 cups water

1 cup dry/uncooked quinoa

1¼ pounds yams, peeled and cut into ½-inch chunks (about 3 cups)

1 medium yellow or white onion, chopped (about 2 cups)

1 medium red bell pepper, seeded and chopped (about 1½ cups)

2 cups coarsely chopped greens (kale, collards, or Swiss chard)

1 tablespoon finely chopped garlic (4 to 5 medium cloves)

1 can cooked black beans (15 ounces; about 1½ cups), drained and rinsed

1 cup loosely packed cilantro, chopped

1 medium, ripe avocado, chopped (optional)

For the dressing:

⅓ cup lime juice

1 tablespoon taco seasoning or Mexican seasoning blend (see Note)

1. Bring the water and quinoa to a boil in a medium saucepan over high heat, uncovered. Reduce the heat to low, then cover and simmer for 20 minutes. Remove from heat and set aside for 10 minutes with the lid still on.

2. Place the yams into a pot and cover them with water. Bring to a boil over high heat, uncovered, and cook for about 10 minutes, or until the yams are tender but not falling apart. Drain and set aside.

3. Heat 1 tablespoon of water in a large frying pan over medium-high heat. When the water starts to sputter, add the onion and bell pepper. Cook while stirring for 3 to 5 minutes, adding a little water, as needed, until the onions and peppers soften. Stir in the greens and garlic, adding a little water as needed, and cook for 2 to 3 minutes, or until the greens have wilted.

4. Place the cooked quinoa and yams into a large bowl, and add the cooked vegetables, black beans, cilantro, and avocado (if using).

5. For the dressing, mix the lime juice and Mexican seasoning in a small bowl with a fork, and then stir into the salad.

NOTE

To make your own Mexican spice blend, use a combination of chili powder, paprika, cumin, granulated garlic, granulated onion, and/or a pinch of cayenne pepper.

4-BEAN SALAD

In addition to beans, this salad features corn, peas, and red onion. The dressing is a tangy and mildly spicy vinaigrette. This is a colorful, hearty salad, perfect for any of the three P's: potlucks, parties, and picnics!

Shopping tip: To avoid excess sodium, look for canned and/or frozen beans, peas, and corn with no added salt (or cook your own from scratch).

PREPARATION
about 25 minutes

COOKING TIME
10 to 15 minutes

SERVES
8 (makes about
10 cups salad and
1 cup dressing)

For the salad:

3 cups precooked green beans (cut into 1-inch pieces; or 2 14.5-ounce cans, drained and rinsed)

1 can cooked black beans (15 ounces; about 1½ cups), drained and rinsed

1 can cooked kidney beans (15 ounces; about 1½ cups), drained and rinsed

1 can cooked garbanzo beans (15 ounces; about 1½ cups), drained and rinsed

1½ cups peas (thaw first if frozen)

1½ cups corn kernels (thaw first if frozen)

½ cup finely chopped red onion

Tomato Vinaigrette:

1 medium tomato, chopped (including seeds; about ¾ cup)

⅓ cup vinegar (I like apple cider)

2 tablespoons mustard (I like Dijon or stone ground)

1 teaspoon ground cumin

1 medium clove garlic

1. Place all of the salad ingredients (green beans, black beans, kidney beans, garbanzo beans, peas, corn, and onion) into a large bowl.

2. Place all of the vinaigrette ingredients (tomato, vinegar, mustard, cumin, and garlic) into a blender, and blend until smooth. Stir into the salad.

NOTES

A little chopped fresh parsley or basil is also nice in this salad.

If you're feeling decadent, add 1 chopped ripe avocado.

From the blog

"It is hard to believe that this dressing does not have any oil in it; my husband and I did not miss it at all! Flavorful and satisfying!" —*Lisa*

SALAD DRESSINGS

SALAD DRESSING BASICS

This chapter includes recipes for a variety of dressings, as well as a "road map" so that you can get creative and come up with your own dressings.

Bottled dressings from the grocery store usually contain an abundance of oil, salt, and/or sugar, as well as other ingredients that you want to avoid if good health is your goal, such as corn syrup, MSG, caramel coloring, thickeners, and preservatives.

In particular, removing oil from your salad dressing equation is one of the most impactful, healthy changes you can make. Oils provide little flavor (a dressing's flavor comes mainly from the other ingredients), and they are extremely high in calories (120 per tablespoon). People who are trying to lose weight will often overlook this seemingly negligible ingredient in their salad dressing, thinking "a little won't hurt." But little bits of high-calorie foods can really add up and have a profound impact on health.

Not only is making salad dressing from scratch the most healthful way to go, it is really easy. There are many benefits to making your own salad dressing, including:

- Making it taste the way *you* like it.

- Knowing exactly what's in it (and what's not).

- Using higher-quality ingredients.

Salad dressings can range from just one ingredient, such as squeezing a lemon or lime over a salad, to two ingredients, such as a bit of mustard and vinegar mixed right into a salad. Or use three to six ingredients,

like the recipes in this chapter, when you're feeling more creative.

There are no hard and fast rules for making plant-based salad dressings; most any plant food that can be blended can be used. As long as the end result is pourable, composed of healthful ingredients, and tastes good to you, it can be salad dressing. It's as easy as blending all of the ingredients until smooth.

Because homemade dressings are made with mostly fresh ingredients, they won't keep as long as store-bought dressings, typically three to five days. But this way you have the opportunity to make a different type of dressing every week if you like, which keeps salads fun and interesting. Store homemade salad dressings in sealed containers in the refrigerator, and always shake or stir them before using.

Spinach-Dijon Dressing (page 79)

SALAD DRESSING ROAD MAP

Use the following salad dressing "road map" to create healthful salad dressings that appeal to you. Don't be afraid to experiment and, when you find a combination that you like, make a note of it so you don't forget. I keep a small tablet in my kitchen for this purpose. Having a short list of favorite homemade dressings can be a lifesaver.

Let's begin with the seven most common salad dressing ingredient categories. Each is described and measurement suggestions are offered to start you off in creating your own combinations. On the following page is a more detailed list of ingredients, within these seven categories, to spur your creativity.

1. Liquids: Use water to thin out your dressing, or add in citrus juice (lemon, lime, grapefruit), or a bit of 100% fruit juice (apple, pineapple). Vinegars are also excellent additions. I like apple cider vinegar best. (Watch out for seasoned vinegars, as they often contain a lot of sugar and salt.) Suggestion: 1 to 2 tablespoons of vinegar; ¼ to ½ cup of water or juice.

2. Fruit: Almost any fruit can be used in salad dressing. I especially love berries, apples, pears, citrus, peaches, and mangos. Dates and raisins are also a great sweet addition. Suggestion: ¼ to ½ cup of cut-up fresh fruit; 1 tablespoon of raisins or 1 date.

3. Vegetables: Using soft, raw vegetables in dressings is ideal, such as cucumbers or tomatoes. Roasting certain vegetables first (if you have the time), such as bell peppers, tomatoes, onions, and garlic, will result in sweeter, more complex flavors. Suggestion: ¼ to ½ cup chopped raw or roasted vegetables (except for garlic).

4. Fats and beans: Using a small amount of higher-fat plant foods can go a long way to create rich, creamy dressings in the absence of oil. Soft nuts are great, such as cashews, walnuts, pine nuts, or pecans. Seeds, such as hemp, sesame, sunflower, or pumpkin, are also tasty additions. (Soaking nuts and seeds in water for 15 to 30 minutes before blending will result in a smoother dressing. Discard the soak water or retain some to use as part of the dressing.) You can also use cooked white beans in place of the above fat options to achieve a creamy texture but without so much richness. Suggestion: 1 tablespoon of nuts or seeds, or 1 to 2 tablespoons of avocado, tofu, or cooked white beans.

5. Fresh herbs: I love fresh herbs in dressings. Try basil, parsley, cilantro, scallions, chives, oregano, dill, mint, or tarragon. Suggestion: 1 to 2 tablespoons chopped (or less for more lively herbs, like oregano, rosemary and tarragon).

6. Dried herbs and spices: Any kind of dried herb, spice, or blend can be a delicious addition to a dressing. Examples include dill, cumin, granulated onion or garlic, and blends like Italian herbs, curry powder, or chili powder. Suggestion: start with ⅛ or ¼ teaspoon, and work up from there.

7. Zing: Add a little kick to your dressings with a tablespoon of finely minced fresh onion or shallot, or ¼ to ½ teaspoon of finely minced fresh garlic. Additionally, you may like to add 1 tablespoon of prepared mustard (Dijon, German, or stone ground), ¼ to ½ teaspoon of freshly minced ginger or citrus zest, a jalapeño (or other) pepper, or some ground black pepper.

The below list is not exhaustive, but it includes the ingredients I enjoy using in dressings that are also easy to find in stores. (All items are to be used raw unless noted otherwise.)

SALAD DRESSING INGREDIENTS

1. Liquids

100% fruit juice:
- apple
- mango
- pineapple
- citrus juice (grapefruit, lemon, lime, orange or tangerine)

vegetable broth or stock (homemade)

vegetable juice (homemade, salt-free):
- beet
- carrot
- celery

vinegar:
- apple cider vinegar
- balsamic vinegar
- brown rice vinegar

water

2. Fruit

apples

apricots

berries:
- blueberries
- raspberries
- strawberries

citrus (flesh, seeded):
- grapefruit
- lemon
- lime
- orange or tangerine

dates (Medjool or Deglet Noor)

mangos

nectarines

papayas

peaches

pears

pineapples

plums

pomegranates

raisins

3. Vegetables

bell peppers

chili peppers

corn

cucumber

fennel

greens (spinach, arugula)

lettuce

mushrooms

tomatoes

4. Fats and Beans

avocados

beans and lentils (cooked):
- black
- garbanzo (chickpeas)
- lentils
- lima
- pinto
- white (navy, great northern, cannellini)

nut butters:
- almond
- tahini (ground sesame seeds)

seeds:
- hemp
- poppy
- pumpkin

-sesame

-sunflower

soft nuts:

-cashews

-pecans

-pignolia (pine nuts)

-pistachios

-walnuts

tofu

5. Fresh Herbs

mild flavor:

-chives

-parsley (curly or
Italian/flat)

medium flavor:

-basil

-cilantro

-dill

-mint

-sage

-thyme

strong flavor (use less):

-oregano

-rosemary

-tarragon

6. Dried Herbs and Spices

basil

caraway

cardamom

celery seed

chili powder

cumin

curry powder

dill weed

fennel

garlic (granulated,
powdered, minced)

ginger

green herb seasoning blends
(like Italian or French)

mustard (seed, powdered)

nutmeg

onion (granulated, powdered,
minced)

paprika (sweet or smoked)

tarragon

7. Zing

black pepper

citrus zest

garlic (fresh)

ginger (fresh)

jalapeños (or other spicy
peppers)

mustard (Dijon, German,
stone ground)

onions (yellow, sweet yellow,
white, red, shallot, green)

seaweed (kelp powder or
granules, dulse)

"The healthiest foods are the foods that come straight out of the garden and are consumed in their natural form or as simply prepared as possible. These foods are fresh fruits, vegetables, starchy vegetables, legumes, and intact whole grains, and should be the focus of any healthy diet." —*Jeff Novick, M.S., R.D.N.*

TOMATO VINAIGRETTE

This sweet and tangy dressing is used with the 4-Bean Salad recipe on page 70, but it's also an easy-to-make "anytime" dressing for green salads.

1 medium tomato, chopped (including seeds; about ¾ cup)

⅓ cup vinegar (I like apple cider)

2 tablespoons mustard (I like Dijon or stone ground)

1 teaspoon ground cumin

1 medium clove garlic

PREPARATION
about 5 minutes

COOKING TIME
0 minutes

MAKES
about 1 cup

1. Place all of the ingredients (tomato, vinegar, mustard, cumin, and garlic) into a blender, and blend until smooth. Store leftover dressing in a covered container in the refrigerator for up to five days and shake before using.

CASHEW-MUSTARD DRESSING

This easy dressing is used with the Tu-No Salad recipe on page 58 but is delicious anytime you want a tangy, garlicky, creamy dressing.

½ cup water

2 ounces raw, unsalted cashews (about ½ cup)

3 tablespoons lemon juice

2 tablespoons mustard (I like Dijon or stone ground)

2 teaspoons vinegar (I like apple cider)

1 medium clove garlic

PREPARATION
about 20 minutes

COOKING TIME
0 minutes

MAKES
about 1 cup

1. Place all of the ingredients (water, cashews, lemon juice, mustard, vinegar, and garlic) into a blender, and set aside for at least 15 minutes (so the cashews can soften).

2. Blend until smooth, adding a little water as needed. Store leftover dressing in a covered container in the refrigerator for up to five days and shake before using.

STRAWBERRY BALSAMIC

Bring on the sweet and tangy!

Shopping tips: Balsamic vinegar comes in a variety of qualities, so read the labels to make sure there is no added sugar or coloring. Balsamic vinegars contain added or naturally occurring sulfur-based compounds (sulphites), which some people are sensitive to. If this is the case, you may use another type of vinegar, such as apple cider.

1 cup sliced strawberries (about 7 medium)

¼ cup water

2 tablespoons balsamic vinegar

1 tablespoon finely chopped onion or shallot

1 tablespoon mustard (I like Dijon or stone ground)

⅛ teaspoon ground black pepper

1. Place all of the ingredients (strawberries, water, vinegar, onion or shallot, mustard, and black pepper) into a blender, and blend until smooth, adding a little water as needed. Store leftover dressing in a covered container in the refrigerator for up to five days, and shake before using.

PREPARATION
about 8 minutes

COOKING TIME
0 minutes

MAKES
about 1 cup

MUSTARD-LIME DRESSING

This dressing accompanies the Cabbage Salad on page 56. I love this dressing because it's really easy to make, and the lime juice is a fun alternative to lemon juice.

½ cup lime juice

¼ cup mustard (I like Dijon or stone ground)

1 medium clove garlic

1. Place the lime juice, mustard, and garlic into a blender, and blend until smooth. Store leftover dressing in a covered container in the refrigerator for up to five days and shake before using.

PREPARATION
less than 5 minutes

COOKING TIME
0 minutes

MAKES
about ⅔ cup

CREAMY CURRY DRESSING

This dressing accompanies the Curried Sweet Potato Salad on page 66, but it is also delicious over a green salad when you want a little something different.

PREPARATION
about 20 minutes

COOKING TIME
0 minutes

MAKES
about 1 cup

1 teaspoon orange zest

½ cup water

2 ounces raw, unsalted cashews (about ½ cup)

¼ cup orange juice

1 teaspoon curry powder

1 medium clove garlic

1. Zest the orange first before juicing it, and set the zest aside.

2. Place all of the remaining ingredients (water, cashews, orange juice, curry powder, and garlic) into a blender, and set aside for at least 15 minutes (so the cashews can soften).

3. Blend until smooth, adding a little water as needed. Stir the orange zest into the blended dressing with a fork (don't blend it). Store leftover dressing in a covered container in the refrigerator for up to five days and shake before using.

NOTE
For a lower-fat dressing, substitute ¾ to 1 cup of cooked white beans for the cashews.

AVOCADO-DILL DRESSING

This creamy, rich dressing has a bright, herby flavor.

- ½ cup water
- 2 ounces raw, unsalted cashews (about ½ cup)
- ½ medium, ripe avocado, chopped
- 3 tablespoons lemon juice
- 1 medium clove garlic
- 2 green onions, white and green parts, chopped
- 2 tablespoons chopped fresh dill

PREPARATION
about 20 minutes

COOKING TIME
0 minutes

MAKES
about 1 cup

1. Place the water, cashews, avocado, lemon juice, and garlic into a blender, and set aside for at least 15 minutes (so the cashews can soften).

2. Blend the ingredients until smooth. Add the green onion and dill, and blend briefly, so you can still see green flecks. Store leftover dressing in a covered container in the refrigerator for up to three days and shake before using.

NOTE
For a lower-fat dressing, substitute ¾ to 1 cup of cooked white beans for the cashews.

SPINACH-DIJON DRESSING

A bright-green, slightly creamy "flavor bomb" of a dressing!

- 2 ounces spinach leaves (about 1 cup chopped and packed)
- ¼ medium, ripe avocado
- ¼ cup water
- 1 tablespoon Dijon mustard
- 1 green onion, white and green parts, sliced
- 1 small clove garlic

PREPARATION
about 10 minutes

COOKING TIME
0 minutes

MAKES
about 1 cup

1. Place all of the ingredients (spinach, avocado, water, mustard, green onion, and garlic) into a blender, and blend until smooth, adding a little water as needed.

Store leftovers in a covered container in the refrigerator for up to three days and shake before using.

PINEAPPLE-MANGO VINAIGRETTE

PREPARATION
about 10 minutes

COOKING TIME
0 minutes

MAKES
about 1 cup

If you like fruity, tangy dressings, you'll love this one!

Shopping tip: If you use canned pineapple, make sure that no sugar or corn syrup has been added.

½ cup chopped fresh, ripe pineapple (or if canned, drain and reserve the juice)

½ cup chopped fresh, ripe mango

¼ cup water (or pineapple juice)

¼ cup chopped basil

2 tablespoons vinegar (I like apple cider)

1. Place all of the ingredients (pineapple, mango, water, basil, and vinegar) into a blender, and blend until smooth but still with tiny specks of basil showing. Add a little water if needed to thin. Store leftover dressing in a covered container in the refrigerator for up to five days and shake before using.

SESAME-CITRUS-GINGER DRESSING

PREPARATION
about 5 minutes

COOKING TIME
0 minutes

MAKES
about 1 cup

This delicious dressing calls for tahini, which is ground sesame seed paste. It can be found near the peanut butter at the grocery store. You will find tahini raw or roasted; either may be used.

½ cup orange juice

¼ cup lemon juice

¼ cup tahini (ground sesame seed paste)

1 teaspoon grated or finely chopped fresh ginger

1 small clove garlic

1. Place all of the ingredients (orange juice, lemon juice, tahini, ginger, and garlic) into a blender, and blend until smooth. Chill for an hour to thicken and set the flavors. Store leftover dressing in a covered container in the refrigerator for up to five days and shake before using.

SWEET MUSTARD DRESSING

This dressing is used in the Macaroni Salad recipe (page 63) and is a little reminiscent of Thousand Island dressing.

Shopping tip: Look for dates in the bulk food section or packaged near the raisins.

PREPARATION
about 20 minutes

COOKING TIME
0 minutes

MAKES
about 1¼ cup

½ cup water

2 ounces raw, unsalted cashews (about ½ cup)

1 ounce pitted dates (2 Medjool or 4 Deglet Noor), chopped

3 tablespoons lemon juice

2 tablespoons mustard (I like Dijon or stone ground)

1 medium clove garlic

1. Place all of the ingredients (water, cashews, dates, lemon juice, mustard, and garlic) into a blender, and set aside for at least 15 minutes (so the cashews can soften).

2. Blend until smooth, adding a little water as needed. Store leftover dressing in a covered container in the refrigerator for up to five days and shake before using.

NOTE
For a lower-fat dressing, substitute ¾ to 1 cup of cooked white beans for the cashews.

RANCH DRESSING

Use this as a salad dressing, or as a dip for french fries or raw, cut-up vegetables.

PREPARATION
about 20 minutes

COOKING TIME
0 minutes

MAKES
about 1 cup

½ cup water

2 ounces raw, unsalted cashews (about ½ cup)

3 tablespoons lemon juice

1 teaspoon vinegar (I like apple cider)

½ teaspoon granulated onion

½ teaspoon granulated garlic

1 green onion, white and green parts, sliced

2 teaspoons chopped fresh dill (or ¾ teaspoon dried)

1. Place the water, cashews, lemon juice, vinegar, and granulated onion and garlic into a blender, and set aside for at least 15 minutes (so the cashews can soften).

2. Blend until very smooth, adding a little water as needed.

3. Add the green onion and dill, and blend for just a few more seconds so that you can still see green flecks in the dressing. Refrigerate for 2 to 3 hours (or overnight) for the best flavor. Store leftover dressing in a covered container in the refrigerator for up to five days and shake before using. If the dressing is too thick, stir in a little water.

NOTE
For a lower-fat dressing, substitute ¾ to 1 cup of cooked white beans for the cashews.

MAIN DISHES

MAIN DISH BASICS

Traditionally, a meal's main dish is the heaviest, most filling one on the table because it focuses on some type of meat (beef, port, fowl, fish, or seafood), and is often prepared with oil and/or dairy products (cow's milk, cream, butter, or cheese). All of these health-harming foods contribute to our feeling overly full and bloated.

When we subtract these ingredients from the "main dish" equation and make a couple easy substitutions (while maintaining the key flavors), we end up with a main dish that still looks and smells familiar, and tastes great. Don't be concerned that it may not taste exactly like the traditional dish. I often hear from my students that they like the health-promoting dishes *even better* than the ones they usually eat. They like that they can actually taste the vegetables and other flavors since they're not overloaded with fat and salt. Many people will miss meat, cheese, oil, and salt when first transitioning their diet, but after a month or so, their taste buds will adapt, and they will no longer crave these things in the same way.

Let's look at one recipe, Tu-No Casserole (page 100), as an example of how we can still enjoy a favorite main dish without compromising our health. Traditional tuna casserole is usually made with oil, milk, cheese, and canned tuna. Instead, we'll use water instead of oil for cooking the onion and mushrooms on the stovetop, a plant-based milk in the sauce instead of dairy, a few blended cashews instead of cheese, and garbanzo beans instead of tuna, with some kelp granules to add seafood flavor. This dish includes enough familiar tuna casserole ingredients—like pasta, mushrooms, and peas—that it will be reminiscent of the tuna casserole you are used to.

It's not difficult to enjoy a dish like this since so much of it strikes a familiar chord. I've never heard anyone say, "Nope, I need actual tuna," or "I've just *got* to have cow's milk." We just want good food. All the dishes in this chapter have been developed to give you the flavor you look for in the dishes you've come to love without the health-compromising ingredients.

Salt is also a featured ingredient in most traditional main dish recipes, but I have left it out of the recipes in this chapter (and book). I think you will find that the vegetable, herb, and spice combinations provide very satisfying flavors. And if you are craving salt, understand that this craving will decrease the more you avoid salt, both in cooking and at the table.

All of the recipes in this chapter are easy to make and are suitable for any night of the week. Some (like Enchilada Casserole, Lentil-Rice Loaf, and Mushroom Risotto) entail a bit more preparation and are thus great for special meals. Others (including Quinoa Curry with Mixed Vegetables, Pizza Pasta, and Baked Potatoes) are more suited to nights when you don't feel much like cooking.

If you are hesitant about sharing these recipes with others who are not on the same health-promoting path, for fear they will reject your "healthy" dishes, don't tell them—or at least not until afterwards. I bet you that your dish will get rave reviews.

PIZZA PASTA

With traditional pizza ingredients, including onions, garlic, mushrooms, and fresh basil, this dish tastes great, and it also cooks up quickly.

Shopping tips: If you avoid wheat products, look for rice and/or quinoa pasta. To avoid excess sodium, look for canned diced tomatoes with no added salt.

PREPARATION
about 15 minutes

COOKING TIME
20 minutes

SERVES
4 (makes about
7 cups)

3 cups dry/uncooked fusilli or penne pasta

10 medium brown or white mushrooms, sliced (about 4 cups)

1 medium yellow or white onion, chopped (about 2 cups)

1 tablespoon finely chopped garlic (4 to 5 medium cloves)

2 cans diced tomatoes (14.5 ounces each; about 3 cups total)

1 teaspoon dried oregano

1 cup loosely packed fresh basil, chopped

1 ounce walnuts or raw, unsalted cashews, ground (about ¼ cup; for optional garnish)

1. Cook the pasta according to the package instructions. Drain and rinse with cool water, return the pasta to the pot, and set aside.

2. Heat 1 tablespoon of water in a large frying pan over medium-high heat. When the water starts to sputter, add the mushrooms and onions, and cook while stirring for about 5 minutes, adding a little water as needed to prevent sticking. Stir in the garlic, and cook for 1 to 2 minutes more.

3. Stir in the diced tomatoes (with accompanying liquid) and oregano, then cover and cook for 10 minutes, stirring once or twice.

4. Stir the tomato sauce into the pot of pasta, along with the chopped basil. Serve as is, or topped with finely ground cashews or walnuts (using a rotary cheese grater to create a parmesan-like topping).

VEGGIE BURGERS

Instead of using bread or buns (which are overly processed), I eat these veggie burger patties, halved, in romaine lettuce leaves (making a "burger boat"). They also make great leftovers, crumbled onto a green salad or baked potato, or hearty traveling or hiking snacks.

Shopping tips: To avoid excess sodium, look for canned beans and tomato paste with no salt added. Instead of buying ketchup, which is full of salt and sugar, consider making your own (page 152); it's easy!

PREPARATION
about 20 minutes

COOKING TIME
50 minutes (rice),
10 to 15 minutes
(patties)

SERVES
10 (makes 10
patties)

1 cup water

½ cup dry/uncooked short-grain brown rice

1 can cooked kidney beans (15 ounces; about 1½ cups), drained and rinsed

1 cup old-fashioned rolled oats

½ large yellow or white onion, chopped (about 1½ cups)

6 medium white or cremini mushrooms, chopped (about 2½ cups)

¼ cup tomato paste or ketchup

2 teaspoons granulated garlic

2 teaspoons dried oregano

1½ teaspoons chili powder

1 teaspoon granulated onion

1 teaspoon ground cumin

1 teaspoon dried basil

Optional extras: tomato, avocado, onion, lettuce, ketchup, and/or mustard

PREPARATION NOTE

While it's not necessary, cooking the rice the night before and refrigerating it will make the burger mix firmer and easier to shape. Or make the entire recipe and refrigerate it the day before cooking, which allows the flavors to blend thoroughly.

1. Bring the water and rice to a boil in a medium saucepan over high heat, uncovered. Reduce the heat to low, then cover and simmer for 50 minutes. Remove from the heat and let stand for 10 minutes with the lid still on.

2. Add to a large bowl: the cooked rice, beans, oats, onion, mushrooms, tomato paste or ketchup, garlic, oregano, chili powder, granulated onion, cumin, and basil. Stir until the ingredients are evenly mixed.

3. So as not to overload the food processor, transfer only half of the burger mix into it and pulse a few times, just until everything sticks together. (If you do not have a food processor, see Notes.) Place this processed mixture into another bowl. Process the remaining half of ingredients in the same way, and then add to the first batch.

4. Shape the mixture into patties 3 to 4 inches wide and about ½ inch thick. Preheat a nonstick frying pan over medium heat. (If you do not want to use a nonstick pan, see Notes.) Depending on the size of your pan, cook 2 to 4 patties at a time, cooking each side for 5 to 8 minutes or until browned.

Serve on romaine lettuce leaves with traditional burger toppings, such as tomato, avocado, onion, ketchup, and/or mustard.

NOTES

No food processor? No problem. Just mash your beans first with a handheld bean masher or fork, use quick-cooking rolled oats, and finely chop the onion and mushrooms.

If you do not own a nonstick pan (or don't want to use one), bake the patties on a baking sheet lined with parchment paper at 400°F for 10 minutes each side. They will not brown in the same way as in a frying pan, but they will still taste great!

Serving suggestion: I love making these burgers with Potato Salad (page 62), 4-Bean Salad (page 70), and Baked French Fries (page 139).

From the blog
"These burgers taste normal! This recipe is now an official favorite in my collection. Thanks!" —*RNesel*

From the blog

"I drive for a living, so it is really great to have something as good and portable (and healthy) as this. This is one of those things that actually tastes just as good, if not better, on the second day. Better than any fast-food place on the road!" —Lynn

ENCHILADA CASSEROLE

This filling and flavorful casserole is perfect for a family meal, when company visits, or just when you want delicious leftovers for the week. Instead of using cheese as a thickener and topping for this casserole, I use corn tortillas.

Shopping tips: To avoid excess sodium, look for canned tomatoes and beans with no salt added, and corn tortillas with no oil (and having five or fewer ingredients).

PREPARATION
about 25 minutes

COOKING TIME
12 minutes (stove-top), 15 minutes (oven)

SERVES
6 to 8 (makes about 7½ cups)

1 medium yellow or white onion, chopped (about 2 cups)

1 medium red bell pepper, seeded and chopped (about 1½ cups)

1 tablespoon finely chopped garlic (4 to 5 medium cloves)

2 teaspoons chili powder

1 teaspoon dried oregano

1 can diced tomatoes (14.5 ounces; about 1½ cups), undrained

1 can cooked black beans (15 ounces; about 1½ cups), drained and rinsed

1 medium zucchini, sliced (about 2 cups)

1 cup corn kernels

5 cups coarsely chopped greens (kale, collards, or Swiss chard)

3 to 4 six-inch corn tortillas, cut into ½-inch squares

1 to 2 six-inch corn tortillas, cut into small rectangular "chips"

Chopped cilantro and/or avocado for garnish (optional)

1. Heat 1 tablespoon of water in a large frying pan or soup pot over medium-high heat. When the water starts to sputter, add the onion and bell pepper, and cook while stirring for about 5 minutes. Reduce the heat to medium, and add the garlic, chili powder, and oregano, and cook for 2 minutes more, adding a little water as needed.

2. Stir in the tomatoes, beans, zucchini, corn, greens, and the 3 to 4 cut-up corn tortillas, then cover and cook for 5 minutes, stirring halfway through.

3. Preheat the oven to 375°F. Set aside a 9×13-inch casserole dish.

4. Place about 1 cup of the cooked vegetables into a blender and blend briefly (add a little water if the mixture is too thick to blend). Stir this back into the cooked vegetables.

5. Spoon the mixture evenly into the casserole dish and scatter the remaining 1 to 2 cut-up corn tortillas on the top. Bake uncovered for 15 minutes. Let stand for 5 minutes before serving.

THAI VEGETABLES WITH PASTA SHELLS

Garlic, ginger, green onion, and tahini give this dish a distinctive flavor. And the pasta with the hearty vegetables—broccoli, cabbage, carrots and mushrooms—will fill you up!

Shopping tip: If you avoid wheat products, look for rice and/or quinoa pasta.

PREPARATION
about 30 minutes

COOKING TIME
25 minutes

SERVES
4 (makes about 7 cups)

1 cup dry/uncooked pasta shells

¾ cup water

2 tablespoons tahini (ground sesame seed paste)

1 tablespoon finely chopped garlic (4 to 5 medium cloves)

1 tablespoon finely grated or chopped fresh ginger

2 cups small broccoli florets

2 cups sliced carrots (1 to 2 medium)

8 medium white or cremini mushrooms, sliced (about 3 cups)

2½ cups thinly sliced green cabbage

1 cup peas (thaw first if frozen)

1 cup loosely packed fresh cilantro or basil, chopped

4 green onions, white and green parts, sliced

Sesame seeds to garnish (optional)

1. Chop and prepare all of the ingredients before you start cooking, as this dish cooks up quickly. Cook the pasta according to the package instructions. Drain and rinse with cool water, and set aside.

2. While the pasta is cooking, blend the sauce ingredients (¾ cup water, tahini, garlic, and ginger) in a blender until smooth. Set aside.

3. Place about ½ cup of water into a large frying pan or soup pot set to medium-high heat. When the water starts to boil, add the broccoli, carrots, and mushrooms, and cook while stirring for about 5 minutes. Add the

cabbage and peas, and cook while stirring for 5 minutes more, or until the broccoli and carrots are tender (adding a little water, as needed, to prevent sticking).

4. Add the sauce, cooked pasta, cilantro, and green onions to the pot of vegetables, and cook while stirring for 2 minutes. Remove from the heat, and serve hot or warm, topped with a sprinkling of sesame seeds, if desired.

NOTE

A new jar of tahini will have a layer of oil on top due to separation after sitting. I pour this off and discard it instead of stirring it in.

LENTIL AND RICE LOAF

This flavorful loaf is perfect for the holidays or anytime you want a hearty main dish. It can be made with fresh or dried herbs. Make two loaves while you're at it and freeze one for leftovers. This is delicious with Creamy Mushroom Gravy (page 160) or Better Ketchup (page 152).

Shopping tips: To avoid excess sodium, look for canned beans with no salt added (or cook your beans from scratch). Look for salt-free tomato paste and poultry seasoning (don't worry, it does not contain poultry).

PREPARATION
about 25 minutes

COOKING TIME
50 minutes (rice and lentils),
55 minutes (baking the loaf)

SERVES
6 to 10 (makes about ten ¾-inch slices)

1¾ cups water

½ cup dry/uncooked brown-green lentils

½ cup dry/uncooked short-grain brown rice

2 teaspoons poultry seasoning

1 teaspoon granulated onion

1 medium yellow or white onion, chopped (about 2 cups)

5 medium white or cremini mushrooms, chopped (about 2 cups)

1 large rib celery, sliced (about ½ cup)

1 tablespoon freshly chopped garlic (4 to 5 medium cloves)

¾ cup old-fashioned rolled oats

1 can tomato paste (6 ounces)

2 ounces pecans or walnuts, chopped (about ½ cup; optional)

1 tablespoon minced fresh sage (or 1½ teaspoons dried rubbed sage)

2 teaspoons minced fresh thyme (or 1 teaspoon dried)

1½ teaspoons minced fresh rosemary (or ¾ teaspoon dried)

1. Place the water, lentils, rice, poultry seasoning, and granulated onion into a medium saucepan over high heat. When it begins to boil, reduce the heat to low, then cover and simmer for 45 minutes. Remove from the heat and let stand for 10 minutes with the lid still on. (Prepare your remaining ingredients while the rice and lentils are cooking.)

2. Place 1 tablespoon of water into a medium frying pan over high heat. When the water starts to sputter, add the chopped onion, mushrooms, and celery, and cook while stirring for 3 to 5 minutes, adding a little water, as needed. Add the garlic and stir for 2 minutes more until the vegetables have softened. If you're using dried herbs, stir them in with the garlic; if using fresh herbs, you will add them in step 4. Remove from the heat.

3. Preheat the oven to 350°F. Line a standard size loaf pan (9×5×3 inches) with parchment paper.

4. Place the oats, tomato paste, and nuts (if using) into a large bowl. If you're using fresh herbs (sage, thyme, and rosemary), add them to the bowl as well. When the cooked vegetables, rice, and lentils have cooled for at least 10 minutes, add them to the bowl, and stir until all of the ingredients have been mixed thoroughly.

5. Place half of the mixture into a food processor. Pulse about three times then scrape down the sides. Pulse another three times until evenly blended but still somewhat chunky, then spoon into the loaf pan. Place the remaining half of the mixture into the food processor and pulse in the same way. Then add this portion to the loaf pan as well. Press the mixture firmly and evenly into the pan.

6. Cover the pan with aluminum foil and cook for 40 minutes. Remove the foil, and cook for 15 to 20 minutes more, or until the top is browned and the edges look crispy. Remove from the oven, and let cool for 10 minutes before slicing and serving. Serve as is or with Creamy Mushroom Gravy (page 160) or Better Ketchup (page 152).

From the blog

"Just made this for dinner, and it was delicious! My mother was a bit worried about a new recipe idea, especially since we had guests over. They ended up asking for the recipe!" —*Kseinya*

QUINOA CURRY WITH MIXED VEGETABLES

Frozen vegetables have come a long way, and are a healthy and delicious meal addition. This is a hearty dish that provides great leftovers.

Shopping tips: Look for frozen bags of 100% vegetables (no added salt or oil), and tahini that has just one ingredient: ground sesame seeds.

PREPARATION
about 15 minutes

COOKING TIME
20 minutes

SERVES
2 to 4 (makes about 5 cups)

1½ cups water

¾ cup dry/uncooked quinoa

1 teaspoon granulated onion

½ teaspoon curry powder (use "medium" or "hot" if you like things spicy)

1 bag frozen mixed vegetables (16 ounces; I like "stir-fry" or "Thai style")

¼ cup water

1 tablespoon finely chopped garlic (4 to 5 medium cloves)

1 teaspoon finely grated or chopped fresh ginger

1 teaspoon curry powder

2 tablespoons tahini (sesame seed paste)

½ medium, ripe avocado (optional)

White sesame seeds (for garnish; optional)

1. Bring the 1½ cups of water, quinoa, granulated onion, and the ½ teaspoon of curry powder to a boil in a medium saucepan over medium-high heat, uncovered. Reduce the heat to low, then cover and simmer for 15 minutes. Remove from the heat and let stand for 10 minutes with the lid still on.

2. Empty the bag of frozen vegetables into a colander and rinse under warm water to thaw.

3. Place the thawed vegetables and the ¼ cup of water into a soup pot over medium-high heat. When the water starts to sputter, stir in the garlic, ginger, and 1 teaspoon of curry powder. Cook while stirring for 1 to 2 minutes.

4. Remove the pot from the heat, and stir in the cooked quinoa and tahini (adding a little water, as needed, for thorough mixing). Serve as is or topped with diced avocado and/or sesame seeds.

NOTE

You can also use 2½ cups of cooked short-grain brown rice in place of the cooked quinoa. For uncooked rice, use the same measurements as quinoa, but simmer for 50 minutes.

MUSHROOM-BASIL AU GRATIN

This dish is 100% comfort food, and is a cross between potatoes au gratin and lasagna. Along with the potatoes, there are layers of mushrooms, onions, Swiss chard, and fresh basil. The cashew sauce makes the dish rich and creamy. (This recipe requires the use of a mandolin to get the potato slices very thin.)

PREPARATION
about 35 minutes

COOKING TIME
35 minutes

SERVES
6 to 8

Shopping tip: If you prefer not to expose your food to aluminum foil, look for Reynolds Wrap Pan Lining Paper, with foil on one side and parchment paper on the other.

For the casserole:

1¼ pounds russet potatoes (2 to 3 medium), peeled and thinly sliced (see step 2)

1 medium yellow or white onion, halved and thinly sliced (about 1½ cups)

½ pound medium white or cremini mushrooms, thinly sliced (about 1½ cups)

4 cups coarsely chopped Swiss chard

1½ cups chopped fresh basil (about 40 medium leaves)

1 ounce raw, unsalted cashews, ground (about ¼ cup; for garnish)

For the sauce:

2 cups unsweetened nondairy milk (I like soy milk)

2 ounces raw, unsalted cashews (about ½ cup)

1 tablespoon dried Italian herb seasoning

1 teaspoon granulated onion

½ teaspoon granulated garlic

1. To make the sauce, place all of the sauce ingredients (milk, cashews, Italian seasoning, and granulated onion and garlic) into a blender, and set aside for at least 15 minutes (so the cashews can soften).

2. To slice the potatoes thinly and uniformly (like potato chips), use a mandolin slicer set to ⅛-inch thickness or less. Place the prepared potatoes, onion, mushrooms, chard, and basil each into their own bowl.

3. Preheat the oven to 375°F. Set aside a 13×9-inch baking dish.

4. Blend the sauce until smooth.

5. Prepare the casserole by creating layers as follows:

a. Pour a thin layer of sauce into the dish so it coats the bottom evenly.

b. Layer one-third of the potatoes across the bottom of the dish, only slightly overlapping them. Use the thickest and largest potatoes on the bottom.

c. Continue to layer evenly, in this order: half of the onions, half of the mushrooms, half of the basil, and half of the chard. Pour about half of the remaining sauce over this first layer.

d. Add a second full layer, just as in steps b and c, starting with the layer of potatoes (use about half of the remaining potatoes, using the small or odd-shaped ones for this interior layer, and reserving the most uniform ones for the top).

e. Finish the casserole with a final layer of potatoes, creating a nice-looking "roof" to your casserole (if it gets too tall, just press everything down with your hands). Pour the remaining sauce evenly over the top.

6. Cover the dish with a glass lid (if it has one), or cover with aluminum foil (making sure it doesn't touch the surface of the food) and seal the edges. Bake for 30 minutes.

7. Remove the foil (be careful of the hot steam). Use a rotary cheese grater with ¼ cup of cashews to add a parmesan-like dusting across the top. Then cook uncovered for 5 minutes more, or until the potatoes are tender when pierced with a knife and the edges are lightly browned. Let stand for 5 minutes before serving. Serve as is or with chopped fresh basil.

MUSHROOMS AND KALE WITH FRESH ROSEMARY

PREPARATION
about 10 minutes

COOKING TIME
20 minutes

SERVES
2 to 4

This is one of my favorite go-to meals since it can be made quickly and easily all in one pot, and with a minimum of ingredients. Steaming the fresh rosemary infuses the mushrooms, kale, and yams with its great flavor.

Shopping tip: If you haven't tried Japanese yams (sometimes called Japanese sweet potatoes), look for them at your grocery store; they are my favorite in this dish.

¾ cup water

½ teaspoon granulated garlic

1½ pounds yams and/or sweet potatoes (about 2 medium), peeled or unpeeled, cut into ½-inch-thick rounds

1 large bunch curly kale (about 10 ounces), ends trimmed and coarsely chopped

4 small portabella mushrooms (see Note)

2 sprigs fresh rosemary (each about 7 inches long)

1. Add the water and granulated garlic to a soup pot over medium-high heat. Add the sliced yams and/or sweet potatoes, and bring to a boil, uncovered.

2. Add the kale, followed by the whole mushrooms. Lay the sprigs of rosemary on top then reduce the heat to medium-low. Cover and cook for 15 to 20 minutes, or until the potatoes are tender, occasionally checking that the yams or sweet potatoes are not sticking to the bottom of the pot (if so, add a little water and stir gently).

3. Remove all of the rosemary and discard. Serve immediately.

NOTE

Small portabella mushrooms are called "portabellinis," and are 3 to 4 inches in diameter. But if you can't find them, you can use two regular portabella mushrooms.

EGGPLANT STIR-FRY

This dish lets the flavors of summer vegetables shine through a very light sauce of almond butter and Italian herbs. It cooks up quickly and is as colorful as it is delicious. (See photo on page 196.)

Shopping tips: I like using the dark purple, slightly pear-shaped eggplants since they don't need to be salted to draw out any bitterness. Look for almond butter made with 100% raw almonds (no salt, oil, sugar, or additives).

PREPARATION
about 25 minutes

COOKING TIME
15 minutes

SERVES
2 to 4 (makes about 6½ cups)

½ cup chopped red onion

1 small eggplant (about 8 ounces), peeled and cut into ½-inch cubes (about 2 cups)

1 tablespoon finely chopped garlic (4 to 5 medium cloves)

1 tablespoon dried Italian herb seasoning

1 teaspoon ground cumin

2 cups green beans, cut into 1-inch pieces

1 cup corn kernels

1 medium carrot, sliced (about ¾ cup)

2 ribs celery, sliced (about ⅔ cup)

½ cup water (for step 3)

½ cup water (for step 4)

2 tablespoons almond butter

2 medium tomatoes, chopped (about 1½ cups)

1. Heat 1 tablespoon of water in a large frying pan or soup pot over medium-high heat. When the water starts to sputter, add the onion, and cook while stirring for 2 minutes, adding a little water, as needed.

2. Add the eggplant, garlic, Italian seasoning, and cumin, and continue to cook and stir for 2 to 3 minutes, adding water as needed.

3. Stir in the green beans, corn, carrot, celery, and ½ cup of water. Reduce the heat to medium, then cover and cook, stirring occasionally, for 8 to 10 minutes, or until the carrots and beans are tender.

4. While the vegetables are cooking, with a fork or whisk, mix the almond butter into ½ cup of water. Remove the cooked vegetables from the heat, and stir in the almond butter-water mixture and the chopped tomatoes. Serve immediately.

TU-NO CASSEROLE

This hearty casserole calls for garbanzo beans instead of tuna—a surprising but wonderful substitution—and sliced mushrooms instead of the traditional can of dairy- and salt-heavy Cream of Mushroom soup.

Shopping tips: If you avoid wheat products, look for rice and/or quinoa pasta. To avoid excess sodium, look for canned beans with no added salt (or cook your beans from scratch).

PREPARATION
about 30 minutes

COOKING TIME
12 minutes (stove-top), 40 minutes (oven)

SERVES
8 to 10 (makes about 7½ cups)

For the casserole:

1½ cups dry/uncooked elbow macaroni or small-shell pasta

8 medium white or cremini mushrooms, sliced (about 3 cups)

1 medium yellow or white onion, chopped (about 2 cups)

2 cups cooked peas

2 cans cooked garbanzo beans (15 ounces each; about 3 cups total), drained and rinsed

For the sauce:

2½ cups unsweetened nondairy milk

2 ounces raw, unsalted cashews (about ½ cup)

2 teaspoons granulated onion

½ teaspoon granulated garlic

½ teaspoon ground white pepper

3 to 4 teaspoons kelp granules (for a seafood flavor; optional)

1. Place all of the sauce ingredients (milk, cashews, granulated onion and garlic, white pepper, and kelp granules, if using) into a blender, and set aside for at least 15 minutes (so the cashews can soften).

2. Cook the pasta according to the package instructions. Drain and rinse with cool water, return the pasta to the pot, and set it aside.

3. Preheat the oven to 375°F. Set aside a 13×9-inch baking dish.

4. Heat 1 tablespoon of water in a frying pan over medium-high heat. When the water starts to sputter, add the mushrooms and onions, and cook while stirring for 3 to 5 minutes, or until the onions have softened and are lightly browned, adding a little water, as needed. Add the onions and mushrooms, along with the peas, to the pot of cooked pasta.

5. Place the garbanzo beans into a food processor, and pulse just until the beans are broken up but not mushy (or use a fork or handheld bean masher). Add them to the soup pot.

6. Blend the sauce ingredients until smooth, and stir into the pot. (The mixture may be soupy, but it will firm up during cooking.)

7. Spoon the mixture evenly into the baking dish, and bake uncovered for 35 to 40 minutes, or until the top is lightly browned. Let stand at least 5 minutes before serving.

From the blog
"The thought that I can make something that resembles my mom's tuna casserole makes my heart sing." —*Teresa*

From the blog

"I just made this for dinner, and it was fantastic! Who knew all that oil and cheese would never be missed!" —*Christina*

PESTO PASTA

Ah, lovely pesto! But don't you need olive oil and cheese to make pesto? No way! These ingredients are traditional but they can simply be omitted, resulting in a sauce that is lighter and fresher tasting, but still has plenty of that famous basil and garlic punch!

Shopping tip: If you avoid wheat products, look for rice and/or quinoa pasta.

PREPARATION
about 15 minutes

COOKING TIME
7 to 12 minutes
(for pasta)

SERVES
4 (makes about
1⅓ cups of pesto
sauce and 6½ cups
of pasta)

For the pasta:
1 package spaghetti pasta (12 ounces)
1 ounce cashews, walnuts, or pine nuts, ground (about ¼ cup; for optional garnish)

For the Pesto Sauce:
⅔ cup water
3 ounces cashews, walnuts and/or pine nuts (about ¾ cup)
2 tablespoons lemon juice
2 teaspoons finely chopped garlic (2 to 3 medium cloves)
2 ounces fresh basil (about 2 cups chopped)

1. Cook the pasta according to the package instructions. Drain and rinse with cool water, return the pasta to the pot, and set aside.

2. To make the pesto, place all of the sauce ingredients (water, nuts, lemon juice, garlic, and basil) into a food processor, and process for 1 to 2 minutes, adding a little water, as needed. (You can also use a blender, which blends more quickly and results in a smoother sauce.)

3. Stir the pesto sauce into the pot of cooked pasta. Serve immediately as is or topped with ground nuts (use a rotary cheese grater to create a parmesan-like topping).

NOTE
Some lightly cooked vegetables, such as onion, mushrooms, and/or summer squash, are delicious added to this dish, as are chopped fresh tomatoes.

BAKED POTATOES WITH TOPPINGS

PREPARATION
about 5 minutes

COOKING TIME
about 60 minutes

SERVES
4

It's time to separate the oh-so-satisfying baked potato from its traditional, less-than-healthful toppings of butter, sour cream, and bacon bits. I love potatoes and eat them every day, changing the type of potatoes and toppings that I use to keep things interesting.

4 medium-large (about ¾ pound each) russet potatoes, scrubbed and unpeeled

1. Preheat the oven to 425°F. Set aside a baking sheet or dish.

2. You can poke the potatoes with a knife a couple of times if you wish, but I have not found it to make a difference. Do not wrap the potatoes in aluminum foil; simply place them onto the baking sheet or dish and bake for 50 to 60 minutes, or until a knife is easily inserted into the center.

3. After baking, make a lengthwise slit in the top of each potato, going about halfway down. Squeeze each potato at the ends toward the center to open it up. You can use a knife or fork to loosen the potato flesh inside. Finish the potato by topping it with any combination of vegetables or other toppings listed on the following page.

NOTES

You can also bake yams or sweet potatoes. They come in all sizes, so check for doneness at about 45 minutes and then at intervals of 5 to 10 minutes.

Other white potatoes: If you want to use another variety of white potato besides russet, try Yukon Golds. They have thin skins and are less starchy and are creamier in texture, with a naturally buttery flavor. They are generally smaller than russets, so they may not need to cook as long.

From the blog

"My husband and I are so happy we don't have to stop eating baked potatoes; they are so easy and delicious. He had a heart attack a couple months ago (he's only 34), so obviously bacon bits, sour cream, and butter are out. I can't believe I never thought of salsa on baked potatoes!" —*Simonne*

POTATO TOPPING IDEAS

Boiled or Steamed Vegetables

asparagus

broccoli

Brussels sprouts

cabbage

carrots

cauliflower

corn kernels

eggplant

greens (kale, collards, Swiss chard)

green beans

mushrooms

peas

zucchini

Raw Vegetables

avocados

bell peppers

cabbage

carrots

celery

corn kernels

green onions

greens (lettuce, spinach, arugula)

mushrooms

onions (white, yellow or red)

sprouts

tomatoes

Prepared Toppings

Avocado-Garbanzo Dip (page 156)

Barbecue Sauce (page 151)

beans or lentils (cooked)

Better Ketchup (page 152)

Broccoli-Garlic Sauce (page 157)

Creamy Mushroom Gravy (page 160)

diced tomatoes (canned)

Fresh Tomato Salsa (page 153)

Guacamole (page 162)

Hummus (page 159)

hot sauce

leftover soups or stews

Marinara Sauce (page 112)

mustard

Pesto Sauce (page 103)

sautéed mushrooms and onions

SOS-free salad dressings

Southwest Stew (page 126)

Tzatziki Sauce (page 161)

Veggie Burgers, crumbled (page 86)

Fresh Herbs (chopped)

basil

chives

cilantro

dill

garlic

oregano

parsley

thyme

Dried Herbs and Spices
(Look for blends that are salt- and sugar-free. See page 197 for more information on dried herbs and spices.)

chili powder

curry powder

granulated garlic

granulated onion

poultry seasoning

salt-free ethnic seasoning blends (Italian, Mediterranean, Asian, French, Mexican, Cajun, Jamaican)

Nuts and Seeds *(Use a rotary cheese grater to top your potato with a dusting of nuts or seeds.)*

cashews

hemp seeds

pecans

pine nuts

pumpkin seeds

sesame seeds

sunflower seeds

walnuts

QUINOA POLENTA WITH VEGETABLES AND BARBECUE SAUCE

I like to make this dish on special occasions or when I'm feeling in the mood to cook, as it requires three preparations: the polenta, the cooked vegetables, and the barbecue sauce. But it's really tasty and pretty.

PREPARATION
about 25 minutes

COOKING TIME
20 minutes
(stovetop),
15 minutes (oven)

SERVES
4

For the quinoa polenta:

2½ cups water

½ cup medium- or coarse-grind cornmeal

½ cup dry/uncooked quinoa

2 teaspoons granulated garlic

1½ teaspoons granulated onion

1½ teaspoons dried oregano

1 teaspoon chili powder

For the vegetables:

8 medium white or cremini mushrooms, sliced (about 3 cups)

1 medium yellow or white onion, chopped (about 2 cups)

1 medium zucchini, sliced (about 2 cups)

1 medium red bell pepper, seeded and chopped (about 1½ cups)

1 tablespoon finely chopped garlic (4 or 5 medium cloves)

For the barbecue sauce:

1 recipe Barbecue Sauce (page 151)

Note: *To save time, you can make the Barbecue Sauce the day before serving it, which will also enhance the flavor.*

From the blog

"I made this recipe this week, and it immediately became one of our favorites! I'm not always a big fan of polenta, but with the quinoa it is super." —*Kathleen*

1. To make the quinoa polenta, bring all of the ingredients (water, cornmeal, quinoa, grandulated garlic and onion, oregano, and chili powder) to a boil in a medium saucepan over medium-high heat, stirring occasionally. Reduce the heat to low, then cover and simmer for 20 minutes, stirring occasionally.

2. Preheat the oven to 400°F. Line an 8×8-inch square baking dish with parchment paper.

3. Spread the thick, cooked mixture evenly into the bottom of the dish and bake uncovered for 15 minutes.

4. To cook the vegetables, heat 1 tablespoon of water in a large frying pan or soup pot over medium-high heat. When the water starts to sputter, add the mushrooms, onions, zucchini, and bell pepper, and cook while stirring for 3 to 5 minutes, adding a little water as needed. Add the garlic, and cook while stirring for 1 to 2 minutes more. Remove from the heat.

5. After removing the cooked quinoa polenta from the oven, cut it into four squares and place each one on a plate. Spoon the cooked vegetables over the top of each square, and top with a spoonful of the barbecue sauce (or you can serve the sauce on the side).

NOTE

Polenta is a great blank canvas, so experiment by adding:

- Your favorite dried herbs and spices to the cooking polenta.

- Your favorite vegetables to the frying pan.

- A can of drained and rinsed black beans to the cooking vegetables.

- Fresh vegetables on top, such as sliced cherry tomatoes or avocado.

MUSHROOM RISOTTO

This classic Italian rice dish is creamy and hearty, getting its big flavor from a variety of mushrooms, as well as garlic, balsamic vinegar, and tarragon.

PREPARATION
about 20 minutes

COOKING TIME
50 minutes

SERVES
4 to 6 (makes about 6 cups)

7 cups water

1 cup chopped shallots, leeks, or yellow or white onion

6 medium white or cremini mushrooms, sliced (about 2½ cups)

6 medium shiitake mushrooms, sliced (about 2¼ cups)

1 medium portabella mushroom, sliced into small pieces (about 2 cups)

1 tablespoon finely chopped garlic (4 or 5 medium cloves)

1½ cups dry/uncooked Arborio rice

¼ cup balsamic vinegar (use ⅛ cup if you prefer a milder flavor)

1 teaspoon granulated onion

2 tablespoons finely chopped fresh tarragon, plus a little more for garnish

1 teaspoon lemon zest (optional)

1 ounce raw, unsalted cashews, ground (about ¼ cup for garnish; optional)

1. Bring the 7 cups of water to a low boil in a medium saucepan over medium heat. Reduce the heat so the water is steaming but not boiling. Leave it on the stovetop.

2. On a separate burner, heat 1 tablespoon of water in a 4- to 5-quart, heavy-duty saucepan over medium-high heat. When the water starts to sputter, add the shallots (or leeks or onions), and cook while stirring for 3 to 5 minutes until soft, adding a little water, as needed, to prevent sticking.

3. Add all of the mushrooms and garlic, and continue stirring for about 3 minutes, adding water as needed. Add the rice and stir until the edges of the rice are translucent, about 3 minutes. Add the balsamic vinegar and granulated onion, and stir until you can no longer see any vinegar in the bottom of the pot.

4. Pour in 1 cup of the hot water, stirring until it has been almost completely absorbed (2 to 3 minutes). Continue to add 1 cup of water at a time, stirring nearly continuously. This gradual technique is the key to getting the rice to release its starch, thereby making the dish creamy. This process takes 30 to 40 minutes and uses 6 to 7 cups of the hot water. The risotto is ready when the rice is soft but still has a bit of chew to it.

5. Stir in the tarragon and lemon zest (if using). If desired, garnish with chopped tarragon and/or cashews (grind nuts with a rotary cheese grater, which gives the effect of parmesan cheese). When reheating leftovers, stir in a little water or unsweetened nondairy milk, as the risotto will have thickened considerably.

KHICHADI

Khichadi (pronounced "kich-ah-ree") is an Indian comfort food that features rice and lentils. This recipe also calls for a variety of spices that will fill your kitchen with a wonderful aroma!

Shopping tip: Lentils sold as "red" actually range in color from gold to orange to rosy red. They can be found in most natural grocery stores as well as ethnic grocery stores.

PREPARATION
about 35 minutes

COOKING TIME
45 minutes

SERVES
6 to 8 (makes about 9 cups)

For the rice and lentils:

3½ cups water

¾ cup dry/uncooked brown basmati rice

¾ cup dry/uncooked red lentils

1 teaspoon ground cumin

1 teaspoon ground coriander

½ to 1 teaspoon crushed red pepper flakes (these are spicy; optional)

¼ teaspoon turmeric

¼ teaspoon ground cardamom

⅛ teaspoon ground cloves

For the vegetables:

1 medium yellow or white onion, chopped (about 2 cups)

1½ teaspoons finely chopped garlic (about 2 medium cloves)

1 teaspoon finely grated or chopped fresh ginger

3 cups water

½ pound Yukon Gold potatoes, cut into ½-inch chunks (about 1½ cups)

1 medium yam, cut into ½-inch chunks (about 2 cups)

2 ribs celery, sliced (about ⅔ cup)

1¼ cups cooked peas (if frozen, rinse under warm water)

4 cups coarsely chopped greens (I like curly kale)

1. Bring the 3½ cups water, rice, lentils, and spices (cumin, coriander, red pepper flakes, turmeric, cardamom, and cloves) to a boil in a soup pot over high heat, uncovered. Reduce the heat to low, then cover and simmer for 45 minutes.

2. About 15 minutes before the rice and lentils are done cooking, heat 1 tablespoon of water in a large frying pan over medium-high heat. Once the water starts to sputter, add the onion, and cook while stirring for 3 minutes, adding a little water, as needed. Add the garlic and ginger, and cook while stirring for 1 minute.

3. Add the 3 cups of water, potatoes, yams, and celery to the frying pan, and return to a boil, uncovered. Reduce the heat to medium-low, then cover and cook for 7 minutes. Stir in the peas and greens, then cover and cook for 3 minutes more, or until the potatoes are tender.

4. Stir the cooked vegetables into the pot of cooked rice and lentils.

NOTES

If you don't want to bother with all of the individual dried herbs and spices (cumin, coriander, red pepper flakes, turmeric, cardamom, ground cloves), you may replace them with 2 to 3 teaspoons of your favorite curry powder.

If you're not in the chopping mood, you can also make a meal of just the lentils, rice, and herbs and spices after cooking them all together in step 1.

From the blog
"The combination of seasonings creates an intoxicating aroma. I can't remember the last time the kitchen smelled this good." —*Michelle*

SPAGHETTI WITH MARINARA SAUCE

PREPARATION
about 25 minutes

COOKING TIME
35 minutes

SERVES
4 (makes about
4½ cups sauce)

For the pasta, you can use whole-grain pasta or raw or lightly cooked zucchini "noodles" (you will need a mandolin or spiral slicer).

Shopping tip: Buy salt-free canned tomatoes and tomato paste.

For the pasta:

1 package spaghetti pasta (12 ounces) or 6 medium zucchini
    (about 7 inches each)

1 ounce walnuts, cashews, or pine nuts, ground (about ¼ cup; for optional garnish)

For the Marinara Sauce:

8 medium cremini or white mushrooms, sliced (about 3 cups)

1 medium yellow or white onion, chopped (about 2 cups)

1 tablespoon finely chopped garlic (4 or 5 medium cloves)

2 cans diced tomatoes (14.5 ounces each; about 3 cups total), undrained

1 can tomato paste (6 ounces)

2 teaspoons dried Italian herb seasoning

½ cup loosely packed fresh basil, chopped

1. Heat 1 tablespoon of water in a large frying pan or soup pot over medium-high heat. When the water starts to sputter, add the mushrooms and onions, and cook while stirring for about 5 minutes, adding a little water, as needed, to prevent sticking. Stir in the garlic and cook for 1 minute.

2. Stir in the diced tomatoes (including liquid), tomato paste, and Italian herbs. Reduce the heat to low, then cover and simmer for 25 to 30 minutes, stirring occasionally.

3. While the sauce is simmering, prepare the noodles. If you are using whole-grain pasta, cook it according to the package instructions. Drain and rinse with cool water, and set aside. If you are making zucchini noodles, see step 4.

4. Use a mandolin or spiral slicer to create thin, matchstick-sized zucchini strands. If you want to cook the zucchini "noodles" slightly (you can also eat them raw), place them into a pot of low-boiling water, and cook for 1 to 3 minutes, or until they are tender but not falling apart (undercooked is better than overcooked). Drain and set aside.

5. Stir the basil into the sauce. You can add the cooked pasta or zucchini noodles to the simmering sauce, or keep the noodles and sauce separate, ladling the sauce over each plate of noodles just before serving. Serve as is or topped with finely ground nuts (use a rotary cheese grater to create a parmesan cheese-like topping).

SOUPS AND STEWS

SOUP AND STEW BASICS

Plant-based soups and stews are delicious and filling, and they are one of the easiest healthy meals you can prepare since everything comes together in one big pot. They also yield a lot of food, so there are always plenty of leftovers. Soups and stews are easy to freeze, and they taste great upon reheating.

Many of the soups and stews in this chapter will be familiar to you, such as corn chowder, minestrone soup, potato soup, and split pea soup. But they have been given a makeover, removing any traditional ingredients that don't support good health, such as meat (beef, pork, fowl, fish, or seafood), dairy products (cow's milk, cream, butter, or cheese), and oil.

Traditional soup and stew recipes are often very high in salt as well. But even without adding any salt, the dishes in this chapter taste great, with their flavors coming from an abundance of naturally flavorful foods, and fresh and dried herbs and spices. When we give our taste buds a break from salt (and oil) at every meal, we start to taste the wonderful foods beneath them.

Another great thing about cooking plant-based soups and stews is that it's hard to mess them up. They're very open to interpretation when it comes to herbs and spices, and the vegetables and beans you can use. I have learned that few people follow recipes exactly; rather, they modify dishes according to their tastes or what they have on hand. So have fun with your soup pot, and set out to prepare soups and stews that make *your* taste buds happy.

SPLIT PEA AND YAM SOUP

Sweet yams and earthy greens add another level of enjoyment to traditional split pea soup. This recipe is easy to make and yields a large pot of soup, perfect for a family dinner or lunches for the week.

PREPARATION
about 15 minutes

COOKING TIME
55 minutes

SERVES
6 to 8 (makes about 10 cups)

8½ cups water

2 cups dry/uncooked split peas

1 medium yellow or white onion, chopped (about 2 cups)

1 medium yam, peeled and chopped (about 1½ cups)

1 medium white potato, peeled and chopped (about 1½ cups)

2 ribs celery, sliced (about ⅔ cup)

1½ teaspoons dried oregano

1 teaspoon granulated garlic

½ teaspoon ground cumin

¼ teaspoon ground celery seed

5 cups coarsely chopped Swiss chard (or other greens)

1. Bring the water and split peas to a boil in a soup pot over medium-high heat, uncovered.

2. Reduce the heat to medium-low, cover, and cook for 30 minutes, stirring occasionally (so the peas don't stick to the bottom of the pan).

3. Stir in the onion, yams, potatoes, celery, oregano, garlic, cumin, and celery seed, and bring to boiling over medium-high heat.

4. Reduce the heat to medium-low and continue to cook uncovered, stirring occasionally, for about 20 minutes, or until the potatoes are soft.

5. Stir in the greens and cook for 5 minutes more.

From the blog

"I made this soup today. I had some doubts about the flavor without any salt, but it is quite delicious." —*Lilly*

TOMATO-RICE SOUP

Tomatoes and rice go together famously. This flavorful and easy-to-prepare soup makes a meal all on its own. White beans and fresh basil give it that extra "something something."

Shopping tip: To avoid excess sodium, look for salt-free canned beans and diced tomatoes.

PREPARATION
about 25 minutes

COOKING TIME
45 minutes

SERVES
6 to 8 (makes about 10 cups)

1 medium yellow or white onion, chopped (about 2 cups)

6½ cups water

1 can cooked navy or white beans (15 ounces; about 1½ cups), drained and rinsed

¾ cup dry/uncooked long-grain brown rice

2 cans diced tomatoes (14.5 ounces each; about 3 cups total), undrained

2 ribs celery, sliced (about ⅔ cup)

5 medium white or cremini mushrooms, sliced (about 2 cups)

1 tablespoon dried Italian herb seasoning

1½ teaspoons granulated garlic

3 cups chopped Swiss chard

½ cup chopped fresh basil

1. Heat 1 tablespoon of water in a soup pot over medium-high heat. When the water starts to sputter, add the onion and cook while stirring for about 3 to 5 minutes.

2. Add the water, beans, rice, diced tomatoes (including juice), celery, mushrooms, Italian seasoning, and granulated garlic, and bring to a boil, uncovered. Reduce the heat to low then cover and cook for 30 minutes.

3. Stir in the chard then cover and cook for 10 minutes more, until the chard has wilted. Stir in the basil toward the end of cooking.

NOTES

You may also use other greens in this soup, such as beet greens, collard greens, and kale.

If you want to use fresh tomatoes instead of canned, add 1½ pounds of fresh tomatoes (peeled or unpeeled), chopped, in step 2.

BEEFLESS STEW

This hearty stew includes large chunks of potato, carrot, celery, and onion, and portabella mushrooms stand in for the beef. Garlic, paprika, and fresh rosemary provide excellent flavor. This is one of my most popular recipes—especially with husbands!

Shopping tip: To avoid excess sodium, look for salt-free tomato paste.

PREPARATION
about 30 minutes

COOKING TIME
45 minutes

SERVES
6 to 8 (makes about 10 cups)

1½ large yellow or white onions, chopped into ¾-inch pieces (about 3 cups)

3 medium carrots, sliced lengthwise and cut into ¾-inch pieces (about 2¼ cups)

3 ribs celery, cut into ¾-inch pieces (about 1 cup)

2 medium portabella mushrooms, cut into ¾-inch pieces (about 4 cups)

1½ tablespoons finely chopped garlic (about 6 medium cloves)

5 cups water

2 pounds white potatoes, peeled and cut into ¾-inch chunks (about 6 cups)

⅓ cup tomato paste (half of a 6-ounce can)

1 tablespoon dried Italian herb seasoning

1 tablespoon paprika

2 teaspoons finely chopped fresh rosemary

1½ cups cooked peas (if frozen, rinse under warm water)

½ cup fresh parsley, chopped

1. Heat 1 tablespoon of water in a soup pot over medium-high heat. When the water starts to sputter, add the onions, carrots, and celery, and cook, stirring frequently, for about 8 minutes, adding water, as needed.

2. Stir in the mushrooms and garlic, and continue to cook while stirring for 5 minutes more, adding water as needed.

3. Add the water, potatoes, tomato paste, Italian seasoning, and paprika, and bring to a boil, uncovered. Reduce the heat to medium-low and stir in the rosemary.

Cover and cook for 25 to 30 minutes, stirring occasionally, or until the carrots and potatoes are very tender.

4. Add the peas and cook for 5 minutes more.

5. Place 2 cups of the stew (broth and vegetables) into a blender, and blend just briefly. Stir the mixture back into the pot to thicken the stew. Stir in the parsley.

POTATO SOUP

Potato soups are traditionally very creamy and high in fat. This easy recipe, however, maintains a creamy consistency but keeps the fat low. The addition of Swiss chard adds a nice salty flavor.

PREPARATION
about 20 minutes

COOKING TIME
40 minutes

SERVES
6 (makes about 8 cups)

1 medium yellow or white onion, chopped (about 2 cups)

5 cups water

2 pounds white potatoes, peeled and cut into ¾-inch chunks (about 6 cups)

2 teaspoons dried basil

1½ teaspoons granulated garlic

1 teaspoon dried dill

1 teaspoon ground coriander

½ cup unsweetened nondairy milk (at room temperature)

3 cups coarsely chopped Swiss chard (or other greens)

1. Heat 1 tablespoon of water in a soup pot over medium-high heat. When the water starts to sputter, add the onion and cook while stirring for 3 to 5 minutes, adding a little water, as needed.

2. Add the water, potatoes, basil, granulated garlic, dill, and coriander, and bring to a boil, uncovered. Reduce the heat to medium, and cook uncovered for 20 to 25 minutes, or until the potatoes are very tender.

3. Turn the heat to low. Add the nondairy milk and blend the soup to your desired consistency with an immersion blender.

(If you don't have an immersion blender, carefully ladle all or a portion of the soup into a blender, and blend to your desired consistency before returning it to the pot. Or you can use a handheld potato masher right in the pot.)

4. Stir in the greens, and simmer for 5 to 10 minutes more, or until they have wilted.

NOTE

Leeks are also delicious in this soup.
Substitute 1 large leek (white and light green parts, thinly sliced and rinsed) for the onion.

MINESTRONE SOUP

Minestrone is known in Italy as "the big soup," chock full of kidney beans, mushrooms, potatoes, carrots, zucchini, tomatoes, and pasta. Fennel, garlic, and basil also add to the Mediterranean flair of this famous soup.

Shopping tip: Fresh fennel can be found in most produce sections. It looks like a cross between cabbage, celery, and dill. Its sweet licorice taste mellows during cooking. I use the white bulb only (not the green, frilly fronds). If you don't have fennel, celery may be used in its place.

PREPARATION
about 30 minutes

COOKING TIME
45 minutes

SERVES
6 to 8 (makes about 12 cups)

1 medium yellow or white onion, chopped (about 2 cups)

¾ cup chopped fresh fennel (or 3 ribs celery, chopped)

1 tablespoon finely chopped garlic (4 or 5 medium cloves)

1 teaspoon whole fennel seeds

¼ to ½ teaspoon crushed red pepper flakes (optional; these are spicy)

6 cups water

2 cans diced tomatoes (14.5 ounces each; about 3 cups total), undrained

1½ pounds white potatoes, peeled and chopped (about 4½ cups)

2 medium carrots, sliced (about 1½ cups)

1 can cooked red kidney beans (15 ounces; about 1½ cups), drained and rinsed

6 medium white or cremini mushrooms, sliced (about 2½ cups)

1 medium zucchini, sliced (about 2 cups)

½ cup chopped fresh basil

½ cup chopped fresh parsley

2 cups cooked small-shell or elbow pasta (about 1½ cups dry)

1. Heat 1 tablespoon of water in a soup pot over medium-high heat. When the water starts to sputter, add the onion and fresh fennel, and cook while stirring for 3 to 5 minutes, adding a little water as needed.

2. Stir in the garlic, fennel seeds, and red pepper flakes, and cook while stirring for 1 to 2 minutes.

3. Stir in the water, tomatoes (with liquid), potatoes, carrots, and kidney beans, and bring to a boil, uncovered. Decrease the heat to medium-low and cook for 25 minutes.

4. Stir in the mushrooms and zucchini, and cook for 5 minutes, or until the potatoes and carrots are tender. Add the basil, parsley, and cooked pasta, and cook for 1 to 2 minutes more.

CURRIED FRENCH LENTILS

PREPARATION
about 25 minutes

COOKING TIME
45 minutes

SERVES
6 to 8 (makes
about 9½ cups)

This is one of my favorite go-to meals since it's so easy to prepare all in one pot and is very flavorful. It can be eaten alone as a stew, over cooked brown rice, or spooned into steamed corn tortillas with cooked brown rice. (Shown on facing page topped with grated cashews.)

Shopping tip: French green lentils (also known as "Le Puy" lentils) are small, speckled, and dark green in color. Look for them packaged in the bean aisle or in the bulk dry goods section of the grocery store.

6 cups water

1 cup dry/uncooked French green lentils

1 medium yellow or white onion, chopped (about 2 cups)

1 medium yam or sweet potato, peeled and chopped into ½-inch chunks (about 1½ cups)

2 cups small cauliflower florets

2 ribs celery, sliced (about ⅔ cup)

1 can diced tomatoes (14.5 ounces; about 1½ cups), undrained

1 tablespoon yellow curry powder

2 teaspoons dried Italian herb seasoning

1 teaspoon granulated onion

1 teaspoon granulated garlic

4 cups coarsely chopped Swiss chard (or other greens)

1. Bring the water and lentils to a boil in a soup pot over medium-high heat, uncovered. Reduce the heat to medium-low and cook uncovered, stirring occasionally, for 20 minutes.

2. Stir in the onion, yam or sweet potato, cauliflower, celery, diced tomatoes (including the juice), curry powder, Italian seasoning, and granulated onion and garlic. Cover and simmer at a low boil for 15 minutes.

3. Stir in the greens, then cover and cook for 5 to 10 minutes more, or until the lentils and yams or sweet potatoes are tender.

NOTES

If you don't have cauliflower, you can use broccoli instead.

If you're a mushroom fan, add about 6 sliced medium white or cremini mushrooms in step 2.

If you want to turn this thick stew into a soup, simply add 1½ to 2 cups of water in step 2.

From the blog

"Awesome, or as my boyfriend said, 'party in my mouth!'" —Lubna

BROCCOLI SOUP

This soup has a lot going for it: It's easy to make, it has a minimum of ingredients, it's creamy without added fat, and it has great flavor even without added salt.

Shopping tips: Any type of potato will work, but I like Yukon Golds best since they are naturally creamy.

PREPARATION
about 20 minutes

COOKING TIME
25 minutes

SERVES
6 to 8 (makes about 10 cups)

6 cups water

1½ pounds white potatoes, peeled and chopped (about 4½ cups)

1 medium yellow or white onion, chopped (about 2 cups)

2 teaspoons ground coriander

2 teaspoons granulated garlic

1 teaspoon granulated onion

1 teaspoon salt-free poultry seasoning

1½ pounds broccoli (about 2 heads), cut into small florets

4 cups coarsely chopped Swiss chard (or other greens)

1. Bring the water, potatoes, onion, coriander, granulated garlic and onion, and poultry seasoning to a boil in a soup pot over medium-high heat, uncovered.

2. Reduce the heat to medium and add the broccoli. Cover and cook for 15 to 20 minutes, or until the potatoes and broccoli are very tender. Stir in the greens and cook for 3 to 5 minutes more, until wilted.

3. Blend the soup with an immersion blender until smooth. (If you don't have an immersion blender, carefully ladle the soup into a blender and blend before returning it to the pot.)

NOTES

You can also use the broccoli stems; just be sure to peel them first, as the outer skin can be very tough.

If you do not have poultry seasoning on hand, you can use any type of salt-free seasoning blend.

From the blog

"Delicious. Unbelievable there's no salt in this; it's really tasty. Love that it made so much; I can eat it for several days. I used a potato masher, but now I want an immersion blender!" —Rayanne

CREAMY MUSHROOM SOUP

If you have fond memories of canned mushroom soup, you will enjoy this version. The canned soup's appeal is mainly due to its very high salt content. This recipe leaves out the salt but not the flavor.

PREPARATION
about 35 minutes

COOKING TIME
35 minutes

SERVESS
6 to 8 (makes about 10 cups)

1 medium yellow or white onion, chopped (about 2 cups)

1½ pounds white potatoes, peeled and chopped (about 4½ cups)

4 cups water

6 medium cremini or white mushrooms, sliced (about 2½ cups)

1 small yam or sweet potato, peeled and chopped (about 2 cups)

2 ribs celery, sliced (about ⅔ cup)

2 teaspoons dried Italian herb seasoning

1 teaspoon paprika

1 teaspoon granulated garlic

½ teaspoon granulated onion

½ teaspoon ground nutmeg

1 cup water

12 medium cremini or white mushrooms, thinly sliced (4 to 5 cups)

1 cup unsweetened, room temperature nondairy milk

1. Heat 1 tablespoon of water in a soup pot over medium-high heat. When the water starts to sputter, add the onion and cook while stirring for 3 to 5 minutes, adding a little water, as needed, to prevent sticking.

2. Add the potatoes, 4 cups water, 6 sliced mushrooms, yams or sweet potatoes, celery, and herbs and spices (Italian seasoning, paprika, granulated garlic and onion, and nutmeg). Reduce the heat to medium and cook for about 10 to 15 minutes, or until the potatoes are tender.

3. Add the 1 cup of water. Blend the soup with an immersion blender until it is mostly smooth. (If you don't have an immersion blender, carefully ladle the soup into a blender and blend before returning to the pot.)

4. Add the 12 sliced mushrooms and cook over low heat, stirring occasionally, for 15 to 20 minutes until the mushrooms have softened. Remove the pot from the heat and whisk in the nondairy milk.

NOTE
You can use any kind of edible mushrooms in this soup. White and cremini are easy to find in markets and they are the least expensive. You can use all the same type of mushroom or mix it up.

SOUTHWEST STEW

This chunky, satisfying stew is full of beans, greens, corn, mushrooms, and bell pepper, and pairs nicely with Quinoa Cornbread (page 137).

Shopping tips: Look for canned beans, tomatoes, corn, and tomato paste with no added salt. For a spicy stew, use "medium" or "hot" chili powder.

PREPARATION
about 25 minutes

COOKING TIME
35 minutes

SERVES
6 to 8 (makes about 12 cups)

6 medium white or cremini mushrooms, sliced (about 2½ cups)

1 medium yellow or white onion, chopped (about 2 cups)

1 small red bell pepper, seeded and chopped (about 1 cup)

1 tablespoon chili powder

1 tablespoon dried oregano

2 teaspoons granulated garlic

2 teaspoons ground cumin

4½ cups water

¾ pound white potatoes, peeled and cut into ½-inch chunks (about 2 cups)

1 can cooked black beans (15 ounces; about 1½ cups), drained and rinsed

1 can cooked pinto beans (15 ounces; about 1½ cups), drained and rinsed

1½ cups corn kernels

1 can diced tomatoes (14.5 ounces; about 1½ cups), undrained

⅓ cup tomato paste (half of a 6-ounce can)

4 cups coarsely chopped collard greens (or other greens)

1½ cups loosely packed cilantro, chopped (plus extra for garnish)

1. Heat 1 tablespoon of water in a soup pot over medium-high heat. When the water starts to sputter, add the mushrooms, onions, and bell pepper, and cook while stirring for 5 to 8 minutes, adding a little water as needed.

2. Add the chili powder, oregano, granulated garlic, and cumin, and cook while stirring for 1 minute more, adding water as needed.

3. Stir in the water, potatoes, black beans, pinto beans, corn, diced tomatoes, and tomato paste, and bring to a boil, uncovered. Reduce the heat to medium-low, cover, and cook for 10 minutes, stirring once or twice.

4. Stir in the greens, and cook covered for 10 to 15 minutes more, or until the potatoes are tender. Stir in the cilantro, and serve as is or garnished with more chopped cilantro.

NOTES

Tasty additions: Add a small peeled and chopped sweet potato (or yam) in step 3, or serve the final dish over baked sweet potatoes (or yams). Add ¼ cup of dry/uncooked quinoa in step 3. A little chopped avocado on top adds a touch of richness.

From the blog

"I've made this twice now and am absolutely in love with it. I love how potatoes—yay, potatoes!—lend so much richness and depth." —*Erika*

CORN CHOWDER

Fresh rosemary and nutmeg are perfect complements to the sweet corn and hearty vegetables in this soup. This chowder is especially good when made with fresh corn.

Shopping tips: You can use fresh, frozen, or canned corn for this recipe; just make sure that if it's packaged, it hasn't had salt or sugar added. Fresh rosemary is preferred, but if you have only dried, use about ½ teaspoon.

PREPARATION
about 20 minutes

COOKING TIME
30 minutes

SERVES
6 to 8 (makes about 10 cups)

1 medium yellow or white onion, chopped (about 2 cups)

5 cups water

1½ pounds white potatoes, peeled and chopped (about 4½ cups)

2½ cups corn kernels

2 medium carrots, sliced (about 1½ cups)

3 ribs celery, sliced or chopped (about 1 cup)

1 tablespoon dried Italian herb seasoning

1½ teaspoons granulated garlic

1 teaspoon ground nutmeg

1 teaspoon finely chopped fresh rosemary

1. Heat 1 tablespoon of water in a soup pot over medium-high heat. When the water starts to sputter, add the onion and cook while stirring for 3 to 5 minutes, adding a little water as needed.

2. Add the water, potatoes, corn, carrots, celery, Italian seasoning, granulated garlic, nutmeg, and rosemary, and bring to a boil.

3. Reduce the heat to medium-low, cover, and cook for 15 to 20 minutes, or until the carrots and potatoes are tender.

4. To create a creamy soup base, blend the soup with an immersion blender to your desired consistency. (If you don't have an immersion blender, carefully ladle about 3 cups of the soup into a blender and blend briefly before stirring it back into the pot.)

BLACK BEAN AND RICE STEW

This satisfying stew is a breeze to make if you have canned beans and tomatoes on hand, as well as some cooked rice. It's a perfect meal for a cozy night's dinner. And it makes a great taco filling!

Shopping tips: To avoid excess sodium, look for canned beans and tomatoes with no added salt. If you want this dish to be spicy, use "medium" or "hot" chili powder.

PREPARATION
about 25 minutes

COOKING TIME
30 minutes (stove-top), 60 minutes (to precook rice)

SERVES
6 to 8 (makes about 12 cups)

8 medium white or cremini mushrooms, sliced (about 3 cups)

1 medium yellow or white onion, chopped (about 2 cups)

2 ribs celery, sliced or chopped (about ⅔ cup)

1 tablespoon Italian herb seasoning

2 teaspoons chili powder

2 teaspoons ground coriander

1½ teaspoons granulated garlic

1½ teaspoons ground cumin

3 cups water

2 cans diced tomatoes (14.5 ounces each; about 3 cups total), undrained

2 cans cooked black beans (15 ounces each; about 3 cups total), drained and rinsed

1 large white potato, peeled or unpeeled, cut into ½-inch cubes (about 2 cups)

2¼ cups cooked brown rice (see Note)

1. Heat 1 tablespoon of water in a soup pot over medium-high heat. When the water starts to sputter, add the mushrooms, onions, and celery, and cook while stirring for 4 to 5 minutes, adding a little water as needed.

2. Add the Italian seasoning, chili powder, coriander, granulated garlic, and cumin and cook while stirring for 1 minute, adding water as needed.

3. Stir in the 3 cups water, diced tomatoes, beans, potatoes, and rice, and bring to a boil, uncovered. Reduce the heat to medium-low, then cover and cook for 15 to 20 minutes, or until the potatoes are tender, stirring occasionally.

NOTE
To make 2¼ cups of cooked brown rice, bring 1½ cups of water and ¾ cup of dry/uncooked rice to a boil uncovered in a medium saucepan over high heat. Reduce the heat to low, then cover and simmer for 45 minutes for long-grain rice or 50 minutes for short-grain rice. Remove from the heat and let stand for 10 minutes with the lid still on.

HEARTY LENTIL STEW

This vegetable-lentil stew is a breeze to make, and it's very versatile: add in your favorite vegetables or whatever you have in the fridge, plus dried herbs and spices to fit your tastes.

Shopping tip: Brown lentils are the most common variety found in U.S. grocery stores. They are light brownish-green, and can be found packaged in the bean aisle or in the bulk dry goods section of your grocery store.

PREPARATION
about 20 minutes

COOKING TIME
50 minutes

SERVES
6 to 8 (makes about 10 cups)

1 medium yellow or white onion, chopped (about 2 cups)

8 cups water

1½ pounds white potatoes, peeled and chopped (about 4½ cups)

2 medium carrots, sliced (about 1½ cups)

1½ cups dry/uncooked brown lentils, rinsed

3 ribs celery, chopped (about 1 cup)

1 tablespoon dried Italian herb seasoning

1 teaspoon granulated garlic

½ teaspoon ground cumin

3 cups chopped green cabbage

1. Heat 1 tablespoon of water in a soup pot over medium-high heat. When the water starts to sputter, add the onion and cook while stirring for 3 to 5 minutes, adding a little water as needed.

2. Add the 8 cups water, potatoes, carrots, lentils, celery, Italian seasoning, granulated garlic, and cumin, and bring to a boil, uncovered. Reduce the heat to medium-low, then cover and cook for 30 minutes.

3. Stir in the cabbage, then cover and cook for 10 minutes more, or until the lentils are tender.

From the blog
"I just made a double batch of this stew, and it's a hit! Family favorite for sure!" —*Rebecca*

SIDE DISHES

SIDE DISH BASICS

Most traditional side dishes can be transformed easily into health-pro- moting dishes. Just like other meal categories, standard American side dishes are often laden with salt, sugar, oil, and dairy (milk, cream, butter, sour cream, and/ or cheese). All of these ingredients have been overly processed, and are highly concentrated in flavor, which is why they can be so hard to resist.

Yet, by giving your taste buds a short time to adjust to the flavors of dishes without these foods, not only will you come to enjoy them, but you'll start to look forward to them as much as (or more than) the highly salted and dressed foods that you may be accustomed to. It's hard to believe, I know, but hang in there and you'll see what I mean.

On occasion someone has seen me digging into a bowl of steamed vegetables or a big pile of mashed potatoes and asked, "Aren't you going to put anything on that?" But the wonderful truth is that these foods taste amazing all by themselves, without any unhealthy extras stirred in or added on top.

However, this doesn't mean you have to eat your side dishes plain. It just means that you'll want to use more health-promoting accompaniments instead, like a little salt-free seasoning or a dollop of hummus or guacamole. But a great zucchini or batch of green beans from the garden or farmers' market will remind you just how delicious and flavorful steamed vegetables are all by themselves. High-quality produce stands on its own. Even though we've gotten in the habit of adding the typical condiments to them, nothing (or very little) really needs to be added.

In this chapter I'll show you how to make cornbread without milk, butter, eggs, and sugar; flavorful roasted potatoes without salt and oil; mashed potatoes without butter and sour cream; and corn chips and french fries without oil. And recipes aside, a side dish can be almost any plant food, simply prepared, such as a bowl of cut-up tomatoes from the garden with some chopped fresh basil; a can of cooked black beans heated up and spooned over chopped greens; or some steamed broccoli, cauliflower, or asparagus topped with lemon juice and chopped fresh dill.

MASHED POTATOES

Mashed potatoes are the ultimate comfort food. But you may be surprised to find out that they don't need to be loaded with butter, sour cream, and salt to taste great. In this very simple recipe, a little of the cooking water is used to flavor and whip the potatoes.

Shopping tip: I think light and starchy russets make the best mashed potatoes, but other types of white potatoes may be used as well, such as Yukon Gold.

PREPARATION
about 15 minutes

COOKING TIME
20 minutes

SERVES
4 (makes about 4½ cups)

3 pounds russet potatoes, peeled and cut into 1-inch chunks (about 9 cups)

2 teaspoons granulated garlic

1 teaspoon granulated onion

Creamy Mushroom Gravy (page 160; optional)

¼ cup chopped chives, green onions, or parsley (for optional garnish)

1. Place the potatoes into a soup pot and cover them with water. Stir in the granulated garlic and onion, and bring to a boil over high heat, uncovered. Cook for 15 to 20 minutes, or until the potatoes are very tender when pierced with a knife.

2. Ladle 1 cup of the cooking water from the pot into a small bowl, and set it aside. Drain the potatoes and transfer them to a large mixing bowl.

3. Using an electric mixer, beat the potatoes on low speed, adding the cooking water gradually, until you have reached your desired consistency. Top with Creamy Mushroom Gravy and/or garnish with chopped chives, green onions, or parsley.

NOTES

If you prefer chunkier mashed potatoes, do not peel the potatoes and use a handheld potato masher instead of an electric mixer.

To make curried mashed potatoes, add 2 to 3 teaspoons of curry powder along with the granulated garlic and onion in step 1.

To make pistachio mashed potatoes, in step 2, combine ½ cup of the reserved cooking water with ¼ cup raw, unsalted pistachios in a blender, and blend for 1 minute on high speed before mixing in with the potatoes.

QUINOA CORNBREAD

Traditional cornbread gets a total makeover with this recipe, which uses no butter, eggs, cow's milk, salt, oil, or refined sugar, instead getting its moistness from quinoa and its sweetness from dates.

Shopping tips: To avoid excess sodium, use sodium-free baking powder and soda (see page 18). Look for dates in the bulk food section or packaged near the raisins.

PREPARATION
about 25 minutes

COOKING TIME
20 minutes (stove-top), 35 minutes (oven)

SERVES
9 (makes 9 pieces)

1 cup water

½ cup dry/uncooked quinoa

½ cup old-fashioned rolled oats

1½ cups cornmeal

1 teaspoon baking powder

¾ teaspoon baking soda

1¼ cups unsweetened nondairy milk

3 ounces pitted dates (5 to 6 Medjool or 10 to 12 Deglet Noor), chopped

½ cup corn kernels

1. Bring the water and quinoa to a boil in a medium saucepan over high heat, uncovered. Reduce the heat to low, then cover and simmer for 20 minutes. Remove from the heat and set aside for 10 minutes with the lid still on.

2. Grind the oats into flour with a blender. Transfer to a medium bowl, and whisk in the cornmeal, baking powder, and baking soda. Set aside.

3. Place the nondairy milk and dates into the blender, and set aside for at least 15 minutes (so the dates can soften).

4. Preheat the oven to 350°F. Line an 8×8-inch baking pan with parchment paper.

5. Blend the milk and dates until smooth. Stir this mixture into the bowl of dry ingredients, along with the cooked quinoa and corn. Stir just until the dry ingredients disappear.

6. Spread the batter evenly into the pan and bake for 33 to 35 minutes. The cornbread will not rise very much, but when it's done it will have cracks in the top and be lightly browned around the edges. Set aside to cool at least 10 minutes before cutting into 9 pieces.

FALAFEL PATTIES

Traditionally, falafel is shaped into balls and fried in oil, but for this recipe it is pressed into patties and baked (see photo on page 161). Falafel is a Middle Eastern dish whose signature ingredient is ground garbanzo beans. This recipe makes about 8 patties, but double it for families or if you want to freeze some. Serve with Tzatziki Sauce (page 161).

Shopping tip: To avoid excess sodium, look for canned beans with no added salt (or cook your beans from scratch).

PREPARATION
about 25 minutes

COOKING TIME
30 minutes

SERVES
2 to 4 (makes eight 2½-inch patties)

1 can cooked garbanzo beans (15 ounces; about 1½ cups), drained and rinsed

1½ cups chopped kale

1 cup chopped parsley or cilantro

½ cup old-fashioned rolled oats

½ cup chopped yellow or white onion

2 tablespoons lemon juice

2 medium cloves garlic, finely chopped

2 teaspoons ground coriander

2 teaspoons ground cumin

1 teaspoon paprika

Tzatziki Sauce (page 161)

1. Preheat the oven to 375°F. Line a baking sheet with parchment paper.

2. Place all of the ingredients (garbanzo beans, kale, parsley or cilantro, rolled oats, onion, lemon juice, garlic, coriander, cumin, and paprika) into a food processor, and process until the mixture is well blended and starts to stick together. Transfer this to a medium bowl.

3. Form 8 balls (¼ cup falafel for each) and space them evenly on the baking sheet. Flatten each ball with your hand into a patty that is about 2½ inches in diameter and ½ inch thick.

4. Bake for 15 minutes, then gently flip each patty over. Bake for 15 minutes more or until lightly browned on each side. Let cool at least 5 minutes before serving. Serve with Tzatziki Sauce on the side.

From the blog
"I made this for dinner two days ago, and it was incredibly delicious. My husband rated it a 10!" —*Ruth*

BAKED FRENCH FRIES

Once you get hooked on baked fries without oil, you won't want to go back—and there's no guilt since there's no deep-frying. Serve these fries with Better Ketchup (page 152) or Barbecue Sauce (page 151).

3 pounds white potatoes (about 4 large), scrubbed and unpeeled
Better Ketchup (page 152; optional)
Barbecue Sauce (page 151; optional)

PREPARATION
about 10 minutes

COOKING TIME
30 minutes

SERVES
4

1. Preheat the oven to 425°F. Line a baking sheet with parchment paper.

2. To cut the potatoes, use a chef's knife or a french fry cutter (see Note). If using a knife, cut the potatoes into lengths of about 3 × ½ × ½ inch.

3. Spread the fries in one layer (without touching) on the baking sheet. Bake for 15 minutes.

4. Remove the baking sheet from the oven, and use a spatula to loosen and shuffle the fries around. Return the baking sheet to the oven, and bake for 15 to 20 minutes more, or until tender and lightly browned. Serve immediately, plain or with Better Ketchup or Barbecue Sauce.

NOTES

I love my french fry cutter! It makes all of the fries the same size, and it is easy to use. You may need to halve or quarter your potatoes first to fit them through the cutting blade. (Visit my online store to see the inexpensive model that I use.)

In addition to white potatoes, also try yams or sweet potatoes.

HERB-ROASTED POTATOES

If you like a lot of flavor, you will appreciate these hearty roasted potatoes. I peel my potatoes since the herbs and spices stick a little better, but you can also leave them unpeeled. Serve with Better Ketchup (page 152) or Barbecue Sauce (page 151). (At right, served with Better Ketchup and Spicy Beans and Greens, page 142.)

PREPARATION
about 10 minutes

COOKING TIME
10 minutes (stove-top), 30 minutes (oven)

SERVES
2 to 4

2 pounds white potatoes, cut into 1-inch chunks (about 6 cups)

2 teaspoons dried Italian herb seasoning

1½ teaspoons plain or smoked paprika

1 teaspoon granulated onion

½ teaspoon granulated garlic

¼ teaspoon ground black pepper

Dash cayenne pepper (optional)

Better Ketchup (page 152; optional)

Barbecue Sauce (page 151; optional)

1. Preheat the oven to 425°F. Line a baking sheet with parchment paper.

2. Place the potatoes into a pot and cover them with water. Bring to a boil over high heat, uncovered, and cook for about 5 minutes, or until the potatoes are tender when pierced with a knife. Drain, rinse, and set aside. (You can also use a microwave oven or steamer basket to precook the potatoes.)

3. Measure all of the herbs and spices (Italian herb seasoning, paprika, granulated onion and garlic, black pepper, and cayenne pepper, if using) into a small bowl, and mix with a fork.

4. Place the cooked potatoes into a medium bowl, and sprinkle the herbs and spices over them. Toss until the potatoes are evenly coated.

5. Spread the potatoes onto the baking sheet, and bake for 25 to 30 minutes, or until lightly browned. Serve immediately as is or with Better Ketchup or Barbecue Sauce.

NOTE
This recipe is very flexible regarding the herbs and spices you can use, so have fun tailoring it to your tastes.

SPICY BEANS AND GREENS

This simple and nutritious side dish calls for kale, Swiss chard, and Brussels sprouts along with onions, beans, and Mexican seasoning.

Shopping tips: To avoid excess sodium, look for canned beans with no added salt (or cook your beans from scratch). When buying Mexican seasoning, look for blends in the spice aisle, not as a "taco seasoning" packet, as these often contain MSG, aspartame, oil, milk, and excessive amounts of salt and sugar.

PREPARATION
about 15 minutes

COOKING TIME
15 minutes

SERVES
4 to 6 (makes about 6 cups)

1 medium yellow or white onion, chopped (about 2 cups)

1 tablespoon finely chopped garlic (4 to 5 medium cloves)

2 to 3 teaspoons Mexican seasoning blend (or see Note)

1 cup water

1 can cooked cannellini or other white beans (15 ounces; about 1½ cups), drained and rinsed

1 pound Brussels sprouts (about 20), ends trimmed, halved

4 cups coarsely chopped kale (I like curly kale)

4 cups coarsely chopped Swiss chard

1. Heat 1 tablespoon of water in a soup pot over medium-high heat. When the water starts to sputter, add the onion and cook while stirring for 5 minutes, adding a little water as needed.

2. Add the garlic and Mexican seasoning, and cook while stirring for 1 minute more.

3. Stir in the water, beans, Brussels sprouts, kale, and chard. Reduce the heat to medium, then cover and cook, stirring occasionally, for 7 to 10 minutes, or until the Brussels sprouts are tender.

NOTE

Instead of Mexican seasoning, you might try another salt-free seasoning blend, such as Cajun, Caribbean, Mediterranean, curry powder, or chili powder. Start with 1 teaspoon and add more according to your taste.

EASY CORN CHIPS

These oil-free corn chips are easy to make and pair well with the Burrito Bowl (page 53), Guacamole (page 162), Fresh Tomato Salsa (page 153), Spicy Black Bean Salsa (page 155), and Southwest Stew (page 126).

Shopping tips: When buying corn tortillas, you'll find the most healthful brands in the refrigerated section. Strive for the fewest ingredients possible, mainly water, corn, corn flour, and a trace of lime (and no oil).

PREPARATION
about 5 minutes

COOKING TIME
15 minutes

SERVES
8

8 oil-free corn tortillas (6-inch diameter)

1. Preheat the oven to 350°F. Set aside 2 baking sheets lined with parchment paper.

2. Cut each tortilla into 6 triangular pieces, like you're cutting a pizza.

3. Spread the chips evenly, without overlapping, on the baking sheets.

4. Bake for 15 to 17 minutes, or until the chips are almost completely hard (a little softness in the middle is fine since the chips will continue to harden as they cool). The chips should not cook so long as to become overly browned, which will make them too hard.

ROASTED GARBANZO BEANS

These little crunchy snacks remind me of Corn Nuts but without the oil and salt. They are mildly spiced, but you can spice them any way you like (see Note). Eat these plain, or on top of salads or soups in place of croutons.

PREPARATION
about 10 minutes

COOKING TIME
40 minutes (plus 1 hour to cool in the oven)

SERVES
4 to 6 (makes about 2 cups)

2 cans cooked garbanzo beans (15 ounces each; about 3 cups total), drained and rinsed

2 teaspoons granulated or powdered garlic

2 teaspoons granulated or powdered onion

2 teaspoons smoked paprika

1. Place the garbanzo beans into a medium bowl and pat them fairly dry with a couple of paper towels.

2. Toss the garlic, onion, and paprika with the beans until they are evenly coated.

3. Transfer the beans to a large, rimmed baking sheet lined with parchment paper, making sure they are in one layer. Place the baking sheet in the oven and then set the temperature to 375°F. Roast for 20 minutes.

4. Remove the baking sheet and stir the beans, then return the baking sheet to the oven for another 20 minutes.

5. Turn off the oven and leave the beans inside for 1 hour (this helps them dry out more and ensures maximum crispness). Eat warm or cold.

NOTE

Feel free to get creative with the seasonings. If you like hot and spicy snacks, try adding a little cayenne pepper or hot chili powder, or try some curry powder or other herb and spice blends.

BAKED PEARS AND YAMS

This is a great dish to serve in place of candied yams during the holidays, or any time you want a sweet side dish. (Served below with Quinoa Cornbread, page 137, and collard greens and tomatoes.)

Shopping tips: Look for Bosc pears that are ripe but firm. Garnet or jewel yams are preferred in this recipe, but you can also use sweet potatoes or Japanese yams.

PREPARATION
about 15 minutes

COOKING TIME
30 minutes

SERVES
6 to 8 (makes about 6 cups)

2 pounds Bosc pears (about 4 medium), peeled, cored and cut into 1-inch chunks (about 4 cups)

1½ pounds yams, peeled and cut into 1-inch chunks (about 4½ cups)

1 cup water

1 teaspoon cinnamon

⅛ teaspoon ground cloves

1. Preheat the oven to 375°F. Place the cut-up pears and yams into a 2-quart baking dish.

2. Add the water, cinnamon, and cloves, and stir until the pears and yams are evenly coated.

3. Cover the baking dish with a lid or with aluminum foil, and bake for 25 to 30 minutes, or until the yams and pears are tender and soft. Serve immediately. (Leftovers are delicious hot or cold.)

NOTES

For a little more sweetness, use 100% apple juice instead of water in step 2.

Instead of Bosc pears, you can also use Asian pears (also known as apple pears, Chinese pears, and Japanese pears) or apples; however, both usually cook faster than Bosc pears, so I add them to the dish 5 to 10 minutes after the yams begin baking.

RAW CRANBERRY-PERSIMMON RELISH

PREPARATION
about 15 minutes

COOKING TIME
0 minutes

SERVES
6 (makes about
3¼ cups)

The fresh cranberry and persimmon season is short, but even if you make this only a few times for fall and winter meals and holiday feasts, it will be worth it. The sweetness of the persimmon, apple, and tangerine balances the tartness of the raw cranberries like a charm.

Shopping tips: I prefer fresh cranberries (bulk or bagged) although frozen and thawed could also be used. I use Fuyu persimmons in this recipe (they look like orange tomatoes) and tend to steer clear of the larger, acorn-shaped Hachiya persimmons since they are too soft when completely ripe. However, the less common, but very delicious, Amagaki persimmons could be used in place of Fuyus.

1½ cups fresh whole cranberries

2 medium, ripe Fuyu persimmons, chopped

2 tangerines (or 1 orange), peeled, seeded, and chopped

1 medium apple, peeled or unpeeled, cored and chopped

½ teaspoon cinnamon

½ teaspoon ground nutmeg

1. Place the cranberries, persimmons, tangerine or orange, apple, cinnamon, and nutmeg into a food processor, and pulse 10 to 15 times, or until the relish looks like chunky salsa.

2. Transfer the relish to a medium bowl and give it another stir to make sure the cinnamon and nutmeg have been thoroughly mixed in. Serve immediately or chill for later. (If there is too much liquid in the bottom, just drain it off.)

NOTES

Feel free to add other ingredients (after blending in step 1), such as raisins, chopped pears, orange or lemon zest, a handful of pomegranate seeds or raspberries, and/or chopped walnuts or pecans.

If you have leftover relish, add it to the top of a green salad or oatmeal, or blend it with a little vinegar until smooth to make a sweet and tangy salad dressing.

TANGERINE APPLESAUCE

This applesauce is easy to prepare, and it makes a great side dish, snack, or light dessert.

Shopping tips: Softer apples work best for applesauce because they cook down faster. Granny Smith, Fuji, McIntosh, Golden Delicious, Jonagold, Cameo, Jazz, and Gala are all good choices. Use all of one type or a variety.

PREPARATION
about 10 minutes

COOKING TIME
30 minutes

SERVES
4 (makes about
3 cups)

2 pounds apples (about 4 medium), peeled or unpeeled, cored and chopped

1 cup tangerine juice (or orange juice or water)

½ teaspoon cinnamon

¼ teaspoon ground nutmeg

1. Bring the apples, tangerine juice (or orange juice or water), cinnamon, and nutmeg to a boil in a medium saucepan over medium-high heat, uncovered.

2. Reduce the heat to low, then cover and cook at a low boil, stirring occasionally, for 20 to 25 minutes. The applesauce is done when the apples have softened. If your apples are soft but still chunky after cooking, you can serve the applesauce as is, or use a potato masher or food processor to attain a smoother consistency.

SAUCES AND DIPS

SAUCE AND DIP BASICS

The sauces and dips in this chapter are among the keys to successfully transitioning to a health-promoting, plant-based diet. A spoonful of hummus, salsa, or guacamole added to the top of your salad, stew, or baked potato will make you want to dig into your meal with excitement and enthusiasm!

Not unlike traditionally prepared salad dressings, traditional sauces and dips are typically full of fat (oil, butter, or cream), salt, and sugar. They are also often home to generous amounts of sour cream and mayonnaise, which we want to avoid since they are made with cow's milk, cream, oil, and/or eggs.

As with every other chapter in this cookbook, this one shows you how easy it is to avoid health-harming ingredients while still enjoying maximum flavor and satisfaction. Our human taste buds are fairly adaptable if given the opportunity. As long as a healthful dish of food looks and smells like what we're used to eating, and is full of flavor, we'll eat it!

It's time to start rethinking the ingredients we add to our food. There are countless healthy and unhealthy roads to achieving flavor: which road would you rather take? For example, to achieve excellent final flavor, it's not necessary to add:

- Refined brown sugar and anchovies to barbecue sauce.

- Corn syrup, white sugar, and salt to ketchup (one leading brand contains 190 mg of salt per tablespoon).

- Animal fat, butter, and cream to gravy.

- Oil to hummus and other dips.

The beauty of sauces and dips is that they are blended, and the resulting texture alone is very pleasing to the palate. So, as long as we are getting that nice blended or creamy texture, and some delicious plant-derived flavor along with it, that is all we really care about. As far as our taste buds are concerned, where that flavor comes from—dairy sour cream versus white beans or cashews, oil versus almond butter, or brown sugar versus brown raisins—it matters little.

I believe you will find the sauce and dip recipes in this chapter just as pleasing as their traditional counterparts, or even more so, as the wonderful flavors of the ingredients themselves are revealed without the usual heavy blankets of salt and oil. You may find these newer flavors and dishes immediately delicious, or you may find that they grow on you over time once your taste buds clean house and adjust ("neuroadapt") to your new way of eating.

BARBECUE SAUCE

This recipe avoids typical barbecue sauce ingredients that are not health-promoting, mainly anchovies, sugar, and salt. Serve it with Quinoa Polenta with Vegetables (page 106), Veggie Burgers (page 86), or Lentil and Rice Loaf (page 92).

Shopping tips: If using canned tomato paste and/or beans, look for salt-free brands. Make sure your raisins have not had oil or sugar added to them.

PREPARATION
about 10 minutes

COOKING TIME
20 minutes
(optional)

MAKES
about 2 cups

1½ cups water

1 can tomato paste (6 ounces)

½ cup cooked black beans, drained and rinsed

¼ cup brown raisins

2 tablespoons mustard (I like Dijon or stone ground)

1 teaspoon chili powder

1 teaspoon apple cider vinegar

¾ teaspoon granulated garlic

¾ teaspoon granulated onion

1. Place all of the ingredients (water, tomato paste, black beans, raisins, mustard, chili powder, vinegar, and granulated garlic and onion) into a blender, and blend until smooth.

2. At this point, you can serve the sauce as is, or simmer it to deepen the flavors and color. Pour the sauce into a medium saucepan and bring to almost boiling over medium heat. Reduce the heat to low and simmer partially covered, stirring occasionally, for 15 to 20 minutes.

NOTE

For a smoky flavor, add ½ to 1 teaspoon of smoked paprika.

BETTER KETCHUP

PREPARATION
about 8 minutes

COOKING TIME
0 minutes

MAKES
about 1 cup

Ketchup is a straightforward condiment, mainly calling for tomatoes, vinegar, salt, and sugar. For this recipe, the sugar will come from an apple and the salty flavor from the concentrated tomato paste. Serve with Veggie Burgers (page 86), Baked French Fries (page 139), Potato-Veggie Scramble (page 47), or Oil-Free Hash Browns (page 41).

Shopping tip: Look for salt-free tomato paste.

¾ cup water

½ medium apple, peeled, cored, and chopped (about ½ cup)

1 can tomato paste (6 ounces)

1 tablespoon apple cider vinegar

½ teaspoon dried oregano

¼ teaspoon granulated garlic

1. Place all of the ingredients (water, apple, tomato paste, vinegar, oregano, and granulated garlic) into a blender, and blend until smooth. Refrigerate for two to three hours for the best flavor.

NOTES

You can substitute ½ cup of apple juice for the apple (and decrease the water to ½ cup).

You can substitute 1 tablespoon of lemon juice for the apple cider vinegar.

From the blog
"I can't believe I just made ketchup in my kitchen—thank you, it tastes great!!" —*Kate S.*

FRESH TOMATO SALSA

This type of salsa is known for its fresh ingredients and simplicity, made from tomatoes, onion, cilantro, lime juice, and garlic (see Notes for other variations). It can be served along with corn chips or hash browns, or on top of salads or baked potatoes.

Shopping tip: You can use any type of tomato, although Romas are common in salsa recipes and their seeds are easy to remove.

PREPARATION
about 15 minutes

COOKING TIME
0 minutes

MAKES
about 2½ cups

2½ cups chopped Roma tomatoes (about 1 pound or 5 to 6 medium)

1 cup chopped yellow or white onion (about ½ medium onion)

½ cup chopped cilantro or basil

2 tablespoons lime juice

1 medium clove garlic, finely chopped

1. Halve the tomatoes and with a spoon, remove the soft insides that contain the seeds (see Notes). If the seeds and soft centers are not removed, the salsa will be very watery.

2. Chop the seeded tomatoes and place them into a medium bowl. Stir in the onion, cilantro or basil, lime juice, and garlic. This method results in a chunky salsa; for a smoother salsa, pulse very briefly in a food processor or blender. Chill for at least 30 minutes to allow the flavors to blend.

NOTES

To add flair to this basic salsa recipe, add chopped jalapeño, bell pepper, mango, jicama, cucumber, and/or corn kernels. A little dried oregano, ground cumin, black pepper, and/or chili powder are also nice additions.

If you don't want to throw out your tomato seeds/soft centers, save them to blend into a homemade salad dressing.

SPICY BLACK BEAN SALSA

Serve this flavorful chunky salsa with corn chips (page 143), in steamed corn tortillas with rice, or atop salads, or baked potatoes. For a black bean dip, simply blend all of the ingredients in a food processor (see Notes).

Shopping tips: Look for salt-free black beans and corn (if using canned), or make your own from scratch. When fresh corn is not in season, I like to buy it frozen with nothing added.

PREPARATION
about 15 minutes

COOKING TIME
0 minutes

MAKES
about 3 cups

1 can cooked black beans (15 ounces; about 1½ cups), drained and rinsed

1 cup corn kernels (thaw first if frozen)

1 cup chopped tomatoes (1 medium-large)

½ cup packed cilantro, chopped (or parsley)

¼ cup finely chopped red onion

1 tablespoon lime juice

1 tablespoon lemon juice

1 teaspoon chili powder

½ teaspoon regular or smoked paprika

½ teaspoon ground cumin

1 medium clove garlic, finely chopped

1. Place all of the ingredients (black beans, corn, tomatoes, cilantro, onion, lime and lemon juice, chili powder, paprika, cumin, and garlic) into a medium bowl and stir well. Serve immediately or refrigerate for a couple hours to better incorporate the flavors.

NOTES

If you would like a dip rather than a chunky salsa, place all of the ingredients into a food processor and pulse 5 to 6 times so the dip still has some texture. (Makes about 2 cups.)

Also try adding chopped jalapeños, bell pepper, mango, and/or avocado.

From the blog
"I tried this recipe and loved it! I made it to serve along with some Mexican rice to take to a get-together with friends. Leftovers of both were great over chopped salad greens." —*Barbara*

AVOCADO-GARBANZO DIP

This recipe is really easy to make, and is delicious as a topping for baked potatoes and yams, or as a dip for Easy Corn Chips (page 143) or raw, cut-up vegetables. Fresh oregano and lemon juice combine for a unique flavor.

Shopping tips: Look for salt-free beans and mustard (Westbrae Natural sells a good salt-free mustard).

PREPARATION
about 15 minutes

COOKING TIME
0 minutes

MAKES
about 2 cups

1 can cooked garbanzo beans (15 ounces; about 1½ cups), drained and rinsed

2 large, ripe avocados, chopped

¼ cup finely chopped red onion

1 to 2 tablespoons lemon juice

1 tablespoon mustard (I like Dijon or stone ground)

2 teaspoons finely chopped fresh oregano (see Note for other options)

½ teaspoon granulated garlic (or 1 clove garlic, finely chopped)

1. Place the garbanzo beans into a medium bowl, and mash them with a fork or bean masher until they pop open (a quick pulse in a food processor also works well).

2. Add the remaining ingredients (avocados, onion, lemon juice, mustard, oregano, and garlic) to the bowl, mashing the avocado and stirring well until smooth.

NOTE

Instead of fresh oregano, you can also try 2 to 3 tablespoons of finely chopped basil, cilantro, or parsley.

From the blog
"Friggin' yum!" —Dave

BROCCOLI-GARLIC SAUCE

Use this simple yet flavorful sauce over baked potatoes, steamed vegetables, or pasta.

Shopping tip: I prefer Yukon Gold potatoes for this recipe since they are a naturally creamy potato when cooked, but any type of white potato can be used.

PREPARATION
about 10 minutes

COOKING TIME
15 minutes

MAKES
about 2 cups

2 cups chopped broccoli florets
1 medium Yukon Gold potato, peeled and chopped (about 1½ cups)
2 medium cloves garlic, halved

1. Place the broccoli, potatoes, and garlic into a medium saucepan with just enough water to cover. Bring to a boil over medium-high heat.

2. Reduce the heat to medium, and cook for 10 to 15 minutes, or until the potatoes are very tender when pierced with a knife.

3. Use a slotted spoon to transfer the cooked vegetables and ½ cup of the cooking water to a food processor then pulse 4 to 5 times, adding more cooking water as needed. The sauce should have a somewhat coarse texture, with tiny bits of broccoli still visible (overblending can dull the flavors).

NOTE
For a richer sauce, add 1 tablespoon of tahini (ground sesame seed paste) or almond butter to the food processor in step 3.

157

HUMMUS

Hummus is a versatile garbanzo bean dip and spread. While most hummus recipes call for olive oil, this recipe does not, making it low in fat but still high in flavor. Use as a dip for raw, cut-up vegetables or as a topping for baked potatoes and salads.

Shopping tip: Look for salt-free canned garbanzo beans, or make your own from scratch.

PREPARATION
about 10 minutes

COOKING TIME
0 minutes

MAKES
about 1¼ cups

1 can cooked garbanzo beans (15 ounces; about 1½ cups), drained and rinsed

2 tablespoons lemon juice

1 to 2 tablespoons tahini (ground sesame seed paste)

¾ teaspoon ground cumin

1 medium clove garlic, finely chopped

1. Place all of the ingredients (garbanzo beans, lemon juice, tahini, cumin, and garlic) into a food processor, and blend until smooth, adding a little water as needed. Refrigerate for 2 to 3 hours (or overnight) to fully blend the flavors.

NOTES

For an herbed hummus, include ¼ to ½ cup of chopped basil, cilantro, or parsley.

If you are cooking your own garbanzo beans, save the cooking water and use it instead of plain water to thin the hummus. The leftover cooking water from legumes (beans, peas, and lentils) is known as "aquafaba." It adds a delicious flavor to soups and stews when used as a base broth.

CREAMY MUSHROOM GRAVY

This gravy is delicious over Mashed Potatoes (page 135) and Lentil and Rice Loaf (page 92). It's rich and flavorful even without the overly processed ingredients found in many plant-based gravies, mainly salt, soy sauce, nondairy butter, and cornstarch.

Shopping tip: Look for salt-free poultry seasoning (don't worry; it does not contain poultry).

PREPARATION
about 15 minutes

COOKING TIME
6 minutes

MAKES
about 4 cups

2 cups water

1 ounce raw, unsalted cashews (about ¼ cup)

6 medium white or cremini mushrooms, chopped (about 2½ cups)

½ large yellow or white onion, chopped (about 1½ cups)

1 small carrot, thinly sliced (about ½ cup)

1 large rib celery, sliced (about ½ cup)

2 teaspoons finely chopped garlic (2 to 3 medium cloves)

1 teaspoon poultry seasoning

Ground black pepper

1. Place the water and cashews into a blender, and set aside for at least 15 minutes (so the cashews can soften).

2. Place 1 tablespoon of water into a medium saucepan on medium-high heat. When the water starts to sputter, add the mushrooms, onions, carrots, and celery, and cook while stirring for 2 to 3 minutes.

3. Add the garlic and poultry seasoning to the pan, and continue stirring for 2 to 3 minutes, or until the vegetables have softened, adding water as needed.

4. Transfer the cooked vegetables to the blender containing the water and cashews, and blend until very smooth, adding water as needed.

5. Pour the blended gravy back into the same saucepan (or a clean one) on medium-low heat, and simmer briefly just to heat through. Season to taste with black pepper.

From the blog
"I made this today, and it was delicious: creamy, earthy, and the poultry seasoning was perfect! I cannot believe how yummy this was." —*Margarita*

TZATZIKI SAUCE

Yogurt is typically used in Tzatziki (pronounced "sotseeky") sauces, but I use cashews instead, or you could use white beans for a lower-calorie sauce (see Note). Serve this sauce with Falafel Patties (page 138), as a dip with cut-up vegetables, or as a sour cream substitute on baked potatoes.

Shopping tip: I like to use long English cucumbers in this recipe, but any cucumber will work fine.

PREPARATION
about 20 minutes

COOKING TIME
0 minutes

MAKES
about 1 cup

2 ounces raw, unsalted cashews (about ½ cup)

⅓ cup water

2 tablespoons lemon juice

1 small clove garlic

1 cup chopped cucumber (peeled and including seeds)

2 tablespoons fresh dill (or ½ teaspoon dried)

1. Place the cashews, water, lemon juice, and garlic into a blender, and set aside for at least 15 minutes (so the cashews can soften).

2. Blend the sauce until smooth.

3. Add the cucumber and dill, and blend briefly (you want the final sauce to retain some texture). Add a little water if needed. Chill for the best flavor. Store covered in the refrigerator and shake before using.

NOTE

Use ¾ to 1 cup of white beans (drained and rinsed) instead of cashews for a lighter, lower-calorie sauce. If you make your own plant-based yogurt, feel free to use that, or some soft tofu.

GUACAMOLE

Guacamole is an avocado-based dip and spread that can be served with cut-up vegetables, corn chips, salads, veggie burgers, stews, tacos, baked potatoes, and hash browns.

Shopping tips: Look for ripe avocados that yield to gentle pressure but are not mushy or indented, indicating that they are overripe. Leave unripe avocados on your countertop for four or five days to ripen (then eat them or store them in the refrigerator).

PREPARATION
about 15 minutes

COOKING TIME
0 minutes

MAKES
about 2 cups

3 small to medium ripe avocados

½ cup finely chopped yellow or white onion

½ cup chopped fresh cilantro or basil

3 tablespoons lime juice

2 small to medium cloves garlic, finely chopped

½ teaspoon ground cumin

1. Peel and chop the avocados, and mash them with a fork in a medium bowl.

2. Stir in the onion, cilantro or basil, lime juice, garlic, and cumin. Chill for at least 30 minutes to blend the flavors.

BASIC VEGETABLE STOCK

If you like to use vegetable stock instead of water for cooking vegetables on the stovetop or in soups and stews, use this easy recipe (courtesy of Jeff Novick, R.D.). Unlike meat-based stocks, there's no fat-skimming, and you don't need to keep the pot on the stove for hours.

PREPARATION
about 20 minutes

COOKING TIME
25 minutes

MAKES
(variable)

4 cups chopped potatoes, peeled or unpeeled

2 cups chopped carrots, peeled or unpeeled

2 cups chopped celery (leaves are fine to include)

2 cups chopped yellow or white onions

1 cup chopped parsley (stems are fine to include)

1. Wash the vegetables and parsley well. Place all of the ingredients (potatoes, carrots, celery, onions, and parsley) into a large stockpot. Add water to cover, plus an extra couple inches (less water will yield a more concentrated stock, and more water will result in a lighter-flavored stock). Bring to a boil over medium-high heat.

2. Reduce the heat to medium-low and simmer uncovered for at least 20 minutes.

3. Take the pot off the stove and remove all of the vegetables with a slotted spoon. Pour the broth through a fine mesh strainer (or a regular colander lined with cheesecloth) to filter out any pieces. Pour 1- to 2-cup portions of the stock into storage containers (I like canning jars). When cooled completely, the broth may be stored in the refrigerator or freezer.

NOTES

For mushroom flavor, add ½ to 1 pound chopped mushrooms (any variety) in step 1.

What's the difference between stock and broth? Stock is generally left unseasoned and broth is seasoned. Feel free to add some garlic, ginger, or any other favorite seasonings to this stock recipe to create a more flavorful broth.

To use vegetable trimmings, add them (clean) to a plastic bag in your freezer as you accumulate them. Once the bag is full, use the contents to make a batch of broth. Most vegetables can be used, but you should avoid cruciferous vegetables (cabbage, broccoli, cauliflower, Brussels sprouts, and the like) since they can impart a bitter flavor.

DESSERTS

DESSERT BASICS

Plant-based desserts are nothing short of delicious. Familiar recipes, such as carrot cake, fruit cobbler, and oatmeal cookies are all easy to make without health-compromising ingredients. In fact, not once in all my years of teaching have I heard the comment, "Yes, this is good, but I really miss the white sugar and the eggs." People care about the final dessert tasting great; that's it! Let's look at the most common dessert ingredients and how they are used (or not used) in this chapter.

Sugar: Desserts made without overly processed, concentrated sugars—such as white sugar, brown sugar, brown rice syrup, maple syrup, and agave—are just as tasty and sweet. The recipes in this chapter are sweetened using dates, apples, bananas, pineapple, berries, raisins, and apple-sauce—and they taste great.

Dates: Medjool and Deglet Noor are the date varieties I use most often to sweeten desserts. Dates are high in natural sugars and have a flavor reminiscent of brown sugar and maple syrup. They are the perfect dessert sweetener and are also delicious eaten by themselves as a snack. Just be sure to remove the pits; they're very hard. (You wouldn't want to bite down on one or have to fish pit pieces out of your blender.) If you find a dessert not sweet enough or too sweet, feel free to add or subtract a date or two to fit your tastes. All date measurements are given in ounces, as well as by quantity, but since dates can vary in size, ounces will always be the more accurate measure.

Oil: The desserts in this chapter use no oil for two main reasons. First, oils (regardless of extraction method) are the polar opposite of unprocessed foods—they are *highly* refined and processed. Oils are also 100% fat, coming in as the most calorie-dense "food" in existence (the same as beef tallow, pork lard, and vegetable shortening). Instead of oil, the recipes in this chapter use nuts or nut butter to bind the ingredients and provide richness. Soft fruits, like bananas, dates, and applesauce, also help to bind while adding sweetness.

Salt: No salt has been added to any of the recipes. Traditional dessert recipes often call for a little salt (to "brighten" the flavor or cut the sweetness), but since it's such a small amount, you won't really miss it, especially if you are not using salt in your everyday cooking. Some of my dessert recipes, however, do call for baking soda and baking powder, both of which are high in sodium. But fortunately, sodium-free versions of both are available (see Baking Soda and Baking Powder on page 18).

Nuts: Nuts are a common ingredient in baked goods and other desserts, as they provide the richness (fat) that traditionally comes from oil, butter, or shortening. Nuts and seeds are high-fat plant foods and can be easily omitted or reduced, unless they are a foundational ingredient, such as in a frosting. Nuts are also very versatile. If the recipe calls for walnuts but you only have pecans, feel free to use pecans. I tend to use cashews a lot since, being a very soft nut, they don't require a lot of soak time before blending. Instead of using nuts, you can also try using your favorite seed (sesame, sunflower, hemp). All nut measurements are given in ounces (as well as cups or table-spoons) since nuts can come whole, halved, or prechopped. Unsalted, unroasted nuts and seeds are best for health.

Grains: I strive to buy as few prepackaged foods and ingredients as possible. To this end, I do not buy store-bought flours since they are most often highly processed (including bleaching and having much of the fiber removed), though you can find "whole-grain" flours if you look. Years ago I started grinding my own grains into flour with my blender (high-speed blenders, like a Vitamix, work great for this). It is a simple step resulting in fresher flour (and therefore tastier desserts), and you don't end up with bags of flour taking up space.

Given that this is a gluten-free cookbook, no wheat grains or wheat flour is used. Oat and millet flours are my favorite gluten-free grains which, when ground into flour and used together, make delicious cakes and muffins. In baking I don't use the toothpick/knife test for doneness, as these healthier baked goods will be quite moist still at the end of baking and need to cool completely before firming up. I look for a nicely browned top instead.

As is the case with nuts, I've found whole-grain flours to be fairly interchangeable. If you don't have millet but you do have cornmeal, go ahead and try that instead. Since whole-grain flours are often a bit coarser and denser, don't be alarmed if your baked goods do not rise quite as high and have a denser texture.

Milk: Any type of nondairy milk will work in these recipes. Each type of milk has its own subtle flavor, but I've found that once everything is mixed together, the flavor differences are rarely perceptible. I have developed these recipes with plain, unsweetened soy milk in most cases since it's higher in fat (and thus results in a richer dessert). And I can find it with only two ingredients at the store: soybeans and water. If you use presweetened milk, just know that it will make the final dessert even sweeter. And making your own nondairy milk (page 35) will result in even better flavor than store-bought.

Vanilla: Vanilla is another common dessert ingredient. Even though vanilla extract is convenient, many people like to avoid the alcohol or glycerin in it (commercially available brands tend to contain one or the other). So I've also noted the option of using the seeds from a vanilla bean (or pod) in every case. There's nothing like real vanilla seeds straight from the bean. Vanilla beans are a bit pricey but worth it.

Parchment paper: Instead of oiling my baking pans or sheets, I use parchment paper, a food-safe, silicone-coated paper that prevents food from sticking to the pan. And it withstands the high heat of the oven. You can find it in a roll in the aluminum foil aisle. You may also use silicone bakeware, which does not require the use of parchment paper, and is reusable and washable.

CARROT CAKE

This carrot cake is a hit with everyone, and it's great with or without frosting! (Shown on facing page, cupcakes with Vanilla Frosting, page 188, topped with grated walnuts.)

PREPARATION
about 35 minutes

COOKING TIME
45 minutes

SERVES
8 to 10

1½ cups unsweetened nondairy milk

4 ounces pitted dates (7 to 8 Medjools or 14 to 16 Deglet Noor), chopped

½ very ripe banana, sliced

¼ cup raisins

1 teaspoon vanilla extract (or seeds from 1 vanilla bean)

1¾ cups old-fashioned rolled oats

2 teaspoons cinnamon

2 teaspoons baking powder

1 teaspoon baking soda

1 teaspoon ground nutmeg

⅛ teaspoon ground cloves

1½ cups grated carrots (2 to 3 medium)

½ cup raisins

2 ounces walnuts, chopped (about ½ cup; optional)

Vanilla or Lemon Frosting (page 188; optional)

1. Place the nondairy milk, dates, banana, ¼ cup raisins, and vanilla into a small bowl, and set aside for at least 15 minutes (so the dates can soften).

2. Preheat the oven to 350°F. Line an 8×8-inch baking pan with parchment paper.

3. Grind the oats into flour with a blender. Transfer to a medium bowl, and whisk in the cinnamon, baking powder, baking soda, nutmeg, and cloves.

4. Place the milk, dates, banana, raisins, and vanilla in the blender, and blend until smooth.

5. Stir the date mixture into the bowl of dry ingredients. Fold in the grated carrots, ½ cup raisins, and walnuts (if using).

6. Spoon the batter into the pan and spread evenly. Bake for 40 to 45 minutes, or until the top is medium brown. Let cool for 10 minutes before removing from the pan and placing on a cooling rack. Cool completely before serving plain or with frosting.

NOTE

If you'd like 12 cupcakes or muffins, bake in a muffin pan with parchment paper liners at 350°F for 25 to 30 minutes. To bake a standard loaf, decrease the milk by ½ cup, line a 9×5×3-inch loaf pan with parchment paper, and bake at 325°F for 50 to 55 minutes, or until the top is medium brown. Let cool completely before serving.

CARDAMOM-RAISIN RICE PUDDING

This rice pudding features cardamom, an aromatic spice that is used most often in Indian cooking. This dessert is perfect for when you want something sweet and easy to make.

Shopping tips: Cardamom is found in most spice aisles; just be sure to get "ground" unless you want to grind your own seeds (which will be even more flavorful). Look for dates in the bulk food section or packaged near the raisins.

PREPARATION
about 15 minutes

COOKING TIME
65 minutes

SERVES
4 to 6 (makes about 6 cups)

2 cups water

1 cup long- or short-grain brown rice

2 cups unsweetened nondairy milk

3 ounces pitted dates (5 to 6 Medjool or 10 to 12 Deglet Noor), chopped

1 teaspoon vanilla extract (or seeds from 1 vanilla bean)

½ cup brown or golden raisins

1 ounce raw, unsalted almonds, chopped (about ¼ cup; optional)

1 teaspoon cinnamon

½ teaspoon ground cardamom

Chopped or sliced raw, unsalted almonds for garnish (optional)

1. Bring the water and rice to a boil in a medium saucepan over high heat, uncovered. Reduce the heat to low, then cover and simmer for 45 minutes for long-grain rice or 50 minutes for short-grain rice. Remove the pan from the heat and let stand for 10 minutes with the lid still on.

2. Place the nondairy milk, dates, and vanilla into a blender, and set aside (so the dates can soften) while the rice is cooking.

3. When the rice is done, add the raisins, almonds, cinnamon, and cardamom to the pan.

4. Blend the milk, dates, and vanilla until smooth, and stir this mixture into the pan.

5. Cook on medium-low for 10 to 15 minutes to allow the flavors to blend, stirring occasionally to keep the rice from sticking to the bottom of the pan. Add more milk as needed (the pudding will thicken as it cooks). Serve warm or cold in small dessert dishes. Garnish with chopped or sliced almonds if desired.

ZUCCHINI BREAD

This delicious bread is baked as a loaf, but see Notes for instructions on baking as muffins or an 8×8-inch square cake.

Shopping tips: To avoid excess sodium, you may use sodium-free baking soda and powder (see page 18). Look for dates in the bulk food section or packaged near the raisins.

PREPARATION
about 35 minutes

COOKING TIME
65 minutes

SERVES
8 to 10 (makes about ten ¾-inch slices)

7 ounces pitted dates (11 to 12 Medjool or 22 to 24 Deglet Noor), chopped

1 cup unsweetened nondairy milk

2 teaspoons vanilla extract (or seeds from 2 vanilla beans)

1¼ cups old-fashioned rolled oats

¾ cup dry/uncooked millet

1 teaspoon cinnamon

1 teaspoon baking powder

1 teaspoon baking soda

½ teaspoon ground ginger

½ teaspoon ground nutmeg

2 cups unpeeled, grated zucchini (1 to 2 medium)

2 ounces walnuts, chopped (about ½ cup; optional)

1. Place the dates, nondairy milk, and vanilla into a small bowl, and set aside for at least 15 minutes (so the dates can soften). Preheat the oven to 325°F. Line a standard size loaf pan (9×5×3 inches) with parchment paper.

2. Grind the oats and millet into flour with a blender (30 to 40 seconds; millet is hard). Transfer to a medium bowl and whisk in the cinnamon, baking powder, baking soda, ginger, and nutmeg.

3. Pour the soaking ingredients (dates, milk, and vanilla) into the blender, and blend until smooth. Stir this mixture into the bowl of dry ingredients, then stir in the grated zucchini and walnuts (if using).

4. Spoon the batter into the pan and spread evenly. Bake for 65 minutes, or until the top is medium brown. Let cool for 10 minutes before removing from the pan and placing on a cooling rack. Cool completely before serving.

NOTE

If you'd like 12 cupcakes or muffins, bake in a muffin pan with parchment paper liners at 350°F for 25 to 30 minutes. For a square cake, bake in an 8×8-inch pan lined with parchment paper at 350°F for 40 to 45 minutes.

RAW APPLE CRUMBLE

This is one of my oldest and most beloved dessert recipes. It is much easier and faster to make than an apple pie, and it requires no baking.

Shopping tips: Use sweet, juicy apples in this recipe, such as a Gala, Fuji, or Pink Lady. Using a mix of apples provides even better flavor.

PREPARATION
about 25 minutes

COOKING TIME
0 minutes

SERVES
6 (makes about 5 cups)

For the crumble topping:

2 ounces walnuts or pecans (about ½ cup)

1 ounce pitted dates (about 2 Medjool or 4 Deglet Noor), chopped

For the apple filling:

4 medium apples, peeled or unpeeled, cored and chopped (about 4 cups)

1 tablespoon lemon juice

For the applesauce:

2 medium apples, peeled or unpeeled, cored and chopped

2½ ounces pitted dates (4 to 5 Medjool or 8 to 10 Deglet Noor), chopped

¼ cup raisins

2 tablespoons lemon juice

¼ teaspoon cinnamon

¼ teaspoon ground nutmeg

1. To make the crumble topping, place the nuts and dates into a food processor, and process until the mixture resembles Grape Nuts cereal (don't overprocess; it should be loose). Transfer to a small bowl and set aside. (Keep the food processor handy for step 3.)

2. To make the apple filling, toss the chopped apples and lemon juice together in a medium bowl. Set aside.

3. To make the applesauce, place all of the ingredients (apples, dates, raisins, lemon juice, cinnamon, and nutmeg) into the food processor, and process to the consistency of applesauce, adding a little water as needed.

4. Stir the applesauce into the bowl of chopped apples and lemon juice. Serve on small dessert plates or bowls sprinkled with the crumble topping.

NOTES

Try another type fruit in place of one apple in the filling, such as a pear, peach, nectarine, mango, banana, or persimmon, or some berries or pineapple.

If you'd like to bake this dessert, use an 8 × 8-inch baking pan and cook at 350°F for 35 to 45 minutes or until the apples are tender (topping can be added before or after).

SWEET POTATO-PECAN PIE

This pie is perfect for holidays and special occasions, and you can easily make a pumpkin or yam pie from this same recipe (see Notes).

Shopping tips: Sweet potatoes have yellow-tan skin and white flesh. Look for dates in the bulk food section or packaged near the raisins. If you do not like to use aluminum foil in baking, look for Reynolds Wrap Pan Lining Paper, with foil on one side and parchment paper on the other.

PREPARATION
about 30 minutes

COOKING TIME
30 minutes

SERVES
6 to 8 (makes one 8-inch pie)

¼ to ½ cup old-fashioned rolled oats (½ cup will result in a firmer filling)

¾ cup unsweetened nondairy milk

4 ounces pitted dates (7 to 8 Medjool or 14 to 16 Deglet Noor), chopped

1 teaspoon vanilla extract (or seeds from 1 vanilla bean)

1½ cups (packed) baked sweet potato (about 1 pound before cooking; see Notes)

1¼ teaspoons cinnamon

¼ teaspoon ground ginger

⅛ teaspoon ground cloves

1 prebaked Pecan-Date Pie Crust (page 176)

15 to 20 raw, unsalted pecan halves to decorate the outside edge, plus ¼ cup chopped pecans for the center of the pie

1. Grind the rolled oats into flour with a blender and then transfer to a small bowl.

2. Place the nondairy milk, dates, and vanilla into the blender, and set aside for at least 15 minutes (so the dates can soften).

3. Preheat the oven to 375°F. Set aside your prebaked pie crust.

4. Add the baked sweet potato to the blender with the milk, dates and vanilla, and blend until smooth.

5. Add the oat flour, cinnamon, ginger, and cloves to the blender mixture, and blend until smooth, scraping down the sides a couple times. (This will be thick, so use your blender's tamper if it has one, or you can also use a food processor.)

6. Pour the pie filling into the prebaked pie crust and smooth out evenly. Arrange the pecan halves around the outside of the pie and the chopped pecans in the middle.

7. Wrap a few 3-inch-wide strips of aluminum foil around the edge of the pie crust (keeping the edges of the foil from touching the filling) to prevent the crust from overbrowning.

8. Bake for 25 to 30 minutes, or until the crust is a medium brown. Remove the pie from the oven and remove the foil strips. Cool completely before slicing.

NOTES

To bake the sweet potato, place the unpeeled potato on a baking sheet, and bake at 400°F for 60 to 70 minutes, or until very soft when pierced with a knife.

To make this a pumpkin pie, substitute 1 can (15 ounces) 100% cooked pumpkin (not "pumpkin pie mix") or 1½ cups (packed) baked pumpkin.

To make this a yam pie, substitute 1½ cups (packed) baked yams. Yam pie will be darker in color than sweet potato pie.

PECAN-DATE PIE CRUST

This crust tastes like a sweet, crumbly cookie. I use it with the Sweet Potato-Pecan Pie recipe on page 174, but you can use it wherever a sweet, prebaked pie shell is called for.

PREPARATION
about 25 minutes

COOKING TIME
10 minutes

MAKES
one 8-inch
pie crust

1¼ cups old-fashioned rolled oats

2½ ounces raw, unsalted pecans (about ½ cup)

½ teaspoon cinnamon

2½ ounces pitted dates (4 to 5 Medjool or 8 to 10 Deglet Noor), chopped

1½ tablespoons unsweetened nondairy milk

1. Place the oats, pecans, and cinnamon in a food processor, and process until the texture resembles coarse flour.

2. Add the dates, and process for about 1 minute, or until the mixture just begins to clump together. Add the milk and process until the mixture starts to ball up into dough (this will happen quickly).

3. Form the dough into one big ball and place it on a large piece of parchment paper on top of a large cutting board or other flat surface. Press the ball flat with your hands and then place another large piece of parchment paper over the top.

4. Preheat the oven to 375°F. Set aside an 8-inch pie pan.

5. Use a rolling pin to roll out the dough into a circle that is about ⅛ inch thick. The circle should be slightly larger than the upper edge of the pie pan. (If your circle is irregularly shaped, just cut a piece of dough from another area and press it in.)

6. Peel off the top piece of parchment paper and carefully invert the rolled-out crust onto the pie pan. Peel away the remaining piece of parchment paper. Gently ease the crust into the contours of the pan and lightly press into place.

7. Trim away any hanging crust (don't wrap the crust over the edge of the pan since this will make it harder to cut after it's baked). You do not need to poke the crust with a knife.

8. Place a piece of aluminum foil over the entire crust, loosely tucking under the corners. Place on a baking sheet and bake for 10 minutes, or until the edges are very lightly browned.

From the blog
"I think this is the best vegan pie crust I've ever tried since going whole-food, plant-based. Awesome!" —*Teri*

BANANA-WALNUT BARS

These satisfying "go anywhere" bars are dense and filling, a perfect snack for traveling, hiking, or at school or work.

Shopping tip: Look for dates in the bulk food section or packaged near the raisins.

PREPARATION
about 20 minutes

COOKING TIME
35 minutes

SERVES
12 (makes 12 bars)

1 cup unsweetened nondairy milk

3½ ounces dates (6 to 7 Medjool or 12 to 14 Deglet Noor), chopped

2 teaspoons vanilla extract (or seeds from 1 to 2 vanilla beans)

½ cup dry/uncooked millet (will be ground into flour)

½ cup old-fashioned rolled oats (will be ground into flour)

1¼ cups old-fashioned rolled oats

2 teaspoons cinnamon

2 very ripe bananas, sliced (about 1½ cups)

3 ounces walnuts, chopped (about ¾ cup)

1. Place the nondairy milk, dates, and vanilla into a small bowl, and set aside for at least 15 minutes (so the dates can soften).

2. Grind the millet and the ½ cup of oats into flour with a blender. Transfer to a medium bowl.

3. Add the 1¼ cups of oats and the cinnamon to the bowl of flour, and whisk.

4. Preheat the oven to 350°F. Line an 8×8-inch baking pan with parchment paper.

5. Pour the soaking ingredients (milk, dates, and vanilla) into the blender, along with the banana, and blend just briefly (so the banana and dates are still in small bits).

6. Pour the mixture into the bowl of dry ingredients and stir well. Stir in the walnuts.

7. Spoon the batter into the pan and spread evenly. Bake 30 to 35 minutes until nicely browned on top and around the edges.

Cut into 12 bars after cooling for at least 15 minutes.

NOTES

If you don't have millet on hand, you can use more oat flour or cornmeal.

For extra sweetness, add in ½ cup of raisins with the walnuts in step 6.

OATMEAL-RAISIN COOKIES

There's nothing like a soft oatmeal-raisin cookie! Dates and almond butter stand in for more traditional butter, eggs, and refined sugar.

Shopping tips: To avoid excess sodium, you may use sodium-free baking powder. Look for dates in the bulk food section or packaged near the raisins. Almond butter is sold near the peanut butter.

PREPARATION
about 25 minutes

COOKING TIME
14 minutes

SERVES
18 (makes 18 cookies)

7 ounces pitted dates (11 to 12 Medjool or 22 to 24 Deglet Noor), chopped

1 cup old-fashioned rolled oats (will be ground into flour)

1½ cups old-fashioned rolled oats

2 teaspoons baking powder

1 teaspoon cinnamon

¼ cup plus 2 tablespoons almond butter

1½ teaspoons vanilla extract (or seeds from 1 to 2 vanilla beans)

½ cup raisins (plus extra for the tops of the cookies)

2 ounces walnuts, chopped (about ½ cup; optional)

1. Place the dates into a small bowl, cover them with water, and set aside for at least 15 minutes so they can soften. Preheat the oven to 350°F. Line two baking sheets with parchment paper.

2. Grind the 1 cup of rolled oats into flour with a blender. Transfer to a medium bowl, and whisk in the 1½ cups of oats, baking powder, and cinnamon.

3. Drain the dates, reserving the soak water. Place the dates and 2 tablespoons of soak water into a blender, along with the almond butter and vanilla, and blend until smooth.

4. Stir the date mixture into the bowl of dry ingredients until all of the dry ingredients disappear. Stir in the raisins and the walnuts (if using).

5. To get the most uniformly sized cookies, use a 1-tablespoon cookie scooper (or a soup spoon). Place 9 scoops of dough onto each baking sheet. These cookies will not spread out during baking, so press each scoop, with moistened fingers, until it is the size and shape of an already-baked cookie (about 2½ inches wide). Push 2 to 3 raisins into the top of each.

6. Bake for 13 to 14 minutes, or until just starting to brown (or leave in longer if you want cookies that aren't as moist and soft). Remove from the oven and let cool for 5 minutes before transferring to a cooling rack.

NOTE

For a lower-fat, cakier cookie, use ½ cup of applesauce in place of the almond butter.

APPLE CRISP

I like Granny Smith apples in this recipe because they soften nicely but still retain their shape after baking. However, you can use other apples as well.

Shopping tips: Look for dates in the bulk food section or packaged near the raisins. Make sure your raisins have not had oil or sugar added to them.

PREPARATION
about 30 minutes

COOKING TIME
30 minutes

SERVES
6 to 8

For the topping:
3 ounces pitted dates (5 to 6 Medjool or 10 to 12 Deglet Noor), chopped
¼ cup plus 1 tablespoon apple juice
1¾ cups old-fashioned rolled oats
1 teaspoon cinnamon

For the fruit:
1¾ pounds Granny Smith apples (4 to 5 medium), peeled and cored
½ cup raisins

For the fruit sauce:
½ cup old-fashioned rolled oats
1½ cups apple juice
3 tablespoons lemon juice
1 teaspoon cinnamon

1. To start the topping, place the chopped dates and apple juice into a small bowl for at least 15 minutes (so the dates can soften). Place the rolled oats and cinnamon into a medium bowl and stir. Set aside.

2. For the fruit, slice the apples into thin wedges about ⅛ inch thick and then cut them in half crosswise (so they are more bite-sized). Place the cut apples and raisins into a medium bowl, and set aside.

3. Preheat the oven to 350°F. Set aside an 8×8-inch baking pan (no parchment paper is needed).

4. To make the fruit sauce, place the oats into a blender and grind them into flour. Add the apple juice, lemon juice, and cinnamon, and blend once more until smooth.

5. Pour the fruit sauce into the bowl of apples and raisins, and stir (the sauce will be thin, but it will thicken during baking). Transfer this mixture to the baking pan.

6. To finish the topping, transfer the soaked dates and apple juice to the blender, and blend until smooth. Pour this into the bowl of oats and cinnamon, and stir to coat.

7. Spread the topping evenly over the apples, and bake uncovered for 25 to 30 minutes, or until the topping is a deep medium brown. Let cool at least 5 minutes before serving.

NOTE

For a little variation, substitute one of the apples with a cup of blueberries, sliced strawberries, peaches, nectarines, or pears, or chopped pineapple.

PUMPKIN PIE SQUARES

These easy-to-make squares are perfect for dessert or a snack. This is my go-to recipe when I'm in the mood for pumpkin but don't want to spend the time making an entire pumpkin pie. If I'm serving these at a special occasion, I will add Vanilla Frosting (page 188).

Shopping tips: Buy "100% pure pumpkin," not "pumpkin pie mix." Look for dates in the bulk food section or packaged near the raisins.

PREPARATION
about 25 minutes

COOKING TIME
30 minutes

SERVES
16 (makes 16 squares)

7 ounces pitted dates (11 to 12 Medjool or 22 to 24 Deglet Noor), chopped

1 cup unsweetened nondairy milk

1 teaspoon vanilla extract (or seeds from 1 vanilla bean)

1¼ cups old-fashioned rolled oats

2 teaspoons pumpkin pie spice (or cinnamon)

1 can 100% pure pumpkin (15 ounces)

Vanilla Frosting (page 188; optional)

1. Place the dates, milk, and vanilla into a small bowl, and set aside for at least 15 minutes (so the dates can soften).

2. Preheat the oven to 375°F. Line an 8×8-inch baking pan with parchment paper.

3. Grind the rolled oats into flour with a blender. Transfer to a medium bowl and whisk in the pumpkin pie spice.

4. Pour the soaking ingredients (dates, milk, and vanilla) into the blender, and blend until smooth.

5. Pour this mixture into the bowl of dry ingredients, and add the pumpkin. Mix the batter with an electric mixer until it is thick but smooth. (If you don't have an electric mixer, you can use a food processor or a blender along with its tamper.)

6. Spoon the batter into the pan and spread evenly. Bake for 30 minutes. Let cool completely before serving (or chill overnight for firmer snack bars). Serve as is or with Vanilla Frosting.

NOTE

If you'd like to use fresh pumpkin, place a halved small sugar pumpkin (with stem and seeds removed) cut-side down onto a rimmed baking dish lined with parchment paper. Bake uncovered at 375°F for 50 to 60 minutes, or until tender. Let cool before cutting the skin away. Cut the pumpkin into chunks, and mash or blend it until fairly smooth. Use 1½ cups for this recipe.

BLACKBERRY-PEACH COBBLER

While traditional cobblers rely on refined white sugar, butter, and cow's milk, you won't miss these ingredients in this classic dish. I recommend thoroughly reading this recipe before starting, since you will use the blender for multiple steps.

Shopping tips: To avoid excess sodium, you may use sodium-free baking powder. Look for dates in the bulk food section or packaged near the raisins.

PREPARATION
about 30 minutes

COOKING TIME
30 minutes

SERVES
6 to 8

For the biscuit topping:

½ cup unsweetened nondairy milk

2 ounces pitted dates (3 to 4 Medjool or 6 to 8 Deglet Noor), chopped

½ very ripe banana, sliced

1 teaspoon vanilla extract (or seeds from 1 vanilla bean)

1½ cups old-fashioned rolled oats

1½ teaspoons baking powder

¼ teaspoon cinnamon

For the fruit sauce:

1 cup water (or fruit juice)

2 ounces pitted dates (3 to 4 Medjool or 6 to 8 Deglet Noor), chopped

2 tablespoons lemon juice

¼ cup old-fashioned rolled oats

½ teaspoon cinnamon

The fruit:

2 cups fresh or frozen pitted and sliced peaches (about 4 medium peaches)

2 cups fresh or frozen blackberries

1. To start the biscuit topping, place the nondairy milk, dates, banana, and vanilla into a small bowl, and set aside for at least 15 minutes (so the dates can soften).

2. Grind the 1½ cups of rolled oats (for the biscuit topping) and ¼ cup of rolled oats (for the fruit sauce) into flour with a blender. You can grind these together if you like; just measure out 1½ cups and ¼ cup of flour afterwards, and set aside.

3. For the fruit, place the peaches and blackberries into a medium bowl (if frozen, you don't need to thaw first).

4. Preheat the oven to 375°F. Set aside an 8×8-inch baking pan (no parchment paper is needed).

5. To make the fruit sauce, place the water (or juice), dates, and lemon juice into the blender, and blend until smooth. Add the ¼ cup of oat flour and the cinnamon, and blend again until smooth.

6. Pour the fruit sauce into the bowl of peaches and blackberries, and toss. Spread evenly into the pan.

7. To finish the biscuit topping, whisk the remaining 1½ cups of oat flour and the baking powder and cinnamon together in a medium bowl.

8. Pour the soaking ingredients (milk, dates, banana, and vanilla) into the blender, and blend until smooth.

9. Add this mixture to the bowl of dry ingredients and mix well.

10. Spread the batter over the fruit and sauce (in the baking pan), somewhat evenly but with some gaps of fruit in between. Bake uncovered for 25 to 30 minutes, or until the topping is lightly browned. Let cool for at least 10 minutes before serving.

NOTES

Fruit variations: You can also try nectarines, apples, plums, persimmons, blueberries, strawberries, raspberries, or even a few cranberries, or a combination of fruit.

For a nicer presentation, I often use a decorative, deep-dish ceramic pie pan instead of a square baking pan.

From the blog
"I used frozen peaches and blueberries, and it tastes wonderful! The sweetness is just right, and that oaty topping is to die for." —*Annie*

ALMOND-POPPY SEED CAKE

This hearty cake is delicious served plain or with strawberries and Lemon Frosting (page 188).

Shopping tips: To avoid excess sodium, you can use sodium-free baking soda and powder (see page 18). Poppy seeds can be found packaged in the spice aisle or in the bulk spice section.

PREPARATION
about 30 minutes

COOKING TIME
60 minutes

SERVES
8 to 10 (makes about ten ¾-inch slices)

- 7 ounces pitted dates (11 to 12 Medjool or 22 to 24 Deglet Noor), chopped
- 1½ cups unsweetened nondairy milk
- 1½ teaspoons almond extract
- 1¼ cups old-fashioned rolled oats
- ¾ cup dry/uncooked millet
- 2 tablespoons poppy seeds
- 1 teaspoon baking powder
- 1 teaspoon baking soda
- ¼ cup applesauce
- 1 tablespoon lemon zest (from 1 medium lemon; see Zesting, page 24)
- Lemon Frosting (page 188; optional)
- 2 cups sliced strawberries (optional)

1. Place the dates, milk, and almond extract into a small bowl, and set aside for at least 15 minutes (so the dates can soften). Preheat the oven to 325°F. Line a standard size loaf pan (9×5×3 inches) with parchment paper.

2. Grind the rolled oats and millet into flour with a blender (30 to 40 seconds; millet is hard). Place the oat and millet flour, poppy seeds, baking powder, and baking soda into a medium bowl, and whisk.

3. Pour the soaking ingredients (dates, milk, and almond extract) into the blender, and blend until smooth. Add this mixture to the bowl of dry ingredients along with the applesauce and lemon zest, and stir until all of the dry ingredients have been incorporated.

4. Spoon the batter into the pan and spread evenly. Bake for 55 to 60 minutes, or until the top is medium brown. Let cool for 10 minutes before removing from the pan and placing on a cooling rack. Cool completely before serving plain or with Lemon Frosting and sliced strawberries.

NOTE

If you'd like 12 cupcakes or muffins, bake in a muffin pan with parchment paper liners at 350°F for 25 to 30 minutes. For a square cake, bake in an 8×8-inch pan lined with parchment paper at 350°F for 40 to 45 minutes.

VANILLA OR LEMON FROSTING

This is a simple nut-based frosting that can have a vanilla or lemon flavor (see Notes for lemon). Both flavors are great on Carrot Cake (page 168), Pumpkin Pie Squares (page 182), and Almond-Poppy Seed Cake (page 186). The frosting can also be used as a dip for fruit.

Shopping tip: Look for dates in the bulk food section or packaged near the raisins.

PREPARATION
about 8 minutes
(plus 45 minutes to soak)

COOKING TIME
0 minutes

MAKES
about 1½ cups

5 ounces pitted dates (8 to 9 Medjool or 16 to 18 Deglet Noor), chopped

3 ounces raw, unsalted cashews (about ¾ cup)

1 teaspoon vanilla extract (or seeds from 1 vanilla bean)

¾ to 1 cup water

1. Place the dates, cashews, and vanilla into a blender. Add ¾ cup of water. If the water doesn't completely cover the dates and nuts, add more just until it does. Set aside for at least 45 minutes (so the dates and nuts can thoroughly soften).

2. Blend until very smooth, scraping down the sides a couple times. If your blender has a tamper, you may want to use it. (Add a little more water if the mixture becomes too thick to blend.)

NOTES

For lemon frosting, add 2 to 3 tablespoons of lemon juice. Meyer lemons are great in this recipe when they are in season.

For firmer frosting, chill for a couple hours before using.

PART THREE

A LITTLE SUPPORT

15 TIPS FOR MAKING
DIETARY CHANGE EASIER

Here are 15 tips to help make your dietary transition easier and more enjoyable. Read through these upon beginning your journey, as well as later on if you find yourself feeling frustrated or in need of a little refresher.

Try not to worry about doing it "just right." There isn't just one right way; we each apply our own interpretations to how we eat. As long as you're eating an overall varied diet made up of wholesome plant foods, as well as taking in adequate daily calories, you'll be on your way to great health!

1. Repeat what you eat: Most of us—health-minded or not—are creatures of habit. We prepare and eat the same types of dishes over and over again, and there is nothing wrong with this habit. Rotating in a new recipe periodically can be a fun change, but don't feel that you must make a new recipe every day if you're just starting out. There is no rule that says you can't eat the same types of dishes repeatedly; just vary their ingredients a little to keep things interesting.

Whether I'm eating a meal of a big salad, baked potato, or pasta, I might use black beans instead of pinto, grated zucchini instead of grated carrots, thinly sliced cabbage instead of lettuce, asparagus instead of broccoli, or red potatoes instead of white. Find five to 10 dishes that you like, and replicate them almost exactly or mix up the ingredients a little each time. (For more information on menu planning, see page 200.)

2. Tailor recipes to your own tastes: If a recipe calls for a certain ingredient that you are out of or don't like, feel free to change it and do what feels right to you. Get creative if you are comfortable making substitutions and changes. A guideline many cooks use is to make the recipe as written the first time and then note anything you'd like to change for next time. You can write in the cookbook or use sticky notes so you won't forget. Have fun with the recipes and make them your own so that *you* will keep eating them.

3. Adjust how you see your plate: You do not need to have a certain number of items on your plate (such as the traditional three), and there does not need to be a "center-piece" dish (like chicken or fish). Try not to get too locked into what your plate used to look like. While variety is just fine if you want to prepare different dishes, you can also just eat one dish. In a way, plant-based eating can be a wonderful world of one or more side dishes.

For example, eat a breakfast of just fruit or a bowl of oatmeal, a lunch consisting of a big salad topped with beans or a big bowl of soup, or a dinner of baked yams and some steamed asparagus with a little mustard or hummus on the side. Creating simple meals made from plant foods that you love will help you ease into plant-based eating and avoid feeling stressed. To see photos of my own meals, visit the "My Meals" section of my blog (*StraightUpFood.com*) or visit my Facebook page (*Facebook.com/StraightUpFood*) and click "Photos."

4. Plan what you'll be eating next: If the thought of creating a menu and planning your meals doesn't excite you, know that transitioning to a plant-based diet can be made much easier by doing so. You don't want to be caught not knowing what you'll be eating at your next meal. To avoid this, spend a little time planning and writing down what you're going to eat at home and work.

It's so easy to slide off course when we find ourselves in a situation where we're really hungry and have no idea what we're going to eat. One of my favorite books, *The Pleasure Trap,* expertly states the importance of planning our meals: "Hunger causes urgency, and urgency demands short-term solutions that compromise long-term values. Plan for success and you will succeed more often." Keep a notebook in your kitchen with ideas for your favorite meals and recipes, jotting down your ideas for the upcoming week, or create a more formal menu plan that spells out all of your intended meals for the week (see Menu Planning on page 200 and Tips for Eating at Events and While Traveling on page 213).

5. Do some meal preparation ahead of time: If you can carve out an hour or two on the weekend to do some preparation for the week ahead (when, presumably, things will be busier), this will make your midweek meal preparation a breeze. It's such a dream to open the refrigerator to find your next meal already partially prepared.

You can do lots of things to prepare for the week. Examples include washing and cutting up vegetables for salads, making a batch of pasta sauce, cooking a double batch of rice or beans, or making a batch of hummus or salsa to use as dressing, dip, or baked potato topping. Anything you can prepare ahead of time—even if it's just one or two things—will go far to ease the hustle and bustle of mealtimes and shorten the time between being hungry and sitting down to eat.

Broccoli Soup (page 124)

6. Make one-pot or one-dish meals: Whether it's a soup, salad, stew, or stir-fry, preparing everything in just one pot or dish makes life so much easier. One of my favorite one-pot meals is Mushrooms and Kale with Fresh Rosemary (page 98). This recipe's cooking technique can be applied to any potatoes and vegetables you have on hand. Simply put everything in a covered pot with a bit of water in the bottom, and cook for 15 minutes or until tender. A slow cooker or pressure cooker is also great for one-pot soups and stews. Big salads, such as the Burrito Bowl (page 53), full of hearty beans and rice, are also easy to make and very filling.

7. Prepare your ingredients before cooking: Baking and cooking are so much more enjoyable and efficient when we gather and prepare (peel, chop, juice, pit, and so forth) all of our ingredients *before* we begin with step one of the instructions. I have included instructions to prepare all of the ingredients first for recipes where things cook up quickly, but this early prepping is a good rule of thumb for any recipe, especially if you are new to cooking. Reading the recipe in its entirety once or twice first is also very helpful. If you don't know how to prepare or chop a certain food (such as an onion or mango), just search YouTube for a video that explains it.

8. Keep your favorite staples on hand: I always try to keep certain favorite staple foods on hand so I can easily whip up a meal. Everyone's favorite staples will be different, but mine include things like canned beans and diced tomatoes, nondairy milk, grains, pasta, potatoes, yams, greens, and frozen vegetables. If I have only these items in the kitchen, I know I can make a meal that I will enjoy.

For example, I might heat up a can of cooked beans with some frozen vegetables and dried herbs and spices, and eat them alone or put them on top of a baked yam or mashed potatoes. Having a short list of staples comes in handy when you're in the grocery store and feeling unfocused about

what to buy. When my favorite packaged staples are on sale, I stock up, always opting for brands with no salt, sugar, or oil.

9. Keep your favorite dried herbs and spices handy: A simple soup of potatoes and cabbage becomes so much more interesting with the addition of a little dried garlic, onion, and dill. Salt-free blends (such as an Italian herb seasoning of oregano, basil, and thyme, or a Mexican spice blend made of chili powder, paprika, cumin, cayenne, and granulated garlic) are great to add to soups, stews, and salad dressings. Always have plenty of the basics on hand, including dried garlic and onion, curry powder, chili powder, and cumin.

If you've never visited a spice shop before, treat yourself; you can smell everything before you buy. Or pick up a new blend at your grocery store and give it a test drive. If you love it, keep it in permanent rotation; if you don't,

Mashed potatoes with steamed broccoli, collard greens, kale, cucumbers, tomatoes, and Sesame-Citrus-Ginger Dressing (page 80)

try something new next time. (See Using Dried Herbs and Spices on page 197).

10. Invest in a few good kitchen tools: In any effort, using the right tools can make all the difference in the final product as well as how much you enjoy the task. This is so true when it comes to cooking. Three of my most-used kitchen tools are my eight-inch chef's knife, my large cutting board, and my blender. These items don't need to be costly, but they should be of good quality (see Kitchen Tools on page 16).

11. Keep learning: Regularly educating yourself about healthy eating and living will help reinforce your daily habits and remind you why you have chosen to adopt a health-promoting diet. If you don't understand *why* you're doing this, a change in habit can be short lived. As they say, "What we think about comes about." So, stay focused on your goals—and why they are worthy—by reading health-related books, watching videos, and attending lectures, events, and plant-based potlucks in your area.

12. Find support: Change can be hard, so find people to connect with who are also making the same kinds of changes that you are. Even just one online friend with whom you exchange emails, or someone in your neighborhood you can talk with about dietary change, can make a big difference.

Strive to be among people who will support you and your way of eating, not put

Strive to be among people who will support you and your way of eating, not put you down or try to change you.

you down or try to change you. They say that it takes just one caring adult to put a child on the right path, and I think the same is true of adults who are trying to change how they eat for the better. If you can find just one caring person to connect with, and both of you can support each other along the way, you'll be on better footing.

13. Use the Internet to help you: The Internet has been a great resource for me along my healthy eating journey. It's fast and easy, and you can find answers to most *any* question you have, such as, "How do you substitute fresh garlic for dried?" "How do you cook garbanzo beans from scratch?" or "What are collard greens?"

You can also use the Internet to find recipes, read articles about healthy eating, locate a plant-based doctor or healing center, find out where your local plant-based potlucks are held, watch inspiring documentaries about food and health, buy health books, and follow health-minded communities via social media (Facebook, Twitter, YouTube, etc.). Use the Internet to your advantage by creating your own community of support and resources.

14. Have patience: For many of us, it has taken a long time for our ill health to develop, so likewise, it can take time to regain our good health. But this won't take as long as you'd think. The body gives us positive signs that we are doing what it likes within a few days of making changes. For example, digestion and elimination start to work more

Yukon Gold potatoes with steamed spinach, corn, and peas, topped with chopped onion and tomatoes

smoothly, and energy levels often improve within a few short days.

It's easy for the brain to become overly and unnaturally excited when we consume a diet high in animal foods, highly processed and refined foods, and salt, sugar, and oil. It can be difficult to say "no" to these things since our taste buds have come to expect them. But if your goal is to eliminate (or greatly reduce) these items in your diet, the more you avoid them the less you will miss and crave them, and the easier your new way of eating will become.

In time, your taste buds will clean out and become more open to new foods and ingredients. Eventually you will be saying, "This food tastes better now than when I started." While part of this may be due to your becoming a more proficient cook, it's more likely due to your brain having latched onto your new way of eating and now craving it instead of the old way.

15. Be nice to yourself: The sister to having patience with yourself is being kind to yourself. Adopting a new diet is like learning a new language: proficiency comes in stages and requires continued learning and practice. Criticizing yourself every time you fall off the healthy-eating wagon is counterproductive.

Try to view lapses not as failures, but as new information with which to move forward. You might think to yourself, "Okay, so I ate that piece of cake because I was out with my coworkers and I didn't want to be the only one not ordering dessert. To avoid this in the future, I will bring my lunch to work or at least for the next month until I'm feeling more confident about ordering what I want in restaurants." When you make a mistake or fail in your efforts, use that information—don't lose it; this is how we learn and progress.

"Take your health one day at a time. There is no need to be perfect or anxious. This should be a time of exploration and enjoyment. You will likely start to notice your tastes changing within weeks of changing your diet, and they will continue to change. The habits you form will become more and more stable and mindless, and the health benefits of your efforts will quickly start to emerge." —*Thomas Campbell, M.D.,* The Campbell Plan

COOKING WITHOUT OIL

Many reasons for avoiding extracted oils are noted on page 11, so I won't recap them here. But I want to explain briefly how oil can simply be removed from or substituted in everyday meals. If you've always used oil, learning to cook without it can seem awkward at first, but after a while you (and your taste buds) will become used to its absence. In homemade salad dressings, for example, it's easy enough to just leave it out. In stovetop cooking, substituting with water or vegetable stock is very easy. And in baking, many alternatives exist, as you'll read below.

SALAD DRESSINGS

Oil and vinegar salad dressing is so traditional that it may be hard to imagine a salad without it; but you will grow to appreciate the cleaner, fresher taste of the vegetables and greens in your salads without the heaviness of the oil (and I'm sure you won't miss the calories). If I am following a dressing recipe that calls for oil, I simply omit it (or then add a little water or juice to make up for the lost volume). That's it!

For quick homemade dressings without oil I often use some mustard mixed with vinegar or juice (lemon, grapefruit, lime, apple, carrot, celery). For a more complex dressing I add in some soft fruits or vegetables, such as strawberries, mango, or cucumber. For richer, creamy dressings, a very small amount of high-fat tofu, avocado, or nuts may be used (see Salad Dressing Road Map on page 73).

STOVETOP COOKING AND ROASTING

When you are sautéing (cooking while stirring at high heat) vegetables on the stovetop, simply replace the oil with a tablespoon or two of water or vegetable stock. You can use other liquids too, such as fresh vegetable juice or vinegar, but water is the oil replacement I use most. Vegetables release water as they cook, so this is why we usually need to add only a small amount of liquid. Just keep an eye on your pan (I keep a glass of water nearby), as your food can quickly stick or burn if all the water cooks off and you are not paying attention.

Oil-Free Hash Browns (page 41) with Better Ketchup (page 152)

When cooking vegetables, such as onions, celery, mushrooms, and bell peppers, first heat your frying pan or soup pot on medium-high heat with 1 or 2 tablespoons of water in the bottom. When the water starts to sputter, add the vegetables (harder vegetables like carrots and potatoes at first, followed by softer vegetables, like zucchini and greens), keeping them moving for a few minutes until they become tender. Cooking vegetables in this way (at high heat and with little liquid) allows the natural sugars to release and the flavors to intensify.

If you are roasting vegetables in the oven, oil is also not needed. We have been taught that we need to first coat vegetables in oil (or an oil-based marinade), but the oil is simply not necessary. Vegetables will still cook up nicely and brown, creating a wonderful roasted flavor.

Eggplant Stir-Fry (page 99)

BAKING

Oil is used in baked goods to provide moistness as well as to create a rich taste. Instead of oil, however, we can use foods like bananas, applesauce, dried fruit, and dates to add moistness, and high-fat foods, like nuts and seeds, to add richness. In the Carrot Cake recipe on page 168, I use bananas and dates to provide moistness (as well as sweetness) instead of oil. When making Oatmeal-Raisin Cookies (page 178), I use dates and raisins for sweetness, and almond butter for richness. And in the Creamy Mushroom Gravy (page 160), I use cashews instead of butter, cream, and/or animal fat to provide richness.

Instead of oiling your pans for baking cakes, breads, or cookies, use parchment paper, a disposable, silicone-coated, nonstick paper that resists high temperatures. (It's different than wax paper but is found close to it in the grocery store; see Parchment Paper, page 22.) Or you can use food-grade silicone bakeware; muffins pop right out of silicone muffin pans. Silicone baking mats are also available, and are useful for baking cookies and roasting vegetables. Silicone bakeware and silicone mats are washable and reusable.

USING DRIED HERBS AND SPICES

The role of dried herbs and spices is a very important one in SOS-free cooking. Because the standard American diet is so heavily seasoned with salt, oil, and sugar (SOS), we have come to rely on these ingredients for the bulk of our flavor and satisfaction. When salt, oil, and sugar are removed from our food preparations, we really notice their absence.

However, avoiding SOS on a regular basis is easier when you understand two key points: (1) In time your taste buds will adjust to not having these highly concentrated and addictive ingredients, and you won't crave them as you once did. This takes a little leap of faith, but if you give your body time to adjust, you will get there. (2) Flavor comes in many different packages besides salt, oil, and sugar. When you learn to flavor your foods with herbs and spices, you can still enjoy eating to the fullest.

Below are answers to the most frequently asked questions about dried herbs and spices, followed by a list of some of the most commonly used herbs and spices in American cooking.

What's the difference between an herb and a spice? Herbs are made from the leafy green parts of plants and can be either fresh or dried. Herbs include basil, mint, and parsley. Spices are usually dried and come from the bark, bud, fruit, berries, roots, or seeds of a plant and are generally very aromatic. Spices include cinnamon, nutmeg, and cloves.

When would I use fresh vs. dried herbs? Recipes will specify whether an herb is to be used fresh or dried, but I tend to use fresh herbs in salads and dips, as well as toward the end of stovetop cooking (such as fresh basil in marinara sauce or cilantro in a curried stew) so they don't become overcooked and lose their flavor and color. Dried herbs intensify in flavor as they are heated, so they are usually added early in the cooking of soups and stews. I also use dried herbs and spices in salad dressings.

If I'm not using a recipe, how much should I use? Start off small and work your way up. Start with ¼ teaspoon (if cooking for one person) of spices, and ½ to 1 teaspoon of dried herbs. Then taste your dish and add more if you like, keeping in mind that some herbs and spices are more pungent than others (cumin, rosemary, ginger, curry, cayenne) and less may be best to start with. I tend to use two to four different dried herbs and spices when cooking a dish. Pretty soon you'll find your own balance, and seasoning food with dried herbs and spices will become second nature. (Keeping notes as you experiment also helps.)

How do I know which herbs and spices go together? Flavor combinations are endless, but one approach is to use herbs and spices that are used together in regional cooking (Chinese, Thai, Indian, Italian, Mediterranean, Southwestern, etc.). You can find out what these are by reading the ingredient lists on your dried herb and spice blends or by searching online for "herb and spice blends" or, for example, "herbs and spices for Thai cooking." You can even create your own unique blends and keep them in small glass jars. When cooking, I usually start with granulated onion and garlic, a dried green herb or green herb blend, and then add something else, like chili or curry powder.

Where should I buy my herbs and spices? You can buy bottled dried herbs and spices at any grocery store, and many natural groceries and co-ops offer them in bulk (where you can buy just the amount you need). I often buy my dried herbs and spices from one of the two spice shops in my town, and it's a treat to visit them (my idea of "kid in the candy store"). You can smell everything and buy a variety of sizes, and the employees are there to help you. I find the herbs and spices at these shops to be the most flavorful and fresh, but I also buy some from the grocery store when it's more convenient.

How much should I buy? In general, buy in smaller quantities so you can avoid becoming the owner of a bunch of old herbs and spices. I buy larger quantities of those I use most often (like granulated garlic and onion, oregano, cinnamon) and less of those I use less often (like cardamom, tarragon, cloves). The quantities you buy will depend on how much you cook and which herbs and spices you tend to use the most and least. When I'm trying out a new herb or spice, I usually buy a small amount before committing to buying a larger amount.

How should I store them? Dried herbs and spices should be stored in small glass containers out of the light and away from heat and humidity in a cool, dry place. That spice rack by your oven, although convenient, will speed up the aging of your herbs and spices. Instead, keep them in a drawer or cabinet that is not adjacent to your oven. Do not shake your dried herbs and spices over a hot pot or pan since the steam can enter the jar and cause clumping and faster aging. Instead, shake some into your hand then put it into the pot, or dip in a small measuring spoon after removing the plastic sifter that comes fixed to the top of most herb and spice jars (which I always throw out).

How do I know if my herbs and spices are too old? Dried herbs and spices will deteriorate in flavor over time. The best way to tell if herbs are still good is to rub them between your fingers and sniff; if they don't smell like anything, toss them. With spices, shake the jar first, then open it and give the spices a sniff to see if they still have a strong aroma; if not, toss them. If you're eating a plant-based diet and going SOS-free, having a variety of freshly dried herbs and spices on hand is a must. If you ever have a question about a particular herb or spice (how to use it or what it smells and tastes like), just ask the Internet.

How long do dried herbs and spices keep? When properly stored, whole spices, like nutmeg and clove, keep the longest (up to a few years), followed by ground spices, like cumin and cinnamon (about a year or so), then dried herbs, like Italian herb seasoning (six months to a year). It's helpful to write the purchase month and year on your containers. It can be hard to throw out old herbs and spices that you paid good money for, but by doing so and purchasing newer, fresher herbs and spices, your food will taste better, and you'll be more likely to want to eat health-promoting meals. Combination boxes of dried herbs and spices make great gifts, for yourself or others who love to cook. Many spice companies offer salt-free blends and salt-free gift boxes.

What if a recipe calls for an herb or spice I don't like? The herb and spice police are not going to bust you, so go right ahead and substitute with the herbs and spices you like best. Most people don't follow recipes exactly as written anyway if they don't like an ingredient, don't have the one called for, or just want to do their own thing. Feel free to use recipes as starting points to get creative and make food that appeals to you. Herbs and spices are like paints on an artist's palette; their applications are endless. So have fun with them and don't add too much to start with (you can always add more, but you cannot take away).

Which herbs and spices should I buy to get started? This will depend on your own tastes, but below is a general list, based on common home-cooking usage as well as my own. If you're just starting to stock your herb and spice cupboard, I would buy some of the daily items and then add one or two from the frequent and occasional lists to experiment with. As a side note, I prefer granulated onion and garlic since they do not clump when added to soups and stews, but you can use powdered or minced instead if you prefer.

COMMONLY USED DRIED HERBS AND SPICES

I use these almost daily:

cinnamon

garlic (granulated)

Italian herb seasoning

nutmeg

onion (granulated)

I use these frequently:

basil

cardamom (ground)

chili powder

coriander (ground)

cumin (ground)

curry powder

garam masala (a spicy Indian blend)

marjoram

oregano

parsley

other ethnic blends (Thai, Latin, Cajun, Indian)

paprika and smoked paprika

poultry seasoning (a powdered blend of green herbs and spices)

rosemary

thyme

I use these occasionally:

allspice

bay leaf

caraway seed

cayenne pepper

celery seed

Chinese 5-spice

cloves

dill weed

fennel seed

ginger

mustard seed

pumpkin pie spice

saffron

sage

tarragon

turmeric

MENU PLANNING

If you are just starting to transition your diet, it will be helpful to create a weekly menu plan—not a menu like at a restaurant, but more like a calendar. This simple act of writing your meals down as a plan, and placing it where you can easily see it, sets up a line of defense against unhealthy, spur-of-the-moment eating.

Once you've gotten into the rhythm of your new way of eating, you can leave menu planning behind, much like training wheels. However, some home cooks like to work from menu plans all of the time, even after getting the hang of it, since they just make meal preparation easier.

Follow these steps to create your own menu plan:

1. Brainstorm a list of plant-based, SOS-free foods: Come up with ideas for breakfast, lunch, and dinner dishes that you've already made and like, or recipes that appeal to you and you want to try. Brainstorm a couple different breakfasts and three to four different lunches and dinners to start with. (If you don't usually eat breakfast, you can fill in just lunch and dinner.) Brainstorm some snacks as well (see the *Healthy Snacking* eBook on my blog). Check grocery sales before menu planning if you like to catch discounts.

2. Create a menu template: On a piece of paper, fill in the days of the week along the top and your food categories along the left side. You can create this on your computer or a piece of paper. It doesn't have to be fancy, although it should be clear and organized enough so that you'll actually use it. You may want to designate one binder as the keeper of your menu plans and printed recipes. (For a free downloadable basic menu template, visit "Resources" on my blog.)

3. Plug in your meals: Using your brainstormed items, fill in your menu template with as much detail as you need so as not to leave anything to chance. Or if you tend not to use recipes as much and like to cook on the fly, jot down meal ideas more loosely, such as "big salad with vegetable soup" or "oatmeal with fruit." Write down your entries in a way that will help *you* most.

4. Add optional categories: Feel free to add other categories to the bottom of your menu plan, such as beverages, or kids' lunches. You can also add categories for any shifts you intend to make for that day or week, such as "no added salt" or "no coffee" or "take lunch to work." Some people like to add even more health-related goals, such as "walk for one hour after dinner," "drink four glasses of water today," or "sleep at least seven hours." Design your menu plan with you and your life in mind.

5. Write up a shopping list: Right after creating your one-week menu plan, make your shopping list (see Grocery Shopping on page 203), then go shopping for the week.

Once-a-week shopping is easier and more economical than going many times a week. Plus, this way you have everything in the house for the *whole week:* all of your healthy food at your fingertips and ready to roll—no excuses!

6. **Create more menus:** Once you have experience with creating one weekly menu, shopping for it, and making all of the meals, go ahead and create one or two more menus that are different, and rotate them from week to week.

Here are some helpful tips for planning meals:

- **Keep themes in mind:** Many people find it helpful to plan their menu with reoccurring themes in mind, such as designating Mondays as "Mexican food" night, Wednesdays as "soup" night, and Saturdays as "baked potato" night. Asking family members to join in with the planning often helps them get more onboard with a new way of eating.

EXAMPLE OF A PARTIAL-WEEK MENU PLAN

	Sunday	Monday	Tuesday	Wednesday
Breakfast	Potato Scramble with Better Ketchup	Oatmeal with fruit and nondairy milk	Cooked quinoa with fruit and nondairy milk	Baked Oatmeal with Apples and Raisins and nondairy milk
Lunch	Tu-No Salad on spinach leaves	Leftover Enchilada Casserole in steamed corn tortillas	Boiled potatoes with vegetables	Leftover spaghetti
Snack	Bowl of cut-up fruit	Cut-up vegetables with hummus	1 apple or 1 cup of leftover stew	1 banana
Dinner	Enchilada Casserole, Burrito Bowl salad, Guacamole	Beefless Stew with Caesar Salad	Spaghetti with Marinara Sauce, steamed broccoli	Split Pea and Yam Soup
Beverage	4 glasses water	4 glasses water	4 glasses water	4 glasses water
Exercise	1 hour walking	30 minutes of strength training (with weights)	1 hour walking	30 minutes of strength training (with weights)

- **Extend prepared dishes:** With the goal of not starting from scratch at each new meal, make enough food to have leftovers for the next day or two. For example, if you make spaghetti for Tuesday's dinner, slot it in again for Wednesday's lunch.

- **Do some batch cooking:** If you don't like cooking every single day, make double or triple batches of food on the weekend, freezing some of it for the following weeks. Soups and stews freeze very well and are great for batch cooking. You can also batch cook things that can be incorporated into various meals throughout the week, such as spaghetti sauce, salad dressings, beans, and hummus.

- **Repurpose dishes:** In addition to batch cooking, plan to use one dish in several ways throughout the week. For example, if you make Enchilada Casserole on Sunday, you can serve it again on Monday in steamed corn tortillas or on top of brown rice or baked potatoes.

- **Keep notes:** Keep track of the dishes that you loved (I put a star next to these) and those that you probably won't make again (I draw a diagonal line through these). Keep all of your "loved" recipes and ideas in a central place. After a while you'll have a clear picture of all the healthy dishes that you really enjoy, and from this you can create menu plans that make your taste buds sing week after week!

- **Post your menu plan in your kitchen:** I like the idea of keeping the plan on the refrigerator so that it's clear to everyone in the house what's on the menu for that week. It also reminds you of your healthy-eating goals whenever you walk by it.

- **Planning for other types of eaters:** I want to give you some guidance on accommodating other types of eaters in your home since this issue comes up frequently.

  One way to approach this is to avoid making two separate meals by planning adaptable dishes. For example, if your husband wants meat, cook it separately and then just add it to his food. You can make a healthy pot of spaghetti, soup, stew, or baked potatoes, tacos, or a big salad, and then add whatever he wants to his portion only.

  Another route that many home cooks take is to kindly announce that since they are the cook in the house, this is what will be served going forward (discuss your menu with family members), and if anyone wants something different, they are welcome to prepare it themselves or buy something prepared outside of the house.

  If you have young children, and there are two parents in the home, the kids may become more interested in trying new, healthy food if they see both of their parents eating it (as opposed to just one). Young kids like modeling the behavior of their parents. Teenagers can be a bit more tricky. Getting their input on meals (and possibly help with preparation) may help get them more interested. Making healthy versions of dishes they are already used to eating is also helpful. Some health-minded parents strike a balance by stipulating that their older kids eat "our way" at home, and when they are away from home, they can choose whatever they want.

GROCERY SHOPPING

Grocery shopping on a plant-based diet is so much faster and easier because there are many aisles in the store you will no longer be traveling down, such as the snack, cereal, soda, meat, eggs, and dairy aisles.

You will spend most of your time in the grocery store in the produce section. This is where you'll find food still in its natural, unprocessed form, which means it looks like it was just picked from the garden or tree. I view the produce section as "home base," full of fresh, colorful vegetables, fruits, and green herbs.

After I have all of my produce, I make my way to the bulk bin or dry goods section of the store, where I stock up on grains, such as oats, rice, and quinoa, as well as dried legumes (beans, peas, lentils). This is also where I find nuts, seeds, and/or dried fruit. You can also find all of these foods outside of the bulk section in boxes and bags, but I like to buy in bulk because it cuts down on packaging waste, is often less expensive, and I get to choose the quantity I buy.

From the bulk section, I make my way to the frozen food section, where I stock up on bags of frozen vegetables and fruits (with no other ingredients added), including peas, corn, mixed vegetables, strawberries, and blueberries.

The last part of my shopping trip is devoted to anything else that is not found in the produce, bulk, or frozen foods sections. I

I view the produce section as "home base," full of fresh, colorful vegetables, fruits, and green herbs.

call this category "other," and it's usually the smallest section on my grocery list. It might include items such as nondairy milk, mustard, canned beans, canned diced tomatoes, pasta, seasonings, and any nonfood items, such as sponges or garbage bags.

To accommodate this pattern of shopping, I organize my shopping list to match, which makes for an efficient shopping trip. I divide a piece of paper into four sections and label each: "produce," "bulk," "frozen," and "other." (For a free downloadable shopping list template, visit "Resources" on my blog.)

If you're the organized type, you can create a permanent grocery list document on your computer and then fill in all of the foods you shop for most under each category, adding new items to the document as you think of them. An example of this is shown on the following page. Before you leave to go shopping, print out your list and highlight or circle each item you need to buy. Or print out and mark up the list when you first plan your meals, and keep it on your refrigerator until shopping day, adding any additional items you think of.

This way of shopping and list arrangement are just two examples of how you can make your shopping trips easier. Come up with a pattern and list that make the most sense for you and your life. (For a comprehensive list of foods that can be consumed

EXAMPLE SHOPPING LIST

PRODUCE
- ☐ apples
- ☐ bananas
- ☐ broccoli
- ☐ kale
- ☐ mushrooms
- ☐ onions
- ☐ parsley
- ☐ romaine lettuce
- ☐ russet potatoes
- ☐ yams

BULK
- ☐ apricots (dried)
- ☐ black beans (dry)
- ☐ brown rice
- ☐ buckwheat
- ☐ flax seeds
- ☐ quinoa
- ☐ raisins
- ☐ red lentils
- ☐ rolled oats
- ☐ walnuts

FROZEN
- ☐ bell peppers
- ☐ blueberries
- ☐ broccoli
- ☐ corn
- ☐ green beans
- ☐ peas
- ☐ mixed vegetables
- ☐ mushrooms
- ☐ onions
- ☐ strawberries

OTHER
- ☐ beans (canned)
- ☐ cinnamon
- ☐ corn tortillas
- ☐ mustard
- ☐ pasta
- ☐ soy milk
- ☐ tomatoes (diced)
- ☐ tomato paste
- ☐ dish soap

on this diet, visit "Resources" on my blog. For information on reading and understanding packaged food labels, see page 206.)

Here are some helpful tips for grocery shopping:

- **Use cloth or other types of reusable grocery bags instead of paper or plastic:** In addition to using reusable grocery bags, you can also reuse your small paper bags (for things like mushrooms and shallots) and plastic produce bags (if they are not too dirty or wet, although you could wash these out and air dry them). You can even go without bags for certain items that are not misted with water and won't be staying in bags once you are home (onions, potatoes, cucumbers). So much waste is generated from the food we buy; anything we can do to lighten the load is a good thing.

- **Storing food:** For information on storing food, see Freezing Food on page 19 and Refrigerating Food on page 23. You can also search "how to store food" online for more detailed information.

- **Buy outside the box:** To avoid getting in a food rut, try something new from the grocery store each trip, such as a new type of apple, lettuce, grain, or frozen vegetable. Whenever I see a small collection of new produce, I will usually try one or two since these are generally specialty or seasonal items that taste great and are only around for a short while.

- **Beyond the grocery store:** While most of us frequent grocery stores, many people get the bulk of their food from a local farmers' market or CSA (community supported agriculture). And if you have a vegetable garden in your backyard, even better! To find local produce, search the name of your town or county plus "farmers' markets" or "CSAs."

- **Clean out your kitchen:** If you're just starting out with a new way of eating, you may want to do a kitchen, pantry, and refrigerator cleanout. Throw away or give away any foods that you are now avoiding and that might otherwise tempt you off your healthy-eating path. Right after you do this, go shopping for a basketful of healthy foods to fill up your kitchen.

"People who adopt a WFPB [whole-food, plant-based] diet find that most of their health problems were caused or significantly worsened by their old diets and resolve naturally and quickly once the body starts getting the proper fuel. It's like someone who hits their head with a hammer three times a day and finds that nothing cures their headaches. It just makes sense to put down the hammer!" —T. Colin Campbell, Ph.D. with Howard Jacobson, Ph.D., *Whole*

READING FOOD LABELS

Getting into the habit of reading food labels can greatly benefit your health, and it takes only seconds to scan the back of a package. I encourage you to become the investigator of your own food and discover what's behind the curtain!

I strive to avoid packaged foods for the most part, but still buy a handful, such as nondairy milk, canned beans and tomatoes, frozen fruits and vegetables, corn tortillas, and prepared mustard. Even when buying minimally processed foods, it is still important to glance at the ingredient list and Nutrition Facts label.

The importance of reading labels was driven home to me one day while shopping for tomato paste. I found a small can that I had used before, and it contained just one ingredient: tomatoes. As I was putting it into my basket I noticed an almost identical can of tomato paste next to it, the only difference being that it had the words "with Italian herbs" added to the front label. I was intrigued, so I turned the can around to read the ingredient list.

I couldn't believe what I saw! What I thought might be just tomato paste with the addition of basil, oregano, and/or thyme was something very different. The ingredient list had jumped from 1 to 14 ingredients, and the kicker was that there was no mention of herbs anywhere. Being the curious type, I emailed the manufacturer to ask about the herbs, and was told, "We consider the exact spice and natural flavoring ingredients to be proprietary information—part of our special recipe." Not the most satisfying answer.

This is another compelling reason to eat food as close to how nature made it as possible. You never know what's *really* in your food when it is packaged or prepared by a business, whether a food manufacturer or a restaurant. This is not to say that all packaged foods and restaurants are to be avoided. But because their goal is to make money and our goal is to stay healthy, we should always be curious, do our homework, and ask questions.

Aside from the mysterious herbs, this small can of tomato paste's long list of ingredients included many things that compromise good health, such as high fructose corn syrup, partially hydrogenated vegetable oil, hydrolyzed corn gluten, soy and wheat gluten proteins, Romano cheese, and salt. Manufacturers know that most consumers don't read labels but respond to getting more ("with Italian herbs"), and that the addictive nature of sugar (corn syrup), fat (oil, cheese), and salt in their products keeps people coming back for more.

Next time you're buying a packaged food, take a look at the ingredient list; you may be surprised at what you find—possibly

> *I encourage you to become the investigator of your own food and discover what's behind the curtain!*
>
>

a long list of substances you would not otherwise knowingly put into your mouth. Manufacturers also change their ingredients periodically, so check the ingredient list now and then, even if you think you know what's in the product.

This is a good example of how anything—even a simple can of tomato paste—can be turned into a junk food. *Any* food with a label deserves our attention because, as Dr. Michael Klaper likes to say, "The body is always paying attention to what's going into it, even if we're not."

All U.S. food packages contain an ingredient list and a Nutrition Facts label. Understanding both will help you know how much fat, salt, sugar, and calories (among other things) are in your food.

THE INGREDIENT LIST

1. Don't believe the front of the package: Avoid buying food based only on information provided on the front of the package. This is where manufacturers use words and phrases to get us to think that the product is healthier than it is (think "fat-free" or "natural"). Always look to the ingredients list and the Nutrition Facts label on the package to find out exactly what's in the food and how much.

2. Read the ingredients: Scan the ingredients list to make sure it does not include items you are striving to avoid, such as salt, saturated fats, hydrogenated fats, and oils.

INGREDIENTS: Organic black beans, water

This ingredient list for canned black beans is nice and short, and includes no added salt, oil, or sugar.

Similarly, be wary of sweeteners like corn syrup, rice syrup, molasses, or any type of sugar that ends in "ol" or "ose" (sorbitol, dextrose), as well as artificial sweeteners (see point 6 in the Nutrition Facts Label section, which follows). In addition, make sure any grains are whole grains, meaning that the grain has not been stripped of valuable nutrients and fiber (as with white flour).

3. Note the order of ingredients: The ingredients are listed in descending order according to weight, starting with the most used to the least used. Ideally, we want to avoid any added refined salt, oil, or sugar. If you find an otherwise healthful product that does have a little added sugar, just make sure it's not listed as one of the first three ingredients. As for fat and sodium, using the Nutrition Facts label (not the ingredient list) to gauge their amounts will be more helpful to you (see points 4 and 5 in the Nutrition Facts Label section on the next page). This is because even when oil and salt are found at the end of the ingredient list, they can still deliver more sodium and calories per serving than are healthy.

4. Strive for fewer ingredients: Look for packaged foods with few ingredients. I try to buy foods having anywhere from one to five ingredients (such as with canned tomatoes, canned black beans, and frozen strawberries, all of which can be found with just one ingredient, and soy milk made with just two ingredients: soy beans and water). But make sure the few ingredients that are in the food are wholesome (not salt, oil, sugar, and/or white flour).

5. Know what you're eating: If you don't recognize the ingredient names (like hydrolyzed corn gluten, BHT, potassium bromate) and/or do not find the ingredients occurring in nature (like oil, high fructose corn syrup, MSG, artificial coloring and flavoring), it's best to avoid the product. Stick to ingredients that are familiar to you, such as brown rice, oats, tomatoes, peas, and beans.

6. Look for whole grains: Not all grains are created equal. For the most health-promoting grains, be sure that the ingredient list uses one of the following adjectives before the mention of any type of grain: whole, stone ground, cracked, rolled, or sprouted. (Brown rice is the exception and does not need one of these qualifiers to be whole grain.)

THE NUTRITION FACTS LABEL

As you read this section, refer to the example Nutrition Facts label on this page. To make the calculations easy, I created the label with rounded numbers (based on an actual label from a can of "low-sodium" black beans).

1. Serving size: The numbers found on the Nutrition Facts label are all tied to what the manufacturer designates as a "serving size." If you consume the serving size, the stated amounts of nutrients (of primary concern are calories, fat, and salt) on the label are what you'll be getting. But if you consume more than the serving size—which is not hard to do since many are unrealistically small—you'll be getting more of everything.

2. Number of servings per container: Next, you'll want to locate the number of "servings per container." In our example, the serving size listed on the can of black beans is ½ cup, and there are 3 servings (1½ cups) in one can. So eating the whole can of beans by yourself will provide you with 3 times the nutrients stated on the label.

3. Calories per serving: Once you know the serving size and the number of servings in a container, you may want to know the number of calories per serving. The 100 calories listed on our label are for one serving (½ cup). If you eat the whole can (3 servings), the total calories would be 300.

4. Calories from fat: A helpful guideline to follow for fat is to make sure that the calories

Nutrition Facts

Serving Size 1/2 cup (127g)
Servings Per Container 3

Amount Per Serving

Calories 100	Calories from Fat 9

	% Daily Values*
Total Fat 1g	**2%**
Saturated Fat 0g	**0%**
Trans Fat 0g	
Cholesterol 0mg	**0%**
Potassium 280mg	**8%**
Sodium 140mg	**6%**
Total Carbohydrate 17g	**6%**
Dietary Fiber 6g	**24%**
Sugars 0g	
Protein 6g	**12%**

* Percent Daily Values are based on a 2,000 calorie diet. Your Daily Values may be higher or lower depending on your calorie needs.

	Calories	2,000	2,500
Total Fat	Less than	65g	80g
Sat Fat	Less than	20g	25g
Cholesterol	Less than	300mg	300mg
Sodium	Less than	2400mg	2400mg
Total Carbohydrate		300g	375g
Dietary Fiber		25g	30g

from fat are no more than 20% of total calories. So for our black bean example, the calories from fat are 9 out of 100 (9%), which is well below the 20% upper limit.

5. Sodium: To see if you're getting too much sodium, don't look at the "% Daily Value" number; instead, look at the sodium milligrams (mg). A helpful rule of thumb that you can apply is to keep the sodium milligrams equal to or less than the number of calories (the lower the better, of course). In our black bean example, the sodium is 140 mg, which is higher than the number of calories (100).

6. Sugar: Not all sugar needs to be avoided, but current Nutrition Facts labels do not distinguish between the healthy sugars that occur naturally in whole, intact plant foods (like apples and carrots) and the unhealthy refined sugars (such as corn syrup, brown sugar, dextrose, agave, and evaporated can juice) that manufacturers add during processing. (This is changing, however: starting in mid-2018, "added sugars" will be called out separately on food labels.)

We want to limit the amount of concentrated, refined sugars that are added to packaged foods to no more than 5% of calories. However, because the current label does not distinguish between the naturally occurring and the added sugars, we cannot calculate this. Therefore, until the new labels take effect, the only way to know if any sugars have been added to a packaged food is to read the ingredients list. As mentioned on page 207, if you find an otherwise healthful product that does have a little added sugar, just make sure it's not listed as one of the first three ingredients.

This is easier said than done, as there are more than 150 different names for added sugar that can appear on a nutrition label (to find out what they are, search "names of sugar" online). This alone is a great argument for avoiding packaged, processed foods; they're fraught with land mines that only the most educated consumer can avoid.

If you would like more information on label reading, see Resources on page 230 for Jeff Novick's DVD, *Fast Food (volume 3): Shopping School.*

10 TIPS FOR EATING IN RESTAURANTS

Most restaurant food is extremely flavorful as a result of being prepared with concentrated amounts of salt, fat, oil, and sugar (among other things). This is by design so that customers keep coming back. You could vow to never again eat in a restaurant in your efforts to be as healthy as possible, but that isn't very realistic or fun. I eat out less than I used to (much preferring my own food and preparations), but I still enjoy the occasional meal out. Following are 10 tips to help you navigate the challenges of typical restaurant fare.

1. If you have the choice of which restaurant to go to, search for one online that suits how you eat. Restaurants that feature plant-based menu items are everywhere nowadays. To find the ones in your area, simply search online for "vegan restaurants" or "veg-friendly restaurants" and the name of your city or county. *HappyCow.net* (and its accompanying app) is a great international resource for locating restaurants with healthier, plant-based options.

2. If you don't have the choice of restaurant, research the menu of the restaurant you're going to before you get there. You can find most restaurant menus online. Look for something on the menu that fits with the way you eat at home, or as close as possible. If you cannot find a menu online, call the restaurant and ask if they can make you something that fits your diet or modify an existing menu item. Most restaurants today are used to special dietary requests, and many chefs enjoy the challenge of making something different. So don't be afraid to ask for what you want. And if the chef does a great job, tell the server to let them know how much you enjoyed it.

3. If you find yourself sitting in a restaurant that you are unfamiliar with, scan the menu for something that might work for you. If you don't see anything, ask your server if they can make you something simple, such as a baked potato topped with steamed vegetables. Most restaurants have basics like these in their kitchen. Another bonus of ordering this way (besides good health) is that it's often cheaper than the items on the menu. You don't have to feel embarrassed or timid when ordering. When we kindly and confidently ask questions and make requests, we let the restaurant know that this way of eating is important and growing. Your reasonable questions are also a point of education for the server and restaurant, and sometimes even for the people you're dining with.

4. The salad: Of course, there is always the healthy-eater's loyal friend when eating out: the green salad. Most restaurants can pull together a romaine or spinach salad with a variety of raw vegetables and a dressing of simply lemon juice or balsamic vinegar. If they have an oil-free dressing option, order it on the side so you can taste it first and monitor how much ends up on your salad.

Some people even bring their own small container of healthy dressing with them to discreetly pour over their salads.

5. Before ordering, let the server know your dietary needs. None of us wants to be seen as the picky, annoying restaurant customer, but we also want to stay true to our dietary goals and values. Toward this end, cheerfully check in with the server before you order. You might say, "I eat only plant foods, so please let me know if I order anything that has meat, dairy, or eggs in it." In addition, some people associate the term "dairy" only with cow's milk, so you might want to be clear with your server that cheese, butter, and sour cream are also dairy foods you avoid. Similarly, they may not put fish in the "meat" category, so you may want to ask about that as well. In order to be extremely clear, some people carry small cards in their wallets that list the ingredients and foods they do not eat, and give one to the server to pass on to the chef. And if your meal does come with

The healthy-eater's loyal friend: the green salad

something in it or on it that you didn't order, politely send it back.

6. SOS-free: Maintaining an SOS-free (without salt, oil, and sugar) diet in restaurants can be a challenge, to say the least. But if you do find yourself eating out, you can request that no salt, oil, and sugar be added to your food. If these ingredients have already been added during preparation of the food, try to find something else to order. Sometimes even simple items, like vegetables or rice, will have been precooked with salt and oil, so be sure to ask. For example, when I order "home style" potatoes, I ask for them to be cooked dry. And for vegetables, instead of preparing them with oil, I ask if they can be steamed or cooked in water instead.

7. Say "no thanks" or put it on the side. Restaurants pack a lot of flavor (via salt, oil, sugar, butter, lard, animal-based broths, etc.) into dressings, sauces, dips, spreads, and gravies, so feel free to order your food without condiments on top, as well as things like the pat of butter and dollop of sour cream. If you don't want to draw too much attention to your ordering (in the beginning, this is a common concern, but it gets easier in time with practice), just order these things on the side, and then don't eat them. Sometimes I will come across a salad dressing that sounds healthy, but even then, I'll order it on the side just to be safe.

8. Ordering dessert: I often skip desserts (even vegan desserts) when eating out since they are usually made with lots of salt, fat/oil, sugar, and white flour. When I *have* indulged in desserts at restaurants, I often regret it, as I just end up feeling heavy and bloated afterwards since my body is not used to these ingredients. Nowadays I prefer to reserve my occasional desserts for at home where I can control what's in them and, therefore, feel better after eating them. If I am set on something sweet when I'm out, I usually ask for some fruit or split the healthiest dessert on the menu with someone I'm with.

9. Take a break: Going to restaurants is enjoyable because we go with other people and socialize, and we get to eat very stimulating food (due to greater-than-usual amounts of SOS). It's hard to turn down offers for lunch and dinner from friends and family, but if you are serious about going plant-based and SOS-free, you may want to take a break from eating out until you get more comfortable with your new way of eating, which in turn will help you feel more confident navigating restaurant menus and ordering what you want. You might also like to research some restaurants in your area that will work with you.

10. Don't forget, it's just one meal. Years back when I was complaining to a friend about being hungry and there was nothing

I prefer to reserve my occasional desserts for at home where I can control what's in them. (Above, Sweet Potato-Pecan Pie, page 174)

healthy available where we were, he said something that I never forgot: "You know, you don't have to eat." I looked at him like he was crazy, but his point was that it's just one meal. If you miss it or have just a little bit of something that you *can* eat, your life will go on, and you can pick right back up eating as usual at your next meal at home. People can actually go many days without eating. Sure, skipping meals is not as satisfying, but if staying true to your healthy-eating goals is a top priority to you, this is an option for the occasional tricky situation.

EATING AT EVENTS AND WHILE TRAVELING

Similar to eating at restaurants, eating away from home, at various social events, or while traveling, can also be challenging. Anytime you come together with other people (family, friends, coworkers) to socialize and eat—at parties, potlucks, picnics, meetings, or holiday gatherings—you'll want to be prepared if you want to maintain your healthy eating habits. There are many ways to handle these situations with grace so that you don't end up eating food that you don't want to.

BRING YOUR OWN FOOD
Potlucks are the easiest of the "event" scenarios because you can bring any dish you like or at least make a requested dish to your specifications. Whether it's a community potluck or a small dinner party at a friend's house where everyone contributes something, bring plant-based dishes that *you* will enjoy eating so you won't go hungry if all the other dishes have meat and/or dairy in them (which is usually the case, unless you're attending a vegan or plant-based event, but even those are likely to be salt- and oil-heavy). I usually bring two dishes so I have variety for myself. But I also like bringing more than one dish so that I can impress upon others just how delicious healthy eating can be.

COMMUNICATE WITH THE HOST
If you've been invited to a dinner party or other event where all the food will be prepared and provided for you, contact the host to ask about the menu and if there will be any plant-based options. If you feel comfortable asking, you might also request no added oil, although this may be tougher. Many home cooks, chefs, and caterers are used to offering meat- and dairy-free options these days, so your request will not likely be met with surprise or frustration. Some hosts will even enjoy learning about different ways of cooking and eating through your request.

Communicating with the host is also important if you'll be staying at someone else's house, for example, when visiting family or friends out of town. Your host may be interested in cooking to accommodate you, or they may not, in which case you'll want to ask if you can bring some groceries to their house and use their kitchen while staying there. If you don't want to take up too much space, plan on keeping it simple by making meals like a baked potato or rice with steamed vegetables, and oatmeal and fruit for breakfast. I also like to search online to find out where the nearest grocery stores are before I get there so I can do a bit of shopping before arriving at their house.

EAT BEFORE YOU LEAVE HOME
If you know that the event you're attending won't have food that aligns with your way of eating, plan to eat a meal or a snack before you leave home so that you won't arrive at the event really hungry, which dramatically increases the probability that you will eat whatever is in front of you. If only two things

there align with your diet, fill your plate with those things. I've also been known to put a banana into my purse as insurance.

Now, if there's *nothing* there you can eat in good conscience, this isn't the end of the world. You'll be home soon enough and will be able to eat what you want (plus you'll be extra hungry, so it will taste extra good). It's just one meal. Your stomach may be growling but, in this case, try to focus on the social aspect of the event instead of the food.

PLAN AHEAD FOR TRAVELING

Traveling throws us off our everyday routines enough as it is, so we want to minimize its disruption of our way of eating. Toward this end, I bring a small ice chest or a backpack just for my food. This allows me to leave home as prepared as possible, whether I'm taking a day trip, going camping for the weekend, or traveling long distances for business or pleasure.

Great traveling foods include baked potatoes and yams sliced into rounds (these

are tasty cold, too); leftover soups, stews, or pasta (even cold, you will be glad you have them); prepared baked items (like Baked Oatmeal, Carrot Cake muffins, or Banana-Walnut Bars on pages 33, 168, and 177); whole or cut-up vegetables and fruits; granola; and dried fruit. As for packaged items, you might consider rice or corn cakes, or Lärabars (small fruit- and nut-only bars).

If you're driving long distances and want to grab a bite on the road, look online for any health-minded restaurants or grocery stores along your route. Some fast food restaurants (like Wendy's) offer a simple baked potato with vegetables. When you're driving and starving, this simple baked potato will taste so good to you! I personally like to find Whole Foods Markets since I know I can get a good salad at their salad bar, and while I'm there I stock up on some healthy snacks and groceries.

In addition to many restaurants, airports have become increasingly aware of their health-minded customers and are accommodating them by offering more plant-based options on their menus. You can search an airport online to find out what food options are available, and then save time by going there directly instead of hunting around and then settling on something that you really would prefer not to be eating. The Physicians Committee for Responsible Medicine website offers an annual "Airport Food Review" that ranks the 24 healthiest airports in the U.S., listing the healthier restaurants and dishes you will find at each one (go to *PCRM.org* and search "airport food review").

Marinara Sauce (page 112) over corkscrew pasta is a great traveling food, even cold.

MY PATH TO GOOD HEALTH

My attraction to health started in elementary school, where you could often find me checking out library books about nurses and doctors, and marveling at the complexity of the human body in picture books. I pored over our family's set of *Britannica* encyclopedias, especially the volume that illustrated the various organs and systems of the body, each transparent page building upon the previous, eventually revealing a complete body.

Growing up, I had my share of colds, earaches, sore throats, and stomach-aches. By the time I was 13, I had had pneumonia twice. It's no wonder I was so interested in health and the human body. In college I took gross anatomy so I could learn firsthand how it all worked on people who had donated their bodies to science. The class was one of my most difficult but also most unforgettable.

Although I considered a medical path briefly, the time commitment, cost, and discipline it would take intimidated me. I went on to get my BA in psychology and, soon after, an early childhood education teaching credential. I taught elementary school just long enough to realize I wasn't cut out to teach elementary school. I connected well with the children but was overwhelmed by the job. I felt that if I didn't make a career shift, I would melt into a pile of stress and anxiety.

While looking for a new job, I decided to take a hard look at my diet, having become hooked on convenience and fast foods. I could stand to lose a little weight, but mostly I was just sick of feeling tired much of the time. I also knew that it was time for me to figure out how to get dairy foods out of my diet, for they had been the source of painful stomachaches for as long as I could remember.

It was time for me to figure out how to get dairy foods out of my diet, for they had been the source of painful stomachaches for as long as I could remember.

A friend suggested I read a book by Dr. John McDougall, a medical doctor specializing in nutrition who promoted a starch-based diet free of animal foods and oils. Giving up meat was not hard, since eating it had always made me feel heavy and tired. Plus, as an animal lover, giving up meat brought my values of loving animals and living as a compassionate person more into alignment. I had always cared for animals, but until changing my diet and learning more about how poorly farmed animals are treated to become our food, it had never occurred to me that I could simply not eat them. I didn't need permission, I suppose, but Dr. McDougall's books let me know that it was okay not to eat animals. He was the example I needed to take the plunge.

After ditching the animal foods, I felt so good that my new diet soon turned into a *lifestyle*. Within days of cutting out dairy foods, I noticed immediate results, mainly that I no longer got stomachaches after meals. In fact, I felt so good that every once in a while I'd go to a party or a friend's house for dinner and indulge in a little cheese or ice cream, as a special treat for being so good. And a special treat is what I got! It came in the form of a raging stomachache. My body protested dairy to such a degree that I would double over in pain, and start sweating and breathing heavily until I could get to a bathroom and literally expel it from my body. Even small amounts of dairy would throw my now cleaner digestive system into a full-blown tizzy. It was as if my body was scolding me: "Why on earth would you put that into me after we've been doing so well!?" By giving up dairy, I also saw other improvements: my skin looked better, I lost some weight, and my digestion became regular. As for animal foods, I no longer considered them food at all.

As for animal foods, I no longer considered them food at all.

With my health on the right track, and feeling vibrant and excited for what was to come on the job front, I calculated my next step. Having done well in my writing courses all through school, I applied for a job as an associate editor at a local business magazine. This was the kind of job I thought I could really excel at and enjoy, and maybe even build a new career on. Having no journalism experience, I had only my excitement and potential to sell, offering that if they hired me for a month and were not happy, they could send me on my way without paying me

a dime. I got the job and, after a while, was promoted to managing editor. I loved the work: writing, editing, interviewing people, overseeing writers and photographers, and helping produce a useful and beautiful magazine. After a few years, I got a job in the same position but at a larger magazine. Life was very busy but exciting!

However, my love of the work began to take a back seat to the fast pace and my growing list of responsibilities, as our magazine grew and we worked to develop an online presence full of content that would position us as a leader in our field. It's what good business is all about: growing, and staying competitive and valuable to customers. It was exciting to be a part of this evolution, but a lot of the time it felt as if I was riding a bike underwater. It was a constant challenge for me to keep up. But I had asked for it, and I continued to give it my all.

As I pushed on, I began having a hard time falling asleep at night because I was always thinking about what needed to be done the following day at work. When I did sleep, I repeatedly had the same dream: wandering down a dark street, knowing I had to do something but not able to remember what it was. It was maddening, and I felt I was becoming a different person: someone who had to trade doing high-quality work for satisfactory work in order to meet the deadlines.

I was no longer excited by my career, and one day, in utter frustration, I unleashed all my grievances in one fell swoop upon my poor editor. It was so unexpected coming from me that he rolled his chair back slowly, just waiting for me to finish. When I returned to my desk, embarrassed and totally wrung out, I collapsed into my chair and felt an intense, unfamiliar tightening in my chest. I had sensed that I was losing my sanity but was I also losing my health? My body was waving a red flag at me—something was definitely wrong.

After visiting a doctor, I learned that what I had experienced was heartburn, something totally foreign to my existence up until that point. While some people's heartburn is mild, for others it can be so intense that they feel as if they are having a heart attack. Acid reflux caused by stress and the pace I was keeping (you can also get acid reflux from eating certain foods and combinations) was causing the burning in my chest. My doctor prescribed me some medication to calm it, and it worked like a charm, at first. Then it began to lose its effectiveness. I disliked the idea of taking medication to suppress the messages that my body was sending me. So I tried cleaning up my diet even further. I started eating out less and brought my lunch to work. I also exercised more and took classes in stress reduction, breathing, and yoga.

I wasn't ready to give up on my dream job, though, especially since, instead of firing me after my outburst, my boss had hired an assistant for our department. I

> *I disliked the idea of taking medication to suppress the messages that my body was sending me.*

appreciated this so much but eventually realized that the change I needed was to move away from environments that were overly stressful for me. Much like my teaching experience, I had loved many parts of my work, but it occurred to me that the stress, pressure, and pace of both jobs were not good fits with my desire for good health and balance, physically and mentally. An "Ah ha" moment had been served to me on a silver platter: Knowing *what* you love to do is just as important as knowing *how* and *where* you want to do it.

I resigned from my job with hopeful anticipation for what was to come. I relished the reduction of stress in my life. I'd saved some money, and this, combined with working from home as a freelance writer, allowed me some breathing room to research my next step. Not entirely trusting my judgment when it came to career choices at that point, I consulted with a job coach who helped me arrive at my next career. I remember thinking that this—my *third* career path—would be the charm, the golden ticket, the glass slipper that I could slide my foot into and say, "Ahhh! I'm home."

Through our conversations, my job coach learned that I had many varied interests. People throughout my life had noticed the same thing about me, often commenting, "You're quite the Renaissance woman." But while "Renaissance woman" has a nice ring to it, I had come to feel that in my case it described one who couldn't commit and was maybe a little too idealistic. However, three things were clear to me: (1) I knew I wanted to do work I was passionate about, (2) I wanted to help and teach others, and (3) I wanted the freedom to express myself creatively in an environment that was not overly stressful.

I'll never forget my coach asking me this pivotal question early on: "What kinds of books do you read?" Oh, that was easy. I read health and nutrition books mostly. Making my own dietary changes had ignited an interest in the relationship between food and health, which had then snowballed into a full-blown obsession as I devoured books, DVDs, and websites, and attended lectures and cooking classes. Things were coming into focus. With nutrition at the core, I began to get excited and envisioned myself helping others improve their health.

Feeling particularly confident one day, I contacted Dr. McDougall, whose books had helped me a great deal, with the hope of landing a part-time job that would allow me to gain some experience in the field of plant-based nutrition. Geography and timing were on my side, and in 2007 I began working for John and Mary McDougall part time at their 10-day, in-patient nutrition education programs. I helped with administrative tasks and accompanied participants to grocery and cookware stores where they learned to read food labels and stock their kitchens. I'll never forget the first time I met Dr. McDougall in person; he shook my hand and said, "Well, you look healthy!" A better greeting I could not ask for.

It was through the McDougall books and program that I really began to learn the truth about food and its effects on the human body. Like the layers of an onion being peeled away, I gradually began learning things like how to navigate the countless health myths and messages I had grown up with (that we all grow up with), how to read a food label and why this is so important, and why oil and fish are not health foods. As part of the staff, I was able to sit in on presentations by experts in plant-based nutrition, as well as learn from accomplished vegan chefs. I also regularly talked with program participants who spoke of their remarkable health improvements within just days of changing their diet.

In 2010, I was given the opportunity to teach cooking classes at another nearby in-patient facility called TrueNorth Health Center, which specializes in medically supervised water-only fasting and promotes a plant-based diet free of added salt, oil, and sugar (SOS-free). Up until that point, I had enjoyed cooking at home but had no formal culinary training. But ever the Renaissance woman, I jumped in with both spatulas, a bit nervous but knowing that this would be the best way for me to learn. Soon after this, I also began teaching cooking classes at the McDougall Program in addition to my other work there. I was now doing work I was passionate about while teaching and helping others with their health. The slipper fit; what do you know!

Also in 2010, I launched my blog *StraightUpFood.com* so that I could share original plant-based, SOS-free recipes with my students. The website is visited not only by my students, but by people from all corners of the globe who seek excellent health through a plant-based, SOS-free diet. They email me almost every day, often with messages like this one:

> "I never would have dreamed, seven months ago, that I could go dairy- and meat-free (and give up oil as well), but with help from websites like yours, it's all possible. That's why it's so important for you to keep creating and sharing and making it possible for all us newbies! I just wanted you to know how much I appreciate you and thank you so much!" —Deb

This is my job now—to help and connect with others doing what I absolutely love. With my background in writing, and passions for photography and cooking, my blog has become an ideal outlet for my work, a place to express myself creatively on a regular basis. I love that I am able to bring my skills and interests to my work online, in the classroom, and now, with this book, in print.

I may not have fully understood why I was checking out those books in elementary school, but I think I had a sense that helping others to be happy and healthy would be an important aspect of my life's work. And I was right!

NUTRITION DATA

See page 228 for explanations of headings.

Recipe	Notes	Serving size
BREAKFAST		
5-minute Oatmeal	hot whole-grain cereal	1 recipe (337 g), 1 cup
1-Minute Oatmeal	hot whole-grain cereal	1 recipe (277 g), 1 cup
Steel-Cut Oatmeal	hot whole-grain cereal	1 recipe (409 g), 1.25 cups
Quinoa	hot whole-grain cereal	1 recipe (294 g), 1 cup
Brown Rice	hot whole-grain cereal	1 recipe (330 g), 1.25 cups
Millet	hot whole-grain cereal	1 recipe (304 g), 1 cup
Amaranth	hot whole-grain cereal	1 recipe (393 g), 1.25 cups
Buckwheat	hot whole-grain cereal	1 recipe (219 g), 1 cup
Baked Oatmeal w/ Apples and Raisins	w/ nondairy milk, cereal	⅙ recipe (154 g)
Baked Oatmeal w/ Apples and Raisins	w/ nondairy milk, bars	1/16 recipe (58 g), 1 bar
Baked Oatmeal w/ Apples and Raisins	w/ water, cereal	⅙ recipe (115 g)
Baked Oatmeal w/ Apples and Raisins	w/ water, bars	1/16 recipe (43 g), 1 bar
Creamy Rice Cereal	w/out raisins or fruit	½ recipe, (552 g), 1 cup
Almond Milk		⅑ recipe (113 g), ½ cup
Pecan Milk		⅑ recipe (113 g), ½ cup
Oat Milk		⅛ recipe (124 g), ½ cup
Rice Milk		1/12 recipe (135 g), ½ cup
Granola	w/ almonds	⅙ recipe (89 g), ½ cup
Oil-Free Hash Browns	w/ avocado	½ recipe (247 g), 1 potato
Oatmeal-Lemon Pancakes	w/out fruit, nuts, and syrup	¼ recipe (135 g), 3 small pancakes
Waffles	w/ cashews (not almond butter), w/out fruit, nuts, and syrup	¼ recipe, (180 g), 1.5 6-inch classic waffles
Strawberry-Date Syrup		¼ recipe (138 g), ½ cup
Potato-Veggie Scramble	w/out ketchup or salsa	¼ recipe (458 g), 2 cups
Blueberry Muffins	w/ walnuts	1/12 recipe (100 g), 1 muffin
SALADS		
Burrito Bowl		⅙ recipe (304 g), 2 cups
Fruit Salad w/ Fresh Mint		¼ recipe (250 g), 1.25 cups
Cabbage Salad w/ Mustard-Lime Dressing	w/ avocado	⅙ recipe (257 g), 1.5 cups
Spinach-Mango Salad	w/ avocado	⅙ recipe (229 g), 1.5 cups

calories per serving	calorie density (calories per pound)	g fat	% calories from fat	g saturated fat	% calories from saturated fat	sodium mg	g carbohydrate	g protein	g sugar	g fiber	calcium mg
153	206	2.6	15.6%	0.5	2.9%	14	27.4	5.3	0.4	4.1	30
148	243	2.8	17.0%	0.4	2.4%	10	27.3	5.5	0.6	3.8	25
202	224	3.5	16.6%	0.6	2.7%	17	36.1	7.0	0.5	5.4	38
208	321	3.4	14.7%	0.4	1.7%	12	36.4	8.0	3.5	4.0	33
342	471	2.7	7.1%	0.5	1.3%	16	71.4	7.3	0.8	8.8	28
252	376	2.8	10.0%	0.5	1.8%	12	48.6	7.4	1.0	5.7	12
358	414	6.8	17.1%	1.4	3.5%	15	63.0	13.1	1.6	6.5	162
142	294	1.1	7.0%	0.2	1.3%	11	30.7	4.8	0.8	4.2	12
209	616	4	17.2%	0.7	3.0%	10	39.3	7.2	12.3	5.9	31
78	611	1.5	17.3%	0.3	3.5%	4	14.7	2.7	4.6	2.2	11
164	647	2.6	14.3%	0.5	2.7%	4	32.7	4.6	8.0	4.2	15
61	644	1	14.8%	0.2	3.0%	1	12.3	1.7	3.0	1.6	5
346	285	5	13.0%	0.8	2.1%	39	68.2	11.2	23.0	8.0	77
45	181	3.9	77.3%	0.3	5.8%	4	1.7	1.7	0.3	1.0	24
54	217	5.7	95.0%	0.5	8.3%	4	1.1	0.7	0.3	0.8	8
20	73	0.3	13.7%	0.1	4.5%	5	3.4	0.7	0.1	0.5	6
19	64	0.2	9.5%	0	1.4%	5	3.8	0.4	0.1	0.5	5
254	1296	7.2	25.5%	0.7	2.5%	2	44.1	6.4	20.9	6.0	51
204	375	5.5	24.3%	0.8	3.5%	36	36.4	4.2	2.6	7.4	23
223	750	3.6	14.5%	0.5	2.0%	210	45.3	5.6	10.7	5.7	147
247	623	7.4	27.0%	1.1	4.0%	96	40.8	7.1	6.1	5.4	127
85	280	0.1	1.1%	0	0.0%	4	45.72	0.7	19.9	2.3	24
284	282	1.3	4.1%	0.2	0.6%	54	59.2	12.0	9.1	15.4	119
187	849	4.8	23.1%	0.5	2.4%	20	34.8	4.0	16.0	4.3	45
255	381	5.1	18.0%	0.8	2.8%	15	47.0	8.1	3.5	9.3	64
110	200	0.6	4.9%	0.1	0.8%	2	27.7	1.8	20.6	4.9	36
157	277	3.4	19.5%	0.4	2.3%	79	26.6	6.9	8.5	8.4	84
111	220	4	32.4%	0.6	4.9%	33	19.0	2.8	12.1	4.6	76

Recipe	Notes	Serving size
Tu-No Salad	w/ ½ cup cashews and avocado	⅙ recipe (206 g), ¾ cup
Tu-No Salad	w/ ½ cup white beans and avocado	⅙ recipe (212 g), ¾ cup
Caesar-y Salad	w/ ½ cup cashews and avocado	⅙ recipe (146 g), 1.5 cups
Caesar-y Salad	w/ ½ cup white beans and avocado	1⁄16 recipe (139 g), 1.5 cups
Potato Salad	w/ ½ cup cashews and avocado	⅛ salad, 1 cup w/ avocado (395 g)
Potato Salad	w/ ½ cup white beans and avocado	⅛ salad, 1 cup w/ avocado (399 g)
Macaroni Salad	w/ ½ cup cashews and avocado	⅛ recipe (122 g), 1 cup
Macaroni Salad	w/ ½ cup white beans and avocado	⅛ recipe (122 g), 1 cup
Creamy Coleslaw	w/ ½ cup cashews	⅙ recipe (180 g), 1.3 cups
Creamy Coleslaw	w/ ½ cup white beans	⅙ recipe (186 g), 1.3 cups
Curried Sweet Potato Salad	w/ ½ cup cashews and ½ cup almonds	⅛ recipe (186 g), 1 cup
Curried Sweet Potato Salad	w/ ½ cup white beans and ½ cup almonds	⅛ recipe (190 g), 1 cup
Black Bean and Yam Salad	w/ avocado	⅛ recipe (281 g), 1 cup
4-Bean Salad		⅛ recipe (303 g), 1.2 cups
SALAD DRESSINGS		
Tomato Vinaigrette		⅙ recipe (39 g), ¼ cup
Cashew-Mustard Dressing		¼ recipe (66 g), ¼ cup
Strawberry Balsamic		¼ recipe (67 g), ¼ cup
Mustard-Lime Dressing		½ recipe (93 g), ¼ cup
Creamy Curry Dressing	w/ ½ cup cashews	¼ recipe (61 g), ¼ cup
Creamy Curry Dressing	w/ ½ cup white beans	¼ recipe (55 g), ¼ cup
Avocado-Dill Dressing	w/ ½ cup cashews	¼ recipe (84 g), ¼ cup
Avocado-Dill Dressing	w/ ½ cup white beans	¼ recipe (90 g), ¼ cup
Spinach-Dijon Dressing		¼ recipe (46 g), ¼ cup
Pineapple-Mango Vinaigrette	w/ water (not juice)	¼ recipe (74 g), ¼ cup
Sesame-Citrus-Ginger Dressing		¼ recipe (63 g), ¼ cup
Sweet Mustard Dressing	w/ cashews	¼ recipe (61 g), ¼ cup
Sweet Mustard Dressing	w/ white beans	¼ recipe (89 g), ¼ cup
Ranch Dressing	w/ cashews	¼ recipe (61 g), ¼ cup
Ranch Dressing	w/ white beans	¼ recipe (80 g), ¼ cup

calories per serving	calorie density (calories per pound)	g fat	% calories from fat	g saturated fat	% calories from saturated fat	sodium mg	g carbohydrate	g protein	g sugar	g fiber	calcium mg
203	447	6.1	27.0%	0.9	4.0%	105	26.6	9.3	2.4	6.3	82
172	368	2.1	11.1%	0.1	0.5%	104	28.0	9.1	2.0	8.0	89
121	376	7.7	57.3%	1.3	9.7%	66	11.1	4.2	4.2	3.1	36
72	235	3.6	45.0%	0.6	7.5%	66	9.0	2.7	4.0	3.1	34
199	229	6.2	28.0%	1	4.5%	95	33.0	5.3	3.6	4.9	40
175	199	3.1	16.0%	0.5	2.6%	94	34	5.0	3.2	6.0	45
134	499	4.2	28.2%	0.7	4.7%	73	21.1	4.2	6.2	3.0	35
105	391	1.2	10.3%	0.2	1.4%	72	20.8	3.8	5.8	3.5	38
141	356	4.6	29.4%	0.8	5.1%	95	24.7	3.6	14.9	4.1	53
110	269	0.5	4.1%	0.1	0.8%	94	25.8	3.5	14.4	5.3	60
236	576	7	26.7%	0.8	3.1%	57	41.6	5.6	13.1	5.8	65
213	509	4	17.0%	0.3	1.6%	56	42.5	5.3	12.8	6.7	71
224	362	2.3	9.2%	0.3	1.2%	48	49.7	9.7	8.0	11.0	92
289	433	3	9.3%	0.4	1.2%	52	52.5	16.0	8.3	15.9	130
11	128	0.3	0.2%	0	0.0%	59	1.4	0.4	0.7	0.5	9
87	598	6.5	62.7%	1.1	11.4%	89	5.8	3.0	1.2	0.8	13
21	142	0.1	4.3%	0	0.0%	3	4.8	0.4	3.3	0.9	10
36	176	1.1	27.5%	0.1	2.5%	346	7.4	1.5	1.3	1.5	30
89	662	6.3	63.7%	1.1	11.1%	3	6.6	2.8	2.2	0.9	12
42	347	0.3	6.4%	0	0.0%	1	8.2	2.1	1.5	2.8	22
125	676	9.8	71.0%	1.6	11.5%	6	8.1	3.5	1.5	2.0	17
67	338	2.8	37.6%	0.4	5.4%	4	9.0	2.4	0.6	3.8	26
24	237	1.6	60.0%	0.2	7.5%	103	2.0	0.9	0.2	1.1	21
30	184	0.2	6.0%	0	0.0%	1	7.1	0.4	6.0	0.8	11
109	785	8.2	67.7%	1.1	9.1%	18	8.2	2.9	3.3	1.6	69
106	789	6.5	55.2%	1.1	5.4%	87	11.8	3.1	5.9	1.3	17
53	270	0.6	10.2%	0	0.3%	97	11.1	2.0	5.3	2.1	22
84	625	6.3	67.5%	1.1	11.8%	3	5.8	2.8	1.3	0.6	11
31	176	0.3	8.7%	0	0.0%	12	5.8	1.7	0.7	1.4	16

Recipe	Notes	Serving size
MAIN DISHES		
Pizza Pasta	w/ walnuts	¼ recipe (342 g), 1.75 cups
Veggie Burgers		1/10 recipe (119 g), 1 patty
Enchilada Casserole	w/out avocado, w/ 4 tortillas	⅛ recipe (240 g), 1 cup
Thai Vegetables w/ Pasta Shells	w/out sesame seeds	¼ recipe (316 g), 1.75 cups
Lentil and Rice Loaf	w/ pecans	1/10 recipe (150 g), 1 slice
Quinoa Curry w/ Mixed Vegetables	w/ avocado, w/out sesame seeds	¼ recipe (278 g), 1.25 cups
Mushroom-Basil au Gratin		⅛ recipe (198 g)
Mushrooms and Kale w/ Fresh Rosemary		¼ recipe (370 g)
Eggplant Stir-Fry		¼ recipe (327 g), 1.5 cups
Tu-No Casserole		1/10 recipe (240 g), ¾ cup
Pesto Pasta	w/ optional nut garnish	¼ recipe (183 g), 1.5 cups
Baked Potatoes w/ Toppings		¼ recipe (173 g), 1 medium potato
Quinoa Polenta w/ Vegetables and Barbecue Sauce	including barbecue sauce	¼ recipe (621 g)
Mushroom Risotto	w/ optional nut garnish	⅙ recipe (436 g), 1 cup
Spaghetti w/ Marinara Sauce	w/ pasta and optional nut garnish	¼ recipe (480 g)
Spaghetti w/ Marinara Sauce	w/ zucchini and optional nut garnish	¼ recipe (689 g), 1 cup sauce
Khichadi		⅛ recipe (354 g), 1.5 cups
SOUPS AND STEWS		
Split Pea and Yam Soup		⅛ recipe (405 g), 1.25 cups
Tomato-Rice Soup		⅛ recipe (449 g), 1.25 cups
Beefless Stew		⅛ recipe (439 g), 1.25 cups
Potato Soup		⅙ recipe (442 g), 1.3 cups
Minestrone Soup		⅛ recipe (548 g), 1.5 cups
Curried French Lentils		⅛ recipe (364 g), 1.25 cups
Broccoli Soup		⅛ recipe (407 g), 1.25 cups
Creamy Mushroom Soup		⅛ recipe (380 g), 1.25 cups
Southwest Stew		⅛ recipe (432 g), 1.25 cups
Corn Chowder		⅛ recipe (347 g), 1.25 cups
Black Bean and Rice Stew		⅛ recipe (436 g), 1.5 cups
Hearty Lentil Stew		⅛ recipe (460 g), 1.25 cups

calories per serving	calorie density (calories per pound)	g fat	% calories from fat	g saturated fat	% calories from saturated fat	mg sodium	g carbohydrate	g protein	g sugar	g fiber	mg calcium
337	447	6	16.0%	0.5	1.3%	49	61.5	11.5	12.0	6.5	67
131	500	1.6	11.0%	0.2	1.4%	18	25.3	6.2	3.7	4.7	39
145	274	1.1	6.8%	0.2	1.2%	37	26.7	6.2	6.3	7.6	103
194	279	5	23.2%	0.7	3.2%	117	31.9	9.1	8.7	7.2	115
163	493	5.2	28.7%	0.5	2.8%	20	26.2	6.0	4.9	4.4	33
281	459	9.3	29.8%	1.3	4.2%	70	40.7	10.2	2.4	9.2	91
155	355	6	34.8%	1	5.8%	52	21.0	6.7	2.9	3.1	53
225	276	1	4.0%	0.1	0.4%	95	52.9	7.5	12.9	8.9	136
145	201	5.2	32.3%	0.5	3.1%	45	23.4	5.5	8.3	6.6	103
234	443	4.8	18.5%	0.7	2.7%	52	36.2	12.1	5.1	6.7	72
488	1211	15.3	28.2%	2.3	4.2%	10	72.5	16.8	4.0	4.3	74
168	441	0.2	1.1%	0.1	0.5%	24	37.1	4.6	1.9	4.0	31
321	235	3.3	9.3%	0.5	1.4%	181	65.8	13.1	21.2	11.5	114
230	239	3.4	13.3%	0.4	1.6%	20	45.0	8.2	4.7	2.8	32
470	444	6.6	12.6%	0.8	1.5%	72	91.6	19.8	14.7	13.2	164
226	149	6.4	25.5%	0.9	3.6%	72.9	37.5	11.1	22.1	9.8	196
196	251	1.3	6.0%	0.1	0.5%	52	39.9	8.8	4.5	6.0	58
221	248	0.8	3.3%	0.1	0.4%	86	42.3	13.3	6.9	14.7	62
154	156	0.9	5.3%	0.2	1.2%	71	30.8	6.3	4.9	5.8	108
168	174	0.7	3.8%	0.2	1.1%	93	36.9	6.2	9.8	7.5	76
141	145	0.7	4.5%	0.1	0.6%	75	30.7	4.4	4.4	5.4	53
200	166	1.4	6.3%	0.2	0.9%	62	41.0	8.6	8.9	8.2	113
118	147	0.4	3.1%	0.1	0.8%	81	21.9	6.7	5.6	5.2	75
112	125	0.6	4.8%	0.1	0.8%	89	24.4	4.8	4.4	5.5	75
111	133	1	8.1%	0.2	1.6%	40	22.3	5.1	4.6	4.4	44
194	204	1.4	6.5%	0.2	0.9%	66	39.2	9.6	7.1	10.4	141
125	164	0.7	5.0%	0.2	1.4%	46	29.5	4.0	5.0	4.8	43
236	246	1.5	5.0%	0.3	1.1%	59	47.4	9.8	5.7	11.7	121
207	204	1	4.3%	0.1	0.4%	57	41.8	10.2	5.4	9.6	71

Recipe	Notes	Serving size
SIDE DISHES		
Mashed Potatoes		¼ recipe (345 g), 1 cup
Quinoa Cornbread		⅑ recipe (112 g); 1 piece
Falafel Patties		¼ recipe (160 g), 2 patties
Baked French Fries		¼ recipe (340 g)
Herb-Roasted Potatoes		¼ recipe (230 g)
Spicy Beans and Greens		⅙ recipe (258 g), 1 cup
Easy Corn Chips		⅛ recipe (24 g), 1 tortilla
Roasted Garbanzo Beans		⅙ recipe (78 g), ⅓ cup
Baked Pears and Yams		⅛ recipe (228 g), 1 cup
Raw Cranberry-Persimmon Relish		⅙ recipe (141 g), ½ cup
Tangerine Applesauce	w/ tangerine juice	¼ recipe (289 g), ¾ cup
SAUCES AND DIPS		
Barbecue Sauce		⅙ recipe (115 g), ⅓ cup
Better Ketchup		¼ recipe (114 g), ¼ cup
Fresh Tomato Salsa		⅚ recipe (131 g), ½ cup
Spicy Black Bean Salsa		⅙ recipe (110 g), ½ cup
Avocado-Garbanzo Dip		⅛ recipe (94 g), ¼ cup
Broccoli-Garlic Sauce	w/out tahini	¼ recipe (103 g), ½ cup
Broccoli-Garlic Sauce	w/ tahini	¼ recipe (107 g), ½ cup
Hummus		⅕ recipe (91 g), ¼ cup
Creamy Mushroom Gravy		⅙ recipe (174 g), ½ cup
Tzatziki Sauce	w/ ½ cup cashews	¼ recipe (76 g), ¼ cup
Tzatziki Sauce	w/ ½ cup white beans	¼ recipe (96 g), ¼ cup
Guacamole		¼ recipe (140 g), ½ cup
Basic Vegetable Stock	figures estimated from similar, salt-free store brand	¼ recipe (227 g), 1 cup
DESSERTS		
Carrot Cake	w/ walnuts, w/out frosting	⅒ recipe (104 g), 1 piece
Cardamom-Raisin Rice Pudding	w/ ¼ cup almonds in pudding, w/out almond garnish	⅙ recipe (223 g), 1 cup
Zucchini Bread	w/ walnuts	⅒ recipe (107 g), 1 slice

calories per serving	calorie density (calories per pound)	g fat	% calories from fat	g saturated fat	% calories from saturated fat	sodium mg	g carbohydrate	g protein	g sugar	g fiber	calcium mg
276	363	0.3	1.0%	0.1	0.3%	18	63.1	7.7	2.4	4.7	49
170	689	2.3	12.2%	0.3	1.6%	118	34.2	5.1	7.5	3.8	44
163	463	2.2	12.1%	0.4	2.2%	36	28.1	7.9	2.5	6.5	99
269	359	0.3	1.0%	0.1	0.3%	17	61.5	7.3	2.1	4.4	44
165	326	0.5	2.7%	0.1	0.5%	37	37.6	4.2	2.9	6.4	52
111	195	1	8.1%	0.1	0.8%	95	21.6	6.7	4.7	6.6	91
52	984	0.7	12.0%	0.1	1.7%	10	10.7	1.4	0.2	1.3	19
113	658	2.2	17.5%	0.2	1.6%	162	18.8	5.7	3.4	5.3	38
150	299	0.1	0.6%	0	0.0%	49	35.6	1.8	15.1	6.2	41
84	270	0.4	4.3%	0.1	1.1%	2	21.8	0.8	14.3	4.6	21
146	229	0.6	3.7%	0.1	0.6%	2	37.9	0.9	29.7	5.8	28
68	268	0.5	6.6%	0.1	1.3%	90	14.9	2.9	7.3	3.3	30
48	191	0.3	5.6%	0.1	1.9%	27	11.5	1.9	7.6	2.4	20
32	111	0.2	5.6%	0.04	1.1%	6	7.3	1.3	3.9	1.7	19
93	384	0.7	6.8%	0.1	1.0%	16	18.7	4.8	2.0	5.8	40
111	536	5.7	46.2%	0.7	5.7%	35	11.9	3.5	0.8	4.4	31
61	269	0.2	3.0%	0	0.4%	18	13.4	2.5	1.3	2.4	30
83	352	2.2	23.9%	0.3	3.3%	23	14.2	3.2	1.3	2.7	46
100	499	2.3	20.7%	0.2	1.8%	22	14.2	4.8	0.9	3.3	52
57	149	2.3	36.3%	0.4	6.3%	21	7.9	2.5	3.1	1.6	26
85	508	6.3	66.7%	1.1	11.6%	3	5.8	2.9	1.5	0.7	12
34	161	0.3	7.9%	0	0.0%	12	6.3	1.9	0.9	1.6	20
189	613	15.8	75.2%	2.2	10.5%	11	13.3	2.6	1.4	7.5	31
15	30	0	0.0%	0	0.0%	30	3.0	0.0	2.0	1.0	20
187	816	5.7	27.4%	0.7	3.4%	18	32.9	4.7	17.3	4.5	60
250	509	4.9	17.6%	0.6	2.2%	17	47.3	6.9	17.7	6.2	60
205	870	5.7	25.0%	0.7	3.1%	132	35.4	5.4	14.8	4.8	54

Recipe	Notes	Serving size
Raw Apple Crumble		⅙ recipe (121 g), ¾ cup
Sweet Potato-Pecan Pie	w/out crust	⅛ recipe (97 g), 1 slice
Pecan-Date Pie Crust		⅛ recipe (33 g), 1 slice
Banana-Walnut Bars		1/12 recipe (75 g), 1 bar
Oatmeal-Raisin Cookies	w/ almond butter and walnuts	1/18 recipe (36 g), 1 cookie
Oatmeal-Raisin Cookies	w/ applesauce and walnuts	1/18 recipe (37 g), 1 cookie
Apple Crisp		⅛ recipe (204 g)
Pumpkin Pie Squares	w/out frosting	1/16 recipe (61 g), 1 square
Blackberry-Peach Cobbler	sauce made w/ water (not juice)	⅛ recipe (164 g)
Almond-Poppy Seed Cake	w/out frosting and strawberries	⅒ recipe (92 g), 1 slice
Vanilla or Lemon Frosting		⅙ recipe (¼ cup; 68 g), ¼ cup

Recipe: Some recipes are listed more than once if the recipe offers a popular variation (see the Notes column for exact change in recipe).

Notes: The notes help clarify what the data are based on.

Serving size: The serving size is not necessarily the suggested quantity of food you should eat, but it tells you the quantity of food used to calculate the numbers in these tables.

Calorie density: Foods that are higher in calorie density have more calories in a given amount of food (in this case, one pound). Eating foods lower in calorie density allow you to consume more food without taking in more calories. For example, a pound of raw carrots has a calorie density of 186 while a pound of bagels has a calorie density of 1200.

Saturated fat: Eating foods with high concentrations of saturated fats can raise the cholesterol in your blood, increasing your risk of heart disease and stroke.

Recipe breakdowns: Figures were calculated using CRON-o-Meter, a web application for tracking nutrition and health data. Every effort was made to be as accurate as possible, but in some instances exact ingredients were not available (such as some 100% salt-free products). If you would like to calculate the nutrients of any recipe, visit http://cronometer.com.

calories per serving	calorie density (calories per pound)	g fat	% calories from fat	g saturated fat	% calories from saturated fat	sodium mg	g carbohydrate	g protein	g sugar	g fiber	calcium mg
171	642	6.4	33.7%	0.6	3.2%	1	30.5	2.2	23.6	4.1	29
154	721	5.4	31.6%	0.5	2.9%	20	25.4	3.2	13.1	3.9	37
134	1844	7.4	49.7%	0.7	4.7%	0.5	16.5	2.6	6.6	2.8	14
171	1035	6.3	33.2%	0.7	3.7%	3	26.0	4.5	8.6	3.8	21
139	1753	5.8	37.6%	0.6	3.9%	1	20.8	3.3	10.4	2.8	55
110	1350	2.9	23.7%	0.3	2.5%	1	20.6	2.2	10.8	2.4	38
228	507	2	7.9%	0.3	1.2%	4	51.4	3.8	28.1	6.7	30
74	551	0.9	10.9%	0.2	2.4%	3	16.2	1.8	9.4	2.5	19
152	421	1.9	11.3%	0.3	1.8%	4	32.7	3.9	16.0	5.9	72
177	873	2.8	14.2%	0.4	2.0%	132	34.9	2.8	14.6	4.6	70
146	974	6.2	38.2%	1.1	6.8%	3	22.0	3.0	16.6	2.1	21

RESOURCES

Below are some of my favorite resources for continued learning. This is not an exhaustive list, but many of the books, websites, recipe apps, and videos that I have found to be helpful (all are not SOS-free). You can find a more comprehensive resource list by visiting "Resources" on my blog.

FOLLOW STRAIGHT UP FOOD

Recipe blog:
www.StraightUpFood.com

Facebook:
www.facebook.com/StraightUpFood

Pinterest:
www.pinterest.com/StraightUpFood

Instagram:
www.instagram.com/StraightUpFood

Twitter:
www.twitter.com/StraightUpFood

HEALTH AND NUTRITION WEBSITES

Engine 2 Diet: www.Engine2Diet.com

Forks Over Knives:
www.ForksOverKnives.com

Jeff Novick, R.D.: www.JeffNovick.com

Joel Fuhrman, M.D.: www.DrFuhrman.com

McDougall Program: www.DrMcDougall.com

Michael Klaper, M.D.: www.DoctorKlaper.com

National Health Association:
www.HealthScience.org

Nutrition Facts: www.NutritionFacts.org

Physicians Committee for Responsible Medicine: www.PCRM.org

Plantz St.: www.PlantzSt.com

Sustainable Diet: www.SustainableDiet.com

TrueNorth Health Center:
www.HealthPromoting.com

UC Davis Integrative Medicine:
www.UCDIntegrativeMedicine.com

HEALTH AND NUTRITION BOOKS
(many of these also contain recipes)

Eat to Live, by Joel Fuhrman, M.D.

How Not to Die, by Michael Greger, M.D.

Prevent and Reverse Heart Disease, by Caldwell B. Esselstyn Jr., M.D.

The Campbell Plan, by Thomas Campbell, M.D.

The China Study, by T. Colin Campbell, Ph.D. and Thomas Campbell, M.D.

The Engine 2 Diet, by Rip Esselstyn

The Food Revolution, by John Robbins

The Forks Over Knives Plan, by Alona Pulde, M.D. and Matthew Lederman, M.D.

The Healthiest Diet on the Planet, by John McDougall, M.D. and Mary McDougall

The McDougall Program for Maximum Weight Loss, by John McDougall, M.D. and Mary McDougall

The Pleasure Trap, by Alan Goldhamer, D.C. and Douglas J. Lisle, Ph.D.

The Starch Solution, by John McDougall, M.D. and Mary McDougall

Whole, by T. Colin Campbell, Ph.D., with Howard Jacobson, Ph.D.

COOKBOOKS AND GUIDES

A Plant-Based Life, by Micaela Cook Karlsen

Bravo!, by Ramses Bravo

The China Study Cookbook, by Leanne Campbell, Ph.D.

Eat Vegan on $4 a Day, by Ellen Jaffe Jones

The Happy Herbivore, by Lindsay S. Nixon

The Health Promoting Cookbook, by Alan Goldhamer, D.C.

The McDougall Quick & Easy Cookbook, by John McDougall, M.D. and Mary McDougall

The Plant-Based Journey, by Lani Muelrath

The Prevent and Reverse Heart Disease Cookbook, by Ann Crile Esselstyn and Jane Esselstyn

Unprocessed, by Chef AJ

Vegan Under Pressure, by Jill Nussinow, M.S., R.D.

HEALTH AND NUTRITION FILMS AND DVDS

Fat, Sick, and Nearly Dead (documentary)

Forks Over Knives (documentary)

Jeff Novick's Fast Food (DVDs, volumes 1–4): (1) The Basics (2) Burgers and Fries (3) Shopping School (4) Beyond the Basics; by Jeff Novick, M.S., R.D.N.

Losing Weight Without Losing Your Mind (DVD), by Douglas J. Lisle, Ph.D.

McDougall Made Easy (DVD), by John McDougall, M.D. and Mary McDougall

Salt, Sugar and Oil: The Good, the Bad and the Ugly (DVD), by Michael Klaper, M.D.

RECIPE APPS

Forks Over Knives: Healthy Recipes & Delicious Meals Made Easy

The New McDougall Mobile Cookbook

ONLINE PLANT-BASED CERTIFICATION AND SUPPORT PROGRAMS

Plant-Based Nutrition (certification), offered by the T. Colin Campbell Center for Nutrition Studies in partnership with eCornell www.eCornell.com/

The Starch Solution Certification Course, offered by the McDougall Program www.DrMcDougall.com

Sustainable Diet (dietary transition support program), offered by Micaela Karlsen, M.S.P.H. and Kathy Pollard, M.S. www.SustainableDiet.com

ACKNOWLEDGMENTS

It truly takes a village to write a book like this. I thank the following people from the bottom of my heart for all of their support, assistance, and education along this journey.

Thank you to my editor, Laurie Masters (of Precision Revision in the San Francisco Bay Area), and to Tamara Dever and Monica Thomas (of TLC Graphics in Austin, Texas). Aside from their expertise, these three women have shown me much patience and kindness as I have worked on this book.

Thank you to Mike Ball for your wisdom on self-publishing and photography, Micaela Karlsen for assistance with the references, Mary Beth Litrico for calculating the nutritional breakdowns, Paula Whiteside for proofreading, and Ken Hassman for indexing.

I thank John McDougall, M.D., Alan Goldhamer, D.C., Michael Klaper, M.D., and Jeff Novick, M.S., R.D. for being my uncompromising teachers of healthful eating and living. Through their work to advocate a lifestyle that can positively change the game for humans, animals, and the environment, I am continually inspired.

Four big hugs to Christina Gore, Maria Maggi, Angela Glasser, and Tom Fronczak, who offered their thoughts and support through the many practical and emotional phases of creating this book.

A heartfelt thanks to my very honest and helpful recipe testers, as well as my followers on Facebook and my blog—all of whom are so kind and caring, qualities I have come to realize go hand in hand with seekers of good health.

Thank you also to Chef AJ, Avery Dinauer, Katie Mae, John Newcomb, Wanda and Mark Huberman, and everyone at TrueNorth Health Center, The McDougall Program, and the National Health Association. I always keep Ken Rubin, Rosie, and Miles in my heart and thoughts for all of the love and support they gave to me when they were here.

And thank you to my mom, Sue Elliott, who has been my biggest cheerleader along this bookmaking journey, not to mention life's journey.

ABOUT THE AUTHOR

CATHY FISHER is the author of the blog *StraightUpFood.com*, featuring free recipes and articles on eating a plant-based diet with no added salt, oil, or sugar. Cathy teaches cooking classes in Santa Rosa, California at TrueNorth Health Center and the McDougall Program. She is also a contributor and editor for *Health Science*, the member magazine for the National Health Association.

Cathy's recipes have been featured in the books *The Campbell Plan* by Thomas Campbell, M.D., co-author of *The China Study; Color Me Vegan* by Colleen Patrick-Goudreau; *Nutrition CHAMPS* by Jill Nussinow, M.S., R.D., and *A Plant-Based Life* by Micaela Cook Karlsen. Cathy's recipes and articles appear on several popular plant-based websites, including *ForksOverKnives.com, Engine2Diet.com, DrMcDougall.com,* and *HealthScience.org.*

Cathy has been eating a plant-based diet since 1999. She is passionate about her work, and is committed to positively affecting the health and welfare of humans, animals, and the environment through her recipes, writing, and teaching.

REFERENCES

1 **Food sources of energy:** O'Neil, Carol E., Debra R. Keast, Victor L. Fulgoni, and Theresa A. Nicklas. "Food Sources of Energy and Nutrients among Adults in the US: NHANES 2003-2006." *Nutrients* 4.12 (2012):2097-2120. Web.

2 **Nutritional profiles of vegetarians and nonvegetarians:** Rizzo, Nico S., Karen Jaceldo-Siegl, Joan Sabate, and Gary E. Fraser. "Nutrient Profiles of Vegetarian and Nonvegetarian Dietary Patterns." *Journal of the Academy of Nutrition and Dietetics* 113.12 (2013):1610-1619. Web.

3 **Nutritional adequacy of vegetarian diets:** Craig, Winston J., and Ann Reed Mangels. "Position of the American Dietetic Association: Vegetarian Diets." *Journal of the American Dietetic Association* 109.7 (2009):1266-1282. Web.

4 **Protein:** John McDougall, M.D. "When Friends Ask: Where Do You Get Your Protein?" *The McDougall Newsletter*, April 2007. Web.

5 **Calcium:** John McDougall, M.D. "When Friends Ask: Where Do You Get Your Calcium?" *The McDougall Newsletter*, February 2007. Web.

6 **The effects of dietary choice on the environment:** Joyce, Andrew, Sarah Dixon, Jude Comfort, and Jonathan Hallett. "Reducing the Environmental Impact of Dietary Choice: Perspectives from a Behavioural and Social Change Approach." *Journal of Environmental and Public Health* (2012). Web.

7 **Celiac disease and gluten sensitivity:** UCLA Health. "UCLA Division of Digestive Diseases Celiac Disease Program: Celiac vs Gluten-Sensitivity vs Wheat Allergies." *UCLA Health.* n.d. Web.

8 **Effects of ultra-processed foods:** Monteiro, Carlos Augusto, Renata Bertazzi Levy, Rafael Moreira Claro, Inês Rugani Ribeiro de Castro, and Geoffrey Cannon. "Increasing Consumption of Ultra-processed Foods and Likely Impact on Human Health: Evidence from Brazil." *Public Health Nutrition* 14.1 (2011):5-13. Print.

9 **Addiction to overly processed foods:** Gearhardt, Ashley N., Caroline Davis, Rachel Kuschner, and Kelly D. Brownell. "The Addiction Potential of Hyperpalatable Foods." *Current Drug Abuse Reviews* 4.3 (2011):140-145. Print.

10 **Changing tastes**: Keast, Russell S. J. "Effects of Sugar and Fat Consumption on Sweet and Fat Taste." *Current Opinion in Behavioral Sciences.* 9 June (2016):55-60. Print.

11 **The Pleasure Trap**: Lisle, Douglas J., and Alan Goldhamer. *The Pleasure Trap: Mastering the Hidden Force that Undermines Health & Happiness.* Summertown, TN: Book Publishing Co., 2006. Print.

12 **Hidden sources of SOS**: Novick, Jeff. "Is Your SOS-Free Diet Really SOS Free? Identifying Hidden Sources of Salt/Sodium, Oil/Fat & Sugars/Sweeteners." Engine2Diet.com, 13 August 2013. Web.

13 **U.S. overweight and obesity rates**: U.S. Department of Health and Human Services. "Health, United States, 2015." CDC, May 2016 (216-217). Web.

14 **Nutrient requirements**: Food and Nutrition Board, Institute of Medicine, National Academies. "Dietary Reference Intakes (DRIs): Estimated Average Requirements." 2011. Web.

15 **USDA dietary guidelines**: United States Department of Agriculture (USDA) and the Department of Health and Human Services, USA. "Scientific Report of the 2015 Dietary Guidelines Advisory Committee: Advisory Report to the Secretary of Health and Human Services and the Secretary of Agriculture." *Health.Gov*, 2015. Web.

16 **Sugar and glucose**: John McDougall, M.D. "Sugar, Coated with Myths." *The McDougall Newsletter*, September 2006. Web.

17 **Sodium in packaged foods**: Gillespie, Cathleen, Joyce Maalouf, Keming Yuan, et al. "Sodium Content in Major Brands of U.S. Packaged Foods, 2009." *The American Journal of Clinical Nutrition*. 101.2 (2015):344-353. Web.

18 **Prevalence of excess sodium intake**: Jackson, L. Sandra, Sallyann M. Coleman King, Lixia Zhao, and Mary E. Cogswell. "Prevalence of Excess Sodium Intake in the United States—NHANES, 2009-2012." *Centers for Disease Control and Prevention*. 64.52 (January 8, 2016):1393-1397. Web.

19 **Salt leads to weight gain**: Whiteman, Honor. "Salt Could Lead to Weight Gain by Driving Fatty Food Intake." *Medical News Today (MNT)*. 13 March 2016. Web.

20 **Damage from too much salt**: Susic, Dinko, Hassan Fares, and Edward Frohlich. "Salt, Arterial Pressure, and Cardiovascular and Renal Damage." *The Ochsner Journal*. 9.4 (2009):197-203. Web.

21 **Lifestyle impacts on cardiovascular health**: Eckel, Robert H., John M. Jakicic, Jamy D. Ard, et al. "2013 AHA/ACC Guideline on Lifestyle Management to Reduce Cardiovascular Risk: A Report of the American College of Cardiology/American Heart Association Task Force on Practice Guidelines." *Journal of the American College of Cardiology*. 63.25 Part B (2014):2960-2984. Web.

22 **Salt's impact on stomach cancer**: Wang, Xiao-Qin, Paul D. Terry, and Hong Yan. "Review of Salt Consumption and Stomach Cancer Risk: Epidemiological and Biological Evidence." *World Journal of Gastroenterology*. 15(18) (2009 May 14): 2204-2213. Web.

23 **USDA national nutrient database**: *USDA National Nutrient Database for Standard Reference*. USDA Agricultural Research Service National Agricultural Library, 2015. Web.

24 **Health issues related to overweight/obesity**: Centers for Disease Control and Prevention. "The Health Effects of Overweight and Obesity." CDC, 5 June 2015. Web.

25 **Effect of oil on arteries**: Felton, C.V., D. Crook, M.J. Davies, and M.F. Oliver. "Dietary Polyunsaturated Fatty Acids and Composition of Human Aortic Plaques." *Lancet*. 344.8931 (1994):1195-1196. Web.

26 **Leading causes of death**: Centers for Disease Control and Prevention. "Leading Causes of Death." CDC. 27 April 2016. Web.

27 **Impotence and heart disease**: Randrup E., Baum N., Feibus A. "Erectile Dysfunction and Cardiovascular Disease." Postgrad Med. 2015 Mar;127(2):166-72. Epub 2014 Dec 16. Web.

28 **Oxidation damage:** Krajcovicová-Kudláčková M, Dusinská M. "Oxidative DNA Damage in Relation to Nutrition." *Neoplasma*. 2004;51(1):30-3. Web.

29 **Nutrient intakes**: USDA, Agricultural Research Service. "Nutrient Intakes from Food and Beverages: Mean Amounts Consumed per Individual, by Gender and Age, in the United States, 2011-2012." *What We Eat in America, NHANES 2011-2012*. USDA, 2014. Web.

30 **Sugar density**: Novick, Jeff. "A Date With Disaster: The Pleasure Trap of Whole Natural Foods." *JeffNovick. com*, 27 June 2012. Web.

INDEX

Note: Page numbers in **bold** refer to pages with a photograph